THE INDISCRETE IMAGE

Infinitude & Creation of the Human

THOMAS A. CARLSON

THE UNIVERSITY OF CHICAGO PRESS

CHICAGO AND LONDON

THOMAS A. CARLSON is professor of religious studies at the University of California, Santa Barbara. He is the translator of three works by Jean-Luc Marion, most recently of *The Idol and Distance* (2001), and the author of *Indiscretion: Finitude and the Naming of God* (1999), the latter published by the University of Chicago Press.

The University of Chicago Press, Chicago 60637
The University of Chicago Press, Ltd., London
© 2008 by The University of Chicago
All rights reserved. Published 2008
Printed in the United States of America

17 16 15 14 13 12 11 10 09 08   1 2 3 4 5

ISBN-13: 978-0-226-09315-4 (cloth)
ISBN-10: 0-226-09315-8 (cloth)

Library of Congress Cataloging-in-Publication Data

Carlson, Thomas A.
  The indiscrete image : infinitude and creation of the human / Thomas A. Carlson.
    p.   cm.—(Religion and postmodernism)
  Includes bibliographical references and index.
  ISBN-13: 978-0-226-09315-4 (cloth : alk. paper)
    ISBN-10: 0-226-09315-8 (cloth : alk. paper) 1. Theological anthropology—Christianity. 2. Philosophical anthropology. 3. Negative theology.
4. Postmodernism—Religious aspects—Christianity. 5. Heidegger, Martin, 1889–1976. 6. Technology—Religious aspects—Christianity. I. Title.
  BT701.3.C37 2008
  218—dc22

                                                          2007052550

♾ The paper used in this publication meets the minimum requirements of the American National Standard for Information Sciences—Permanence of Paper for Printed Library Materials, ANSI Z39.48-1992.

FOR ASHLEY TURMAN TIDEY

Der Mensch ist jenes Nicht-bleiben-können und doch nicht von der Stelle Können. Entwerfend *wirft* das Da-sein in ihm ihn ständig in die Möglichkeiten und hält ihn so dem Wirklichen *unterworfen*. So geworfen im Wurf is der Mensch ein *Übergang*, Übergang als Grundwesen des Geschehens. Der Mensch ist Geschichte, oder besser, die Geschichte ist der Mensch. Der Mensch ist im Übergang *entrückt* und daher wesenhaft "*abwesend.*" Abwesend im grundsätzlichen Sinne—nicht und nie vorhanden, sondern abwesend, indem er *weg-west* in die *Gewesenheit* und in die *Zukunft*, abwesend und nie vorhanden, aber in der Ab-wesenheit *existent*. *Versetzt* ins Mögliche, muß er ständig *versehenseins* des Wirklichen. Und nur weil so versehen und versetzt, kann er sich *entsetzen*. Und nur, wo die Gefährlickeit des entsetzens, da die Seligkeit des Staunens—jene wache Hingerissenheit, die der Odem alles Philosophierens ist.

Igitur hominem accepit indiscretae opus imaginis . . .

Man is that inability to remain and is yet unable to leave his place. In projecting, the Da-sein in him constantly *throws* him into possibilities and thereby keeps him *subjected* to what is actual. Thus thrown in this throw, man is a *transition*, transition as the fundamental essence of occurrence. Man is history, or better, history is man. Man is *enraptured* in this transition and therefore essentially *"absent."* Absent in a fundamental sense—never simply at hand, but absent in his essence, in his *essentially being away*, removed into *essential having been* and *future*, essentially absencing and never at hand, yet *existent* in his essential absence. *Transposed* into the possible, he must constantly *be in oversight of* what is actual. And only because he is thus in oversight and transposed can he be unsettled. And only where there is the danger of being unsettled do we find the bliss of astonishment—being torn away in that wakeful manner that is the breath of all philosophizing.
—Martin Heidegger, *The Fundamental Concepts of Metaphysics: World, Finitude, Solitude*

He therefore accepted man as the work of an indiscrete image . . .
—Giovanni Pico della Mirandola, *Oration*

CONTENTS

ACKNOWLEDGMENTS

Completion of *The Indiscrete Image* would not have been possible without the generosity of numerous institutions and individuals, to whom I express here, incompletely but no less sincerely, my gratitude.

Portions of chapter 3 have appeared previously in "Locating the Mystical Subject," in *Mystics*, ed. Michael Kessler and Christian Sheppard (Chicago: University of Chicago Press, 2003), and portions of chapters 3 and 5 have appeared previously in "And Maker Mates with Made: World- and Self-Creation in Eriugena and Joyce," in *Secular Theology*, ed. Clayton Crockett (New York: Routledge, 2001). Portions of chapter 4 have appeared previously in "Modernity and the Mystical: Science, Technology, and Human Self-Creation," in *Science, Religion, and the Human Experience*, ed. James Proctor (Oxford: Oxford University Press, 2005), and in "Religion and the Time of Creation: Placing 'the Human' in Techno-scientific and Theological Context," in *Religion: Beyond a Concept*, ed. Hent de Vries (New York: Fordham University Press, 2008). I extend to the publishers of these volumes my thanks for giving a first home to work that now appears here, with permission, substantially revised and resituated.

What appears here as chapter 5 began as a talk I delivered at the Zentrum für Literatur- und Kulturforschung, Berlin, thanks to the gracious invitation extended to me by Joseph Jenkins and the center's director, Sigrid Weigel, to participate in their 2005 conference "What Should Inheritance Law Be?" I am doubly grateful to Professor Weigel for having invited me back to the Zentrum for a month-long fellowship in the summer of 2006, which allowed me the time and focus to complete the penultimate draft of *The Indiscrete Image*. Also most gracious in welcoming me to the Zentrum were Ulrike Vedder, Stefan Willer, and Ohad Parnes, members of the research project with which I was associated, "Erbe, Erbschaft, und Vererbung: Über-

lieferungskonzepte zwischen Natur und Kultur im historischen Wandel."
Uwe Wirth, Dirk Naguschewski, and Heidi Keller provided indispensable
logistical assistance and a hospitable welcome, and Alexander Schwieren
provided not only his warm friendship and lively intellectual engagement
but also many important lessons, during the 2006 World Cup, on the ways
and world of true football.

I am happy here to acknowledge the Regents of the University of California, from whom I received several faculty fellowships for summer research
that directly supported the book's progress. I was also most fortunate, in
the course of my research, to spend the spring and fall quarters of 2004 as
a residential research fellow at the University of California's Humanities
Research Institute in Irvine. I am grateful to the Institute's director, David Theo Goldberg, for his hospitality, and to all of the participants in our
research group, "The Ethics of the Neighbor," especially to Steven Mail-
loux, a spirited and genuinely thoughtful interlocutor. The research group's
convener, Kenneth Reinhard, along with Julia Reinhard Lupton, extended
to me then, and continue to offer, a friendship and hospitality, both intellectual and otherwise, that have helped sustain me in no small way.

At the University of California, Santa Barbara, in the average everyday,
it is often my students who keep me alive intellectually, and for the role
they have played in shaping this book, either through conversations, seminars, and their own writing or through other forms of support, I note, with
gratitude, William Robert, Wendy Wiseman, Arianne Conty, John Lardas
Modern, Kerry Mitchell, Evan Berry, Mark Noble, Matt Schunke, Joshua
Marks, Brett Land, Tino Garcia, Caleb Elfenbein, Aaron Gross, Nathaniel
Rich, Patricia Kubala, Stephanie Stillman, Elizabeth Kerr, Ali Bjerke, and
Colleen Windham.

Among academic colleagues to whom I am happily indebted here in various ways, I want especially to acknowledge and thank the following. Elisabeth Weber and Roger Friedland, irreplaceable friends and collaborators on
the UCSB faculty, have given me hope for thinking amidst the business of
research. Kevin Hart and Cyril O'Regan, reviewers for the University of Chicago Press, gave very generous, insightful, and critical readings of the penultimate draft of *The Indiscrete Image*, which my revisions have managed
to answer only in part. Michael Kessler and Christian Sheppard, by inviting
my participation in "Mystics: An Interdisciplinary Conference on Negative
Theology and Mysticism" at the University of Chicago in 1999, provided
the occasion where I first glimpsed the trajectory of the book at hand. James
Proctor, by inviting me to deliver a Templeton Research Lecture at UCSB in

2002, likewise opened paths that led to the present work. The hospitality of Hent de Vries, through his "Future of the Religious Past" project, sponsored by the Netherlands Organization for Scientific Research, also advanced my work on *The Indiscrete Image* in decisive ways. Dana Hollander, Travis Kroeker, and Jeremy Stolow graciously included me in collaborative projects at McMaster University from which I have derived both benefit and enjoyment. Regina Schwartz and Clayton Crockett, by including my work in *Transcendence* and *Secular Theology*, respectively, opened key moments for the development of my thinking in the direction of this book. John Caputo has continued to provide lively conversation and vital support with his inimitable intellectual energy and good humor. Thomas J. J. Altizer's deep and critical reading of previous work has challenged and inspired me here, as have his own writings on Joyce. Maria José A. de Abreu's brilliant reading of this book's penultimate draft showed me more about it than I had yet seen. Without the teaching of H. Ganse Little Jr., David Tracy, and Bernard McGinn, this book simply would not be. I am likewise indebted to Jean-Luc Marion's groundbreaking work and steady friendship, which recurrently awaken me to the possibility of thought. Jeffrey L. Kosky, stubborn friend and intellectual comrade, has provided on this project, as on countless other things, his invaluable insight and encouragement. And the singular vision and generosity of Mark C. Taylor remain a constant and indispensable source of inspiration. I thank also Carlisle Knowlton Rex-Waller for her fine copyediting of the final manuscript, and Alan Thomas and Randy Petilos at the University of Chicago Press, who throughout this project have yet again provided their astute guidance and most valued confidence.

Among the many friends and family who have carried me through to the project's end, I acknowledge especially Doug Johnson, Stephanie Savage, Todd Alden, Pete Struck and Natalie Dohrmann, Stephanie Hodde, Patty Ruprecht and Cliff Ruprecht, David Carlson and Stephanie Crawford, Jay Carlson and Lisa Carlson, Quincey Tidey Grieve and Tim Grieve, Francie Moore and Peter Hirzel, Linda Moore, Carolyn Chubet, and, above all, my parents, Rosanne Lee Carlson and Joseph Carlson II, whose generosity remains immeasurable.

The time of this work's writing has been the time of departure for several beloved family members, whom the work thus inevitably recalls: my grandparents Antonette Lee and Thomas A. Lee Sr., who showed me love's long patience, along with its joy; my uncle Thomas A. Lee Jr. and my father-in-law, Clayton J. Tidey, who each in his own way, even in the face of darkness, shared deeply in such joy and its life; and my dear mother-in-law, Frances Lee Turman Tidey, who in the dignified labor of her dying, as in that of her life, taught me lessons of birth with which I will never be finished.

Born into this time of departure, and thus creating a new world, Aura Lee Carlson and Frances Lee Carlson now determine everything I manage to understand of love and of possibility, and they do so in concert with Ashley Turman Tidey, to whom I dedicate, with love, the work she has made possible.

Santa Barbara
7 December 2007

⚜

OPENING

═══════════

. . . the river of temporal things . . .

In *Indiscretion: Finitude and the Naming of God* (Chicago, 1999), I aimed to establish and elucidate a striking analogy that captured, and still captures, my imagination—the analogy between the logic of Being-toward-God in traditions of mystical theology, where the relation of soul to God concerns a naming of the unnameable or a thinking of the unthinkable, and the logic of Being-toward-death in Heideggerian and post-Heideggerian thinking about the human as finite, mortal existence, where the individual's relation to death signals the paradoxical possibility of an impossibility. In both directions, according to what I named the "apophatic analogy," the subject of thought and language finds itself always already constituted in relation to a term that conditions all thought and language while ever eluding their full or final capture in the presence of any experience. Figured in terms of their "indiscretion," then, the structure and movement of a negative theology—according to which the endlessly named, conceived, and imagined God remains ultimately ineffable, inconceivable, and unimaginable—could never be securely distinguished from, nor identified with, the structure and movement of a negative anthropology, according to which our finite, mortal existence remains ever a mystery to us.

The present work aims to take up and advance this understanding of the human as incomprehensible to itself by showing such incomprehensibility, or the lack of definition it implies, to be a condition of the creative, and indeed technological, capacity that the human inescapably inhabits but never actually exhausts. While *Indiscretion* pointed to the never realized, and never realizable, possibility of my own impossibility primarily in terms of mortal finitude, *The Indiscrete Image* regards the creative possibility of mortal human existence more in terms of the in-finitude or indetermination of such existence—and of such possibility. In that direction, the work posits and develops an intimate linkage between the indetermination of the human, its relative lack of definition or discretion, and the inexhaustible capacity of the human to create and recreate both itself and its world through processes of birth that may themselves go to the heart of the nature we inhabit. Just as *Indiscretion* moves, in terms of finitude and naming, between the theological and the anthropological, so, then, the current work moves, in terms of infinitude and creation, between the anthropological and the cosmological—thus opening and articulating the ground for a next work concerning the nature of world and its relation to human love.

The Indiscrete Image is framed primarily by Martin Heidegger's influential analysis of technological modernity and its ties to Christian theological tradition, taken as an "ontotheology." Following my introductory first chapter, "Of God or a Salamander," which explains the derivation of the book's title and sketches out the logic and stakes of the "indiscrete image" as it will be developed in the course of the work, I explicate in chapter 2, "I Am," the intimate linkages operative between Heidegger's interpretation of Western metaphysics as an ontotheology of the providential Creator, on the one hand, and, on the other, his critique of technological modernity, whose calculative thinking and productive machinations he believes to close off any genuine creation. Both in the metaphysical conception of God, I argue, and in the metaphysics and mass culture of technoscientific modernity, the core of Heidegger's critique concerns a reduction of all "possibility"— which in its ontological form would remain for Heidegger beyond objectification and calculation, management and control—to the logic of eventual actuality, the delimited possibility for this or that, whose presence might lend itself to the forms of objectification and calculation fundamental to modernity's projects of conceptual and practical management or control.

Having established along these lines the terms and stakes of Heidegger's critical perspectives on theological tradition, technological modernity, and their interplay, I go on to offer in two subsequent chapters alternative readings, first, of theological—specifically mystical—tradition and the understandings of divine creation operative there, and then, in turn, of a technological postmodernity and the forms of human creativity it may give us to think. In chapter 3, "The Living Image," I engage theological traditions where God remains beyond concept or comprehension, at points even to himself, and where such incomprehensibility—mirrored in the human who is created in God's image—is thought of as ground or condition of a creation in which the human essentially participates. Within this lineage of mystical theology, I argue, one can trace a creative subject, whether human or divine, who proves to be creative not in and through the clarity and certainty at which modern thought and culture, according to Heidegger, aim, but in the darkness and incomprehension of a creation *ex nihilo*. Chapter 4, "Of the Indefinite Human," engages more recent theorizations of technological culture, associated notably with the "posthuman," in order to elaborate linkages analogous to those made in theological tradition between creativity and incomprehension. In both traditional mystical contexts and contemporary technological contexts, I argue, the endless or inexhaustible creative capacity of the human can be understood as a function of the human's relative lack of definition or discretion, and hence of its incapacity to comprehend itself or its creation. The image of the human that emerges here, what I am calling "the indiscrete image," goes hand in hand, then, with the ongoing creation of a world that itself remains irreducible to the comprehensible limits, to the principled origins and ends, of any totalizing representation or "world picture."

Diverging thus from Heidegger's analyses of theological tradition and technological modernity, the two alternative lines I develop in chapters 3 and 4 will show themselves to intersect in what I take to be the proto-postmodern thought and writing of James Joyce's *Finnegans Wake*, to whose reading I turn in chapter 5, "Here Comes Everybody." As the chapter's subtitle—"Technopoetics and Mystical Tradition in Joyce"—suggests, I read Joyce's *Wake* to recapitulate, in light of the emerging technomodernity that informs the poetic work of the *Wake*, the structure and movement of a dynamic and mystical cosmos whose center is everywhere and circumference nowhere—a cosmos where, as in the poetic technomodernity the work also evokes throughout, a subject absent or opaque to itself proves, in and through its very own unknowing, ever to create and recreate itself and its world. The intersection or interweaving Joyce realizes between the depths of mystical tradition and the currency of an emerging technological postmodernity opens a path for rethinking not only "tradition" and its presumed delimitations, but also the role these might play in placing or locating—which means in defining—the human.

Thus, in my last full chapter, "To Inherit," I engage one of the more insightful and far-reaching among recent challenges to "the posthuman"—that of Robert Harrison's *Dominion of the Dead* (Chicago, 2003)—in order to argue that the worldly conditions of human placement and heritage on which Harrison focuses in his dismissal of the posthuman prove in fact to require just the sort of prosthetic and distributed networks, and hence the resistance to discrete placement, that condition the technological human in recent posthuman discourse. Returning to the "neotenic" character of the human sketched out in chapter 1, I emphasize that a key condition of human inheritance proves to be the indeterminate, or indiscrete, character of the human who can, and must, assume creative, technological capacity—and hence the capacity for sociality over time—thanks to, and because of, that very indetermination or indiscretion.

To keep open the potential of such creative capacity, I suggest in a brief conclusion, would require that we think the indiscretion of the human as inextricably bound with the resistance of world to picture; that we think the openness of such a world and humanity, in their nature, according to the birth implied by mortality; and that we think the ongoing possibility of birth, and thus the ongoing birth of possibility, as the function of a love that remains of the world. The human as indiscrete image, I conclude, in pointing forward, would be bound, by love, with a world that remains open, thanks to such love, for those who dwell in it.

CHAPTER ONE

Of God or a Salamander:
The Creative Human as Indiscrete Image

If "modernity" is often, and often rightly, construed in terms of the creative capacities invented and assumed by an increasingly self-assertive, self-reliant, or indeed self-creative humanity, it is often taken likewise to involve the eclipse or displacement of Christian tradition's omniscient and omnipotent Creator God. On this take, the newly creative and self-creative subject of modern Western humanism is thought to define and to produce both its world and itself much in the way that God was thought, through a good part of Christian tradition, to conceive and to create both the world and, within the world, his own image—the human creature that God intends to exercise dominion over the world. "Let us make man in our image, after our likeness," God says in Genesis 1:26, "and let them have dominion over the fish of the sea, and over the birds of the air, and over the cattle, and over all the earth, and over every creeping thing that creeps upon the earth." The Christian doctrine of the *imago Dei*, in this version of the story, yields in its modern extensions the human project of a domination, both conceptual and practical, that applies ever more thoroughly, if not absolutely, to the natural and social worlds alike—such that all being, including the human being itself, is subjected, without differentiation or exception, to the logic of conception, organization, production, and exploitation.

In our late modern or postmodern context, the unsettling implications of humanity's inventive or creative capacity, especially as that capacity realizes itself by technological and scientific means, seem to multiply daily, as do anxious responses to our emerging technoscientific worlds, which can seem to represent a human creation that threatens the human itself. From popular and provocative titles such as Francis Fukuyama's *Our Posthuman Future* or Gregory Stock's *Redesigning Humans* to philosophical works such as Jürgen Habermas's *The Future of Human Nature*, Dominique Janicaud's *On the Human Condition*, or Peter Sloterdijk's *Rules for the Human Park*, countless publications, which continue to proliferate, suggest something of this pervasive unease and uncertainty.[1]

Indeed, in the many uneasy and well understandable responses to the rapid and potentially radical technoscientific development we all confront—or, in fact, inhabit—today, nothing less than "the human" in its very "nature" and "life" can seem to be at stake. Furthermore, appeal to the human and to the urgent need for its safeguarding will often be made through appeal to "tradition," above all to religious tradition and to the "values" such tradition is thought to preserve and bequeath, in protection of the human itself, of its proper place, its dignity and definition. If such response can often seem and often believe itself to be founded in some knowledge of what the human is, and thus in an understanding of what exactly of the human would be threatened or altered by technoscientific and related developments, it may in fact be (and this is my bet here) that the anxious and often violent response to the apparent threat of technoscientific intervention into "the human" derives its energy less from the secure knowledge of some human definition and more from an uncomfortable and largely unavowed awareness—intensified by technoscientific development itself—that the human is in the end something for which we lack any clear and certain definition. It would be the technological and scientific threat to stable conceptions or definitions of the human, then, as well as to human existence itself, that engenders any number of anxieties and, in turn, evasive and often violent reactions that seek, precisely, to resecure the boundaries within which one hopes to understand and keep safe what one would want to count, and count on, as "proper" to the human, whose essential nature, life, and value would thus be held as "sacred" in their dignity.[2]

Along these lines, the assertion of an irreducible tension between re-

---

1. Francis Fukuyama, *Our Posthuman Future: Consequences of the Biotechnology Revolution* (New York: Farrar, Strauss, and Giroux, 2002); Gregory Stock, *Redesigning Humans: Our Inevitable Genetic Future* (New York: Houghton Mifflin, 2002); Jürgen Habermas, *The Future of Human Nature*, trans. William Rehg, Max Pensky, and Hella Beister (Cambridge: Polity Press, 2003); Dominique Janicaud, *On the Human Condition*, trans. Eileen Brennan (New York: Routledge, 2005); Peter Sloterdijk, *Regeln für den Menschenpark: Ein Antwortschreiben zu Heideggers Brief über den Humanismus* (Frankfurt am Main: Suhrkamp Verlag, 1999).

2. On such interplay, in all of its complexity and self-contradiction, between the "safe" and the "sacred" as these concern the human (and much else), see especially Jacques Derrida's seminal essay "Faith and Knowledge: The Two Sources of 'Religion' at the Limits of Reason Alone," which appears in English in *Religion*, trans. Samuel Weber (Stanford: Stanford University Press, 1998), and in French in *La religion* (Paris: Éditions du Seuil, 1996), both edited by Jacques Derrida and Gianni Vattimo. Please note that unless stated otherwise, translations of quotations in *The Indiscrete Image* are my own.

ligion and its mystery, on the one hand, and scientific and technological modernity, on the other, operative, for example, in the influential analyses of a theorist of modernity like Max Weber, can appear to be reconfirmed. On one side, a calculative and instrumental rationality would assume—or at least seek—conceptual and practical hold over a disenchanted world, and the human itself would fall under such hold. On the other side, the opacity or mystery of religion, preserving and preserved by tradition and its values, would resist the reach of such rationality and its mechanisms—and thus promise to save the human "itself."

In the latter direction, one can hear exemplary voices from both right and left on the political spectrum, such as those of Leon Kass and Bill McKibben, who both resist technoscientific interference with the human, its nature and inherent dignity, through appeal to heritage and tradition, whether explicitly religious tradition (as with Kass) or tradition accorded an implicitly religious sanctity (as with McKibben). Kass, appointed in 2001 by George W. Bush as first chairperson of the President's Council on Bioethics, whose initial membership included also Francis Fukuyama and Charles Krauthammer, argues that in order "to keep human life human," and in order, correlatively, to "defend life's dignity," we need to resist techno-scientific violation of the human—to protect (or restore) the distinctively human capacity for "wonder and awe at the rich and incredible facts of life, soul, and human awareness," out of respect for the human mystery that is taught and transmitted by tradition, the latter most notably in its biblical form.[3] "We can learn from thinking about Genesis what it means that the earth's most godlike creature is a concretion combining ruddy earth and rosying breath; . . . and why respect for a being created in God's image means respecting *everything* about him, not just his freedom or his reason but also his blood."[4] The appeal Kass makes to a human mystery articulated and protected by biblical tradition, and especially that concerning man as *imago Dei*, is crucial to his reactive view of technology as "an entire way of being in the world, a social phenomenon more than a merely material one, characterized by the effort, through rational analysis, methodical artfulness and correlative organization, to order all aspects of our world toward efficiency, ease and control."[5] As in Weber so in Kass, too, too much control—or already the very assumption, as goal, of control by rational-technical

3. Leon Kass, *Life, Liberty, and the Defense of Dignity* (San Francisco: Encounter Books, 2002), 18, 24–25.

4. Ibid., 20–21.

5. Leon Kass, cited in Gary Greenberg, "After Nature: The Varieties of Technological Experience," *Harper's*, March 2004, 93.

means—disenchants the world and deprives humanity of its constitutive mystery, a mystery for which tradition maintains a respect that we moderns and postmoderns risk losing (if we have not already done so). As I will elaborate, a position like that of Kass underplays in a notable way a profound linkage—also to be found in a tradition that counts itself biblical—between a thought of the human as *imago Dei* and an understanding of the human as inherently technological. Attention to this linkage, I will argue, forces us to reimagine the character of the human both as technological and as traditional—and as the one because also the other.

What a thinker like Kass seeks in the appeal to tradition is a sense of respect for the place and limitation of the human in nature, and as writer Gary Greenberg notes in a lucid review essay, the "platitudes" Kass deploys "about cultivating 'given gifts' and respecting 'human dignity'" tend to involve a pastoral language "meant to evoke a time when we knew where we belonged, when a technologically unmediated life meant that we could be trusted to reject certain challenges to the natural order."[6] Such rhetoric, and the sentiments behind it, can place those on the political and cultural right in an uncomfortable proximity to many from the political and cultural left that emerged in the sixties and remains tied to "green" thought and activism today. For example, the worry of McKibben in his book *Enough* is much like that of Kass and the Council on Bioethics: too much control, an overly thorough programming of the human—in this case by means of genetic engineering—will deprive us of the insurmountable limitation and incalculable chance that McKibben takes as indispensable to being human.[7] And while he asserts that his objections are not religiously grounded, he does make repeated appeal to tradition or heritage broadly, and to religious tradition specifically, as that which keeps in place the limits that allow us to remain, as individuals, genuinely human (and it is worth noting that what counts as "genuinely human" for McKibben amounts in the end to a version of the modern Western liberal individual, which traditionally and historically has been a rather restricted figure). "The idea of restraint comes in large measure from our religious heritage," and without restraint we risk falling into the "meaninglessness" against which previously we would have enjoyed the protections provided by "the church and the village and the family and even the natural world."[8]

---

6. Greenberg, "After Nature," 94.

7. Bill McKibben, *Enough: Staying Human in an Engineered Age* (New York: Henry Holt, 2003).

8. McKibben, cited in Greenberg, "After Nature," 96; McKibben, *Enough*, 46. There is some tension in McKibben's position along these lines, for much of his critique is directed at the disas-

The appeal to tradition, such as that by Kass or McKibben, despite evoking the mystery of the human, often seems to have a fairly good sense of who and what the human might or should be: a definition, in other words, some knowledge or understanding of the limit and place of the human, which would allow us to protect the human by keeping it within its proper bounds. To place the issue within the history of theological anthropology, in such cases the appeal to mystery tends to harbor an anthropology that is in fact more positive or affirmative than negative or apophatic. The latter form—the negative or apophatic associated intimately with the mystical— understands the human to be the image of an incomprehensible God, itself likewise incomprehensible. This view often also understands the human, as I will show, to be creative, and thereby self-creative, on the ground of just such incomprehensibility. In a concise and astute treatment of the relation between cloning and the human in Habermas and Derrida, Eduardo Mendieta very efficiently evokes this traditional distinction between positive and negative readings of the *imago Dei* doctrine:

> If the doctrine of *imago Dei* is taken literally, as proscribing a catalogue of qualities assigned specifically to the human being by God the legislator, then we have . . . a positive philosophical anthropology, of which Leon Kass's is the most recent version. If, however, we take the doctrine of *imago Dei* as announcing man as project and incomplete creation, then we have . . . a negative philosophical anthropology. . . . Positive philosophical anthropology tells us how to be human, and thus, how not to be what would challenge our humanity, while negative philosophical anthropology tells us that the question of humanity's essence is not to be answered . . . but that it is our ability to ask the question that is indicative of how our humanity is always in question, awaiting further reformulations.[9]

---

trous consequences of modern individualism, even as what seems to be at stake in our humanity itself is our individuality.

9. Eduardo Mendieta "We Have Never Been Human, or How we Lost Our Humanity: Derrida and Habermas on Cloning," *Philosophy Today*, SPEP Supplement, 2003, 169–70. As Mendieta effectively shows, from a largely Derridean perspective, if those who oppose technoscientific intervention into human nature do so often in the name of the norms and knowing according to which "responsible" agents necessarily act, those who entertain a more negative anthropology can perhaps relocate the condition and redraw the character of responsibility—to be found rightly in the decision that lacks knowledge or program, according to a lack that may keep history open as ontological possibility. I will revisit and elaborate these questions in what follows. Among recent readers of Derrida, John Caputo is especially notable for eliciting the ethical and political force of our "not knowing who we are." In this direction, see, among his many recent works,

The appeal to mystery, as the example of Kass suggests, does not necessarily mean in the end commitment to the indetermination of the human, or its lack of definition, to its status as question and open work—but it can well mean the reverse. The appeal to such mystery in the name of tradition can likewise entail a rather partial take on what in fact courses through the histories and traditions of theological or philosophical anthropology, where that openness and questionability are more prevalent than many appeals to tradition manage to acknowledge.

Writers like Kass and McKibben, despite their very different political and cultural orientations, share a nostalgia that recalls the critique of technoscientific culture that unfolds in the influential thought and writing of the twentieth-century German philosopher Martin Heidegger. And indeed, in the philosophic register, the most significant analyses of the tension between technology's calculative rationality, or modern metaphysics and culture more broadly, and any "openness to the mystery" do remain those of Heidegger, who offers a most powerful and still deeply relevant account of the will to mastery operative in the modern thought and culture for which being is conceived as objectivity and truth is understood in terms of the certainty about such being achieved by the thinking human subject who, in its thinking, securely represents that being to itself—and thus also secures itself. As Heidegger argues in his important essay of 1938, "Age of the World Picture" ("Die Zeit des Weltbildes")—to whose themes I will return in chapter 2—this logic of mastery is operative as much in modern research science, both natural and historical, as it is in technologized modern thought and culture more broadly:

> Nature and history become the objects of a representing that explains. Such representing counts on nature and takes account of history. Only that which becomes object in this way *is*—is considered to be in being. We first arrive at science as research when the Being of whatever is, is sought in such objectiveness. . . . This objectifying of whatever is, is accomplished in a setting-before, in a representing, that aims at bringing each particular being before it in such a way that man who calculates can be sure, and that means certain, of that being. We first arrive at science as research when and only when truth has been transformed into the certainty of representation.[10]

More Radical Hermeneutics: On Not Knowing Who We Are (Bloomington: Indiana University Press, 2000).

10. Heidegger, "Age of the World Picture," 127 [87].

The modern position sketched here by Heidegger appears first in the thinking of Descartes, the father of modern philosophy for whom we humans "should make ourselves masters and possessors of nature."[11] On the Heideggerian account, of course, there is an intimate linkage between the metaphysics coming to expression in Descartes and the technoscientific modernity that troubles contemporary writers like Kass and McKibben.

By contrast, however, to those who would set in clear and simple opposition technoscientific thought and culture, on the one hand, and religious tradition, on the other, Heidegger sees an essential tie between the technoscientific subject of modernity and the God of Christian metaphysics. The modern subject who would represent to itself all reality so as to become, both conceptually and practically, molder and maker of that reality is heir to a Christian God whose mind served as template for creation. Especially in the linkage between technology and the kind of thinking that understands being as object and truth as the certainty of representation, Heidegger argues, "the *Christian-biblical* interpretation of beings as *ens creatum*" persists, and it does so "regardless of whether this is taken in a religious or a secular way."[12]

Among recent heirs to this Heideggerian understanding of the interplay

11. René Descartes, *Discours de la méthode: Texte et commentaire par Étienne Gilson*, pt. 6 (p. 62 according to the Adam-Tannery pagination): "et ainsi nous rendre comme maîtres et possesseurs de la nature." The English version in vol. 1 of *The Philosophical Writings of Descartes*, ed. John Cottingham, Robert Stoothof, and Duguld Murdoch (Cambridge: Cambridge University Press, 1985), gives "the lords and masters of nature." The larger context of this much cited line is worth quoting:

> But as soon as I had acquired some general notions in physics and had noticed, as I began to test them in various particular problems, where they could lead and how much they differ from the principles used up to now, I believed that I could not keep them secret without sinning gravely against the law which obliges us to do all in our power to secure the general welfare of mankind. For they opened my eyes to the possibility of gaining knowledge which would be very useful in life, and of discovering a practical philosophy which might replace the speculative philosophy taught in the schools. Through this philosophy we could know the power and action of fire, water, air, the stars, the heavens and all the other bodies in our environment, as distinctly as we know the various crafts of our artisans; and we could use this knowledge—as the artisans use theirs—for all the purposes for which it is appropriate, and thus make ourselves, as it were, the lords and masters of nature. This is desirable not only for the invention of innumerable devices which would facilitate our enjoyment of the fruits of the earth and all the goods we find there, but also, and most importantly, for the maintenance of health, which is undoubtedly the chief good and the foundation of all the other goods in this life.

12. Martin Heidegger, *Beiträge zur Philosophie*, vol. 65 of Heidegger's *Gesamtausgabe*, rev. ed. (Frankfurt am Main: Vittorio Klostermann, 1994), 132; English version in *Contributions to Philosophy (from Enowning)*, trans. Parvis Emad and Kenneth Maly (Bloomington: Indiana Uni-

between theological tradition and technological modernity, Mark C. Taylor and Jean-Luc Marion take contrasting directions whose difference is instructive. Taylor inherits and develops in his own way the Heideggerian reading and critique of Christian thought as ontotheology, while he remains less taken, especially in his more recent work, with the Heideggerian resistance to technoscientific culture. Marion remains heir to the Heideggerian resistance toward technoscientific culture and its founding metaphysics, while he diverges from the Heideggerian reading of theological tradition, locating in that tradition an apophatic and mystical lineage that would exceed and unsettle the boundaries and logic of ontotheology as Heidegger defines it.

As Taylor points out in his groundbreaking *Erring* (1984), one of the earliest and most influential works to introduce deconstructive thought into the contemporary field of religion, a modern reading of the "death of God," exemplified in the atheistic humanism of a figure like Ludwig Feuerbach, remains insufficient insofar as it merely repeats the will to mastery already implicit in "traditional" metaphysics taken as ontotheology. That is, it simply substitutes for the omnipotent and omniscient Creator God of Christian metaphysics a newly creative human subject who aspires to a similar omniscience and omnipotence—notably in the technological society dominated by utility and consumption, a society where, as Heidegger puts it, "the impression comes to prevail that everything man encounters exists only insofar as it is his construct. . . . It seems as though man everywhere and always encounters only himself."[13] Atheistic humanism, inverting but not truly subverting the divine-human binary on which so much of Western thought and culture has been founded, does not manage to change in any significant way the founding logic of such thought and culture. "This reversal of divinity and humanity," Taylor writes, is the distinctive mark of humanistic atheism. Instead of simply

> denying the reality of God, the humanistic atheist transfers the attributes of the divine subject to the human self. . . . The humanistic atheist insists that "when it is shown that what the subject is lies entirely in the attributes of the subject; that is, that the predicate is the true subject, it is also proved that if the divine predicates are attributes of

---

versity Press, 1999), 92. Cited parenthetically hereafter as *B*, with English pagination followed by the German.

13. Heidegger, *Question concerning Technology*, 27, quoted in Mark C. Taylor, *Erring: A Postmodern A/theology* (Chicago: University of Chicago Press, 1984), 25.

human nature, the subject of those predicates is also human nature."
This reversal reveals the slave's struggle *against* the master to be a
struggle *for* mastery. By transferring the predicates of divinity to the
human subject, the humanistic atheist inverts, but fails to subvert, the
logic of repression. With this inversion, the problem of mastery and
slavery is relocated rather than resolved. The death of the sovereign
God now appears to be the birth of the sovereign self.[14]

In the development of his atheistic humanism Feuerbach argues along fairly
Hegelian lines, though perhaps less dialectically than Hegel, that this self-
assertion on the part of modernity's newly confident human subject is the
logical extension of Christianity's own contention that man is created *in
imago Dei*. For a postmodern thinker like Taylor, whose "a/theology" is
neither a traditional theism nor a modern atheism, the death of God does
not imply that we simply transfer to humanity attributes formerly ascribed
to God but rather that we recognize in that death an imperative—and an
opportunity—to think beyond the autonomy and self-identity that modern
Western humanism, in its will to mastery, first found in and then sought to
take over from the God of ontotheological tradition.

Along these lines, Taylor's reading of theological tradition, like Heidegger's, remains focused on its metaphysical or ontotheological inclina-
tions, which, as the recent work of other philosophers and theologians
suggests, may not be exhaustive. Indeed, as I will be asserting here, a di-
vergent line of theological reflection can well be noted within "the tradition," according to which the contention that man is created in the image
of God implies not the capacity of man to ground or comprehend himself,
or indeed to assume conceptual or practical mastery over the real, but a
fundamental incapacity of man to comprehend or to master himself or the
world in which he dwells cocreatively with God. Such an interpretation
of the human as *imago Dei* would insist on the necessity of man's ongoing, and never securely founded, self-creation, itself taken as an essential,
cooperative dimension of God's own creative activity. That line of theological reflection, I think, can be read anew today, and quite productively,
in light of recent theoretical discourse, associated with the "posthuman,"
concerning the forms of human self-creation one might envisage currently
by technoscientific means.

14. Taylor, *Erring*, 25, quoting Ludwig Feuerbach, *The Essence of Christianity*, trans. G. Eliot (New York: Harper Torchbooks, 1967), 25.

If a thinker like Marion, along one line of his critical engagement with Heidegger, sheds light on a theological field that a position such as Taylor's, following Heidegger, overlooks, Marion does so while neglecting or denying the creative potential of a technological culture that Taylor in his recent works more productively explores and elucidates. In several important theological texts, as well as in his major phenomenological project, Marion has called into question the Heideggerian account of Christian tradition as an ontotheology that reduces God to the figure or concept of a highest being that is cause and ground of all other beings—a concept whose modern versions appear in the principle of sufficient reason, the moral author of the world, and the like: all first causes that are used by human thought to render the givenness of phenomena intelligible as a whole.[15] In revisiting the traditions of negative and mystical theology stemming from the Pseudo-Dionysius, Marion aims to show that Christian tradition has not always and everywhere reduced God to being or concept (especially that of efficient cause) and, indeed, that God has been evoked—and desired and praised—also as a Goodness beyond Being and hence as inconceivable. Attempting to think God beyond the horizons of being and conception, mystical theology would not in fact subscribe to the logic of ontotheology as analyzed by Heidegger.[16]

Marion thus stands in tension with Heidegger on the question of ontotheology and Christian tradition, but he remains very much in line with Heidegger's aversion to the technoscientific thought and culture that for Heidegger marks an extension of Christian ontotheology within the modern context. That remaining kinship with Heidegger, which I treat in chapter 4, might be related to Marion's underplaying the creative and indeed technological dimensions of the human as it comes to be understood in the same mystical traditions he otherwise reads productively in his resistance to Heidegger on the question of theological tradition. In what follows, my own course moves between and beyond the positions marked out by Taylor, who explores the constructive potential of technoscientific culture but overlooks key aspects of relevant theological tradition, and by Marion,

15. Among Marion's theological texts, see especially *God without Being*, trans. Thomas A. Carlson (Chicago: University of Chicago Press, 1991) and *The Idol and Distance*, trans. Thomas A. Carlson (New York: Fordham University Press, 2001). Among his phenomenological works, see especially *Reduction and Givenness: Investigations of Husserl, Heidegger, and Phenomenology* (Evanston: Northwestern University Press, 1998) and, above all, *Being Given: Toward a Phenomenology of Givenness*, trans. Jeffrey L. Kosky (Stanford: Stanford University Press, 2002.

16. For my discussion of Marion's reading of mystical theology, see "The Naming of God and the Possibility of Impossibility, "chapter 6 of *Indiscretion: Finitude and the Naming of God* (Chicago: University of Chicago Press, 1999).

who constructively appropriates those dimensions of theological tradition while resisting a constructive or even theological reading of technoscientific culture. Along this course, I aim to show, a striking resemblance emerges between the technological subject as reimagined constructively, beyond the Heideggerian critique, in what is now commonly called posthuman discourse, and the mystical subject as imagined in its creative capacity by a theological tradition wrongly, or at least incompletely, understood as ontotheological.

A growing field of contemporary literature calls our attention to the possibility that we are underway with a posthuman mode of being—in and through a technoscientific existence that extends and reshapes the powers of human thought, agency, and imagination (via informational, communications, and other media technology) even as it alters the boundaries and character of human and other life (thanks to biological sciences and technologies, genetic engineering, and the like). Because the term is often used in sweeping and dismissive fashion, a few words on its more precise and productive senses might be in order. In that direction, the work of N. Katherine Hayles is especially helpful, for it defines the posthuman very clearly and concretely by its contrast with the logic that defines the subject of modern Western liberal humanism. If the latter is understood as a discrete, self-possessed, and self-governing individual, who exists as such "by nature" and thus prior to the involvements of social being and its prosthetic supports, the posthuman subject is instead an indeterminate, irreducibly relational, and endlessly adaptive figure whose intelligence and agency are not simply possessed or controlled by the individual or his will, but always already distributed throughout complex networks that exceed, even as they constitute, any individual. Such networks include both human and nonhuman agents, biological and nonbiological elements, natural and cultural dimensions whose complex and open-ended interplay unsettles modern models of the masterful subject even as it binds the human, irreducible to discrete location, ever more intimately with its environment. As Hayles writes in *How We Became Posthuman*,

> if, as Donna Haraway, Sandra Harding, Evelyn Fox Keller, Carolyn Merchant and other feminist critics of science have argued, there is a relation among the desire for mastery, an objectivist account of science, and the imperialist project of subduing nature, then the posthuman

offers resources for the construction of another kind of account. In this account, emergence replaces teleology; reflexive epistemology replaces objectivism; distributed cognition replaces autonomous will; embodiment replaces a body seen as a support system for the mind; and a dynamic partnership between humans and intelligent machines replaces the liberal humanist subject's manifest destiny to dominate and control nature.[17]

From this perspective, to abandon the liberal humanist dream of autonomy and mastery is by no means to abandon the human as such. Quite the contrary, to abandon the liberal humanist position is to open a richer, more flexible, and more adaptive understanding of our place within the world, such that we can "fashion images of ourselves that accurately reflect the complex interplays that ultimately make the entire world one system."[18]

To date, the most informed, creative, and far-reaching inquiry into the religious significance of the worlds related to such posthuman thinking and being can be found in the works of Taylor, for example, *Hiding, About Religion, The Moment of Complexity,* and *Confidence Games.*[19] Passing beyond the Heideggerian critique of technological culture that still shapes *Erring,* these later works show that—and how—the complex adaptive networks we come inevitably to inhabit in technoscientific culture, which Taylor takes to work as "non-totalizing systems that nonetheless act as a whole," call fundamentally into question the metaphysics of the subject on which modern technology, in the Heideggerian account, is based.[20] As we inhabit informational and communications networks that evolve interactively with us, the nonhuman "object" becomes ever more active and intelligent; it ceases to appear susceptible to straightforward calculation and control on the part of a subject who would stand independent of the object so as to assume a hold over it. Likewise, to the degree that the human subject thinks and acts increasingly by means of technological prosthetics that extend "sub-

17. N. Katherine Hayles, *How We Became Posthuman: Virtual Bodies in Cybernetics, Literature, and Informatics* (Chicago: University of Chicago Press, 1999), 288.

18. Ibid., 290.

19. Mark C. Taylor, *Hiding* (Chicago: University of Chicago Press, 1997); *About Religion: Economies of Faith in Virtual Culture* (Chicago: University of Chicago Press, 1999); *The Moment of Complexity: Emerging Network Culture* (Chicago: University of Chicago Press, 2001); and *Confidence Games: Money and Markets in a World without Redemption* (Chicago: University of Chicago Press, 2004).

20. I quote "Returnings," a concise introduction to the virtual turn in Taylor's thought, written as an introductory piece for the Fordham University Press reissue of Taylor's *Journeys to Selfhood: Hegel and Kierkegaard* (New York: Fordham University Press, 2000), xix.

jective" faculties outward into the "objective" world, even as the outward also moves inward, that subject can no longer be defined according to its stable delimitation from an objective world "out there." Insisting on the relational and interactive character of subjects and objects, of humans and machines, of culture and nature, Taylor builds on information and systems theory to rework Hegel's insight concerning the necessarily objective and embodied dimension of spirit, and he argues accordingly that both natural and sociocultural systems are fundamentally informational and communicational processes, which are always already taking place in such a way that "it is no longer clear where to draw the line between mind and matter, self and other, human and machine. *Mind is distributed throughout the world.*"[21]

If Taylor's model of distributed mind draws deeply and explicitly on the Hegelian treatment of objective spirit, it also departs significantly from the Hegelian position by insisting on the unconscious dimensions of a networked subjectivity. Just as Freud and his heirs argue that consciousness and its rationality do not exhaust psychic life, and indeed may constitute a relatively small fraction of it, so Taylor asserts that networked subjects think and act by means of systems not fully accessible to the comprehension or control of conscious subjectivity. In *The Interpretation of Dreams*, then, where Freud understands consciousness as the place where other psychic operations not directly or fully accessible to consciousness "show up" in their effects, we might see a precursor to the process Taylor calls "screening":

> A screen . . . is more like a permeable membrane than an impermeable wall; it does not simply divide but also joins by simultaneously keeping out and letting through. As such, a screen is something like a mesh or net forming the site of passage through which elusive differences slip and slide by crossing and criss-crossing. But a screen is also a surface on which images, words, and things can be displayed. Every surface is actually a screen that hides while showing and shows while hiding. . . . Forever oscillating between differences it joins without uniting, *the meaning of screen* remains undecidable. Far from a limitation, this undecidability is the source of rich insight for understanding what we are and how we know. In network culture, *subjects are screens* and *knowing is screening*.[22]

21. Taylor, *Moment of Complexity*, 230 (emphasis in original).
22. Ibid., 199–200 (emphasis in original).

While the Freudian perspective might seem to locate the unconscious primarily "within" the subject, Taylor emphasizes that the "technological unconscious," fundamental to the screening process of the networked subject, unsettles distinctions between inward and outward. The relation of self to world, or of subject to object, is "always two way: as body and mind extrude into world, world intrudes into body and mind."[23] Something like the Augustinian mind that cannot contain itself, the self in Taylor's network culture is "a node in a complex network of relations" such that "in the midst of these webs, networks, and screens, I can no more be certain where I am than I can know when or where the I begins and ends. I am plugged into other objects and subjects in such as way that I become myself in and through them, even as they become themselves in and through me."[24]

Much in line with Taylor's analysis of networked subjectivity and its technological unconscious, Hayles's critique of the liberal humanist conception of self suggests to us that, for posthuman subjectivities, unknowing and impotence are conditions of intelligence, which proves to be distributed, and of agency, whose location likewise cannot be discretely contained: "Subjectivity is emergent rather than given, distributed rather than located solely in consciousness, emerging from and integrated into a chaotic world rather than occupying a position of mastery and control removed from it."[25] Hayles's account both highlights the intimate partnership between individual and environment, including that between human and machine, and shows that partnership to involve an irreducible gap of unknowing for the subject. Because "the distributed cognition of the emergent subject correlates with . . . the distributed cognitive system as a whole, in which 'thinking' is done by both human and non-human actors," we as "subjects" participate constantly "in systems whose total cognitive capacity exceeds our individual knowledge."[26] In a manner reminiscent of Heidegger's Dasein as

---

23. Ibid., 230–31.

24. Ibid., 231; on Augustine, see 200–202. As I'll suggest in subsequent chapters, the Augustinian perspective finally limits, in ways that other mystics like John Scotus Eriugena do not, the kind of apophatic anthropology that Taylor signals in Augustine's famous passages on memory.

25. Hayles, *How We Became Posthuman*, 291.

26. Ibid., 289, 290. Developing her conclusions on the posthuman subject in and through a discussion of Edwin Hutchins's critique of John Searle's "Chinese Room" argument, Hayles emphasizes that

the prospect of humans working in partnership with intelligent machines is not so much a usurpation of human right and responsibility as it is a further development in the construction of distributed cognitive environments, a construction that has been ongoing for thousands of years. Also changed in this perspective is the relation of human subjectivity to its environment. No longer is human will seen as the source from which

Being-in-the-world, or of the linguistic subject in poststructuralist thought, Hayles's posthuman subject, like Taylor's "nodular subjectivity," constitutes a dynamic point of intersection within a system that operates through that subject at least as much as the subject operates through it. Just as the world works through me as much as I through it, just as language speaks me at least as much as I speak it, so here, distributed networks of intelligence and agency think and act through me as much as I through them, and with effects that can seem mystical. As Derrida points out in his seminal essay on religion, "Faith and Knowledge," we increasingly inhabit a gap between the know-how, or the power, we exploit thanks to our technoscientific systems and the actual knowledge grounding such power, and we do so in such a way that the gap proves, in a significant departure from Weber's disenchanted world, insurmountable—and hence in such a way that our experience can indeed seem increasingly magical or mystical.[27]

The posthuman models that theorists like Hayles and Taylor advance owe much to recent developments in cognitive science and related fields

---

emanates the mastery necessary to dominate and control the environment. Rather, the distributed cognition of the emergent human subject correlates with . . . the distributed cognitive system as a whole, in which "thinking" is done by both human and nonhuman actors. "Thinking consists of bringing these structures into coordination so they can shape and be shaped by one another," Hutchins wrote. To conceptualize the human in these terms is not to imperil human survival but is precisely to enhance it. (289–90)

27. See, e.g., "Faith and Knowledge," 56. Building productively on these Derridean insights, Hent de Vries develops a compelling analysis of the miracle as special effect, and vice versa, and in doing so he argues effectively, contra positions such as that of Weber, or of a certain Heidegger, for the need to consider technicity and religion as inextricably bound with each other. See, in this direction, "In Media Res: Global Religion, Public Spheres, and the Task of Contemporary Comparative Religious Studies," in *Religion and Media*, ed. Hent de Vries and Samuel Weber (Stanford: Stanford University Press, 2001), 28:

there are not only empirical, historical, and technological but also systematic reasons to doubt that magic and the miraculous could ever be (or have ever been) taken out of religion, just as there are reasons to suspect that religion was never fully taken out of reason, secularization, mechanization, technicization, mediatization, virtualization, and so on. . . . We should no longer reflect exclusively on the meaning, historically and in the present, of religion—of faith and belief and their supposed opposites such as knowledge and technology—but concentrate on the significance of the processes of mediation and mediatization without and outside of which no religion would be able to manifest or reveal itself in the first place. In contradistinction to Heidegger's analysis, mediatization and the technology it entails form the condition of possibility for all revelation—for its revealability, so to speak. An element of technicity belongs to the realm of the "transcendental," and vice versa.

See also the remarks on media and religion, from a Derridean perspective, in the introduction to de Vries's important study *Philosophy and the Turn to Religion* (Baltimore: Johns Hopkins University Press, 1999).

like artificial intelligence and robotics, where innovative thinkers and re-
searchers such as Edwin Hutchins and Andy Clark are striving to elucidate
the extent to which, and the manners in which, we are, in Clark's phrase,
"natural-born cyborgs," a phrase whose sense is captured also in French
philosopher Michel Serres's suggestion that "we've always been artificial
for nine-tenths of our intelligence. Certain objects in this world write and
think; we take them and make others so that they can think for us, with
us, among us, and by means of which, or even within which, we think. The
artificial intelligence revolution dates from at least as far back as neolithic
times."[28] In order to explore and explain the logic according to which intelligence emerges and operates by means of systems involving both human
and nonhuman actors, Hutchins, an open-ocean racing sailor as well as a
cognitive scientist, turns to the navigational systems used on large ships—
where multiple actors interact both with one another and with a variety of
interrelated nonhuman devices for measuring, recording, retrieving, com-
puting, and the like, in such a way that the navigational system as a whole
yields an intelligence never attained or controlled by any one single actor
or element within that system. As Hayles points out, Hutchins's study of
such "cognition in the wild" allows him to propose a provocative reinter-
pretation of John Searle's much discussed argument concerning "the Chinese room," which Searle meant to show that machines cannot think: "The
Chinese room," as Hutchins writes, "is a sociocultural cognitive system.
The really nice thing about it is that it shows us very clearly that the cognitive properties of the person in the room are not the same as the cognitive
properties of the room as a whole. There is John Searle with a basket of Chinese characters and a rulebook. Together he and the characters and the rulebook in interaction seem to speak Chinese. But Searle himself speaks not a
word of Chinese."[29] "In Hutchins' neat interpretation," as Hayles glosses,
"Searle's argument is valuable precisely because it makes clear that it is not
Searle but the entire room that knows Chinese. In this distributed cognitive

28. Michel Serres, *Angels: A Modern Myth* (Paris: Flammarion, 1995), 50. See Andy Clark's
Natural-Born Cyborgs: Minds, Technologies, and the Future of Human Intelligence (Oxford: Oxford University Press, 2003), which offers a rich and accessible overview of both current and
near-future developments in smart technology and of its implications for understanding the
human as creature of intelligence. See also an earlier work by Clark, *Being There: Putting Brain,
Body, and World Together Again* (Cambridge: MIT Press, 1997), whose opening page rightly notes
that "the image of mind as inextricably interwoven with body, world, and action" was "already
visible in Martin Heidegger's *Being and Time* (1927)" and "found clear expression in Maurice
Merleau-Ponty's *Structure of Behavior* (1942)."

29. Edwin Hutchins, *Cognition in the Wild* (Cambridge: MIT Press, 1995), 362.

system, the Chinese room knows more than do any of its components, including Searle. The situation of modern humans is akin to that of Searle in the Chinese room."[30] That is, the situation of modern humans (or already, if we follow Clark and Serres, premodern humans) is one in which intelligence and ignorance, agency and impotence, are inextricably tied to one another, within systems that not only exceed but also recurrently reshape their own creators.

⸙

Within his brilliant analyses of the systems and subjects that occupy theorists like Taylor and Hayles, Serres opens a rich perspective from which we can elucidate the self-creative work undertaken by a networked or posthuman subjectivity and, in turn, elaborate the quasi-mystical logic of such work. If still largely underappreciated in English-speaking contexts, notably contexts pertaining to religion, Serres is nonetheless one of the more informed and astute among contemporary writers to be grappling, at times explicitly, with the religious significance of our technoscientific humanity. Serres explores in striking ways the manner in which a universal humanity is emerging concretely today thanks to forms of science and technology that reshape human life and death on a global scale, making us "our own cause, the continuous creator of our world and of ourselves" within a process that Serres names "hominescence."[31] From the thermonuclear bomb through global warming and developments in genetics and biotechnology, life and death themselves, on a global scale, come under the influence—and hence the responsibility—of a collective, technoscientific humanity, which, by reshaping its world, reshapes itself, and by reshaping itself reshapes its world, the two movements being inextricably interwoven within fluid and unpredictable processes of world- and self-creation.

The unknowing dimension of this creative process signals an intimate, dynamic, and productive linkage between a relative indetermination of the human and its striking "totipotence," between the human's apparent lack of essence and its virtually infinite capacity to do or to become. The remarkable capacity of the human continually to create and recreate both its world and itself is a function of the human's relative lack of definition or programming, its capacity to "forget" itself so as constantly to remake itself. The ex-

30. Hayles, *How We Became Posthuman*, 289.
31. Michel Serres, *Hominescence* (Paris: Le Pommier, 2001), 165.

traordinary achievements of modernity's technoscientific machines would, while perhaps seeming to threaten humanity with the mechanical form of existence that troubles Heidegger and his heirs, in fact issue from humanity's remarkably unmechanical, unprogrammed, and hence unpredictable condition. The most programmed of beings, from this perspective, are the least technological, and the most unprogrammed of beings, like the human, prove to be the most technological.

The indeterminate human ground of technological innovation, furthermore, is reinforced in its indetermination by the capacity of technology itself to unsettle the bounds we might take to define the human. The more we innovate technologically, the less determined or programmed we become, and the less determined or programmed we become, the more we can innovate—technologically and otherwise. "The more we turn blank [or white, *blanchissons*]," as Serres writes, "the more we invent; the more we cast off [*appareillons*], the more we externalize, the more we turn blank [*blanchissons*]. The more we produce, the more we become innocent: by this saintliness you will recognize the discoverer."[32] Evoking the self-effacement and anonymity of the saint, whose life becomes productive thanks to its poverty, who finds strength in weakness, or influence through susceptibility, Serres links humanity's innovative and productive capacities to a kind of nullity or self-negation. The saints, perhaps unexpectedly shadowed today in our technological humanity, are those who return to the kind of "deprogramming" that renders them open to all; the saints are those who move toward a "transparent indifference" that "whitens them [*les blanchit*] in such a way that they become invisible, in the image of God."[33]

⋘⦿⋙

As the present work argues, the evocation of the *imago Dei* in relation to an essentially technological humanity, invisible or indefinable, can be seen to

32. Michel Serres, *L'incandescent* (Paris: Le Pommier, 2003), 96.

33. Serres, *Hominescence*, 111. The ethical significance of such radical exposure has been central to the philosophy of Emmanuel Levinas, who embraces also, as I'll point out in chapter 4, the ethical potential of technological existence. (See especially the central chapter "Substitution," in *Otherwise than Being, or Beyond Essence*, trans. Alphonso Lingis [Boston: Martinus Nijhof, 1981], and "Heidegger, Gagarin and Us," in *Difficult Freedom: Essays on Judaism*, trans. Seán Hand [Baltimore: Johns Hopkins University Press, 1997.] Among contemporary heirs of Levinas, Edith Wyschogrod stands out for her emphasis on the figure of the saint in postmodernism, along lines that can be read productively in relation to the figure of the saint evoked here in Serres. See her *Saints and Postmodernism: Revisioning Moral Philosophy* (Chicago: University of Chicago Press, 1990).

have analogues in the deeper histories of theology, most notably in its mystical forms. In what follows, my rereading of mystical theological tradition in the Christian West brings to light an understanding of the *imago Dei* that not only resists the logic of ontotheology but also insists, at the same time, on the creative capacity of a humanity that proves to be creative in just the measure that it does not ground, comprehend, or master itself; in these depths of theological tradition, human ignorance or incomprehension itself comes to light as condition of anarchic and open-ended creativity. Likewise in what follows, my rereading of technological culture as it appears among contemporary theorists yields an image of creative humanity defined, as in mystical tradition, by its lack of definition; the human here proves authentically creative in the measure that it fails to achieve the mastery of world and self no doubt sought within major tendencies of modern thought and culture. Along these lines, which diverge in illuminating ways from the Heideggerian accounts both of ontotheological tradition and of technological modernity, the creative human, imagined theologically or technologically, might be understood to enjoy the possibility of creation, and self-creation, only to the degree that it remains an open work, an ongoing creation without fixed archetype or established place, and hence in a fundamental condition of need—the need to engage in the endless multiplication of images and forms and ways of being human, within a dynamic that can never exhaust the indeterminate, or infinite, possibility that very need opens and sustains. If it is thought here in some tension with Heidegger's accounts of theological tradition and technological modernity, such need might nonetheless be consistent with Heidegger's assertion that "the *moment of vision* [*der Augenblick*] in which Dasein [that is, our finite Being-in-the-world] brings itself before itself as that which is properly binding must time and again stand before Dasein as such. Before itself—not as a fixed ideal or rigidly erected archetype, but before itself as that which must first precisely wrest its own possibility from itself again and take itself upon itself in such a possibility."[34] Beyond the idol that such ideals and archetypes can be, insofar as they set bounds around the human and thus make it definable or comprehensible to itself, the human who occupies my attentions here will elude such bounds, and hence unsettle any idolatrous closure, insofar as it proves to enjoy its existential possibility thanks to its essential indetermination.

34. Martin Heidegger, *The Fundamental Concepts of Metaphysics: World, Finitude, Solitude*, trans. William McNeill and Nicholas Walker (Bloomington: Indiana University Press), 165; for the German see *Die Grundbegriffe der Metaphysik: Welt-Endlichkeit-Einsamkeit*, vol. 29/30 of *Gesamtausgabe* (Frankfurt am Main: Vittorio Klostermann, 1983), 247. Hereafter cited parenthetically as *FC*, with English pagination followed by the German.

While Heidegger highlights, explicitly, the ontotheological over the mystical in his treatment of theological tradition, and while he remains resistant to what he takes as the inauthentic machinations of technomodernity's anonymous mass culture, he also offers, along another angle, the means to rethink such anonymity and inauthenticity themselves as creative ground.[35] In the next chapter, I seek to elucidate this ground through an engagement with Heidegger on theological tradition and technological modernity in order then to develop, in the two subsequent chapters, paths for rethinking the creative human as mystical and as technological. Those paths intersect in my reading of James Joyce in chapter 5, where we can sense, in the mass culture of the technomodernity that so worried Heidegger, a creative ground that reverberates with the mystical. The human and cosmic images of mystical tradition, I will argue, and the understanding of these in terms of a creation *ex nihilo*, are as vital as are the technologies and media of modern mass culture to the movement of Joyce's *Finnegans Wake*. In that work, a subject absent to itself—buried in the death of sleep, or the sleep of death, or a drunken dream—becomes the ground or body of an open-ended creation that is also self-creation, an ongoing birth that awakens us to our nature.

Through my reading of the *Wake*, furthermore, I will suggest that the interweaving in Joyce between technological modernity's mass culture and the depths of mystical tradition is only one instance of a more general logic according to which "tradition" always gives far more, and thus also far less, than either its self-proclaimed proprietors and protectors or its avant-garde overcomers can ever actually measure or contain. Both parties—which means all of us—always inherit, in fact, and in principle, an inescapable depth of memory, an overwhelming sway of tradition, to which we inevitably remain blind. If we are at a loss whenever we ask "what man is," this is perhaps because the relevant knowledge, as Heidegger suggests at one

---

35. This is not, of course, to ignore the important role of mystical theology in the development of Heidegger's thought, from the engagement with Augustine and the medieval mystics in his early seminars on phenomenology of religion, through the notable influence of Meister Eckhart in his later thought. In addition to the texts gathered in Heidegger's own *Phenomenology of Religious Life*, trans. Matthias Fritsch and Jennifer Anna Gossetti-Ferenci (Bloomington: Indiana University Press, 2004), see also John Caputo's *The Mystical Element in Heidegger's Thought* (Athens: Ohio University Press, 1978), and for a Heideggerian reading of Eckhart, Reiner Schürmann's *Meister Eckhart, Mystic and Philosopher* (Bloomington: Indiana University Press, 1978). Both John van Buren and Theodore Kisiel shed helpful light also on the religious element in Heidegger's early development. See van Buren, *The Young Heidegger: Rumor of the Hidden King* (Bloomington: Indiana University Press, 1994), and Kisiel, *The Genesis of Heidegger's Being and Time* (Berkeley: University of California Press, 1993).

point, is set down "not in anthropology, psychology, characterology and so on, but rather in the whole history [*Geschichte*] of man—not in something like biographical history [*biographische Historie*], and not at all in historiography [*Historie*], but rather in that originary tradition handed down [*in jener ursprünglichen Überlieferung*] which lies within all human acting as such, whether this is recorded and reported or not" (*FC*, 281 [407]). Our human self-unknowing is, I argue, historical or traditional in this originary sense. It is something we receive in our very being, and the traditions of our history, the truth within which we always already live and move and have our being, a truth which itself lives and moves and has its being through us, are, as much as the source of any identity, the ground and body of this most profound unknowing. Perhaps no writer better than Joyce brings to expression this dimension of unknowing in the sway of tradition, the depths of the unrecorded or unreported spoken silently in any actual memory. Perhaps also, then, no writer better than Joyce demonstrates how it is no easier to escape tradition than it is to protect it. His writing thereby suggests that something akin to the posthuman may course much more deeply through our traditions and histories than either the technophilic utopians or the technophobic guardians may want to acknowledge.

The choice, then, may not be so neat between posthuman abstractions and the traditional grounds of humanism. In a beautiful and challenging book, *The Dominion of the Dead*, which I take up in chapter 6, Robert P. Harrison, by supplementing the "truth" of Heidegger's philosophy with the "philological certainty" of eighteenth-century Italian thinker Giambatista Vico, develops a definition of the human in terms of its burial, and hence its retention of memory, in an earthly "place." To the degree that emerging technologies uproot us from the earth and thereby endanger human dwelling in any real place, Harrison argues, to the degree that technological being thus threatens the very conditions of human burial and human memory, "each one of us must choose an allegiance: either to the posthuman, the virtual and the synthetic, or to the earth, the real, and the dead in their humic densities."[36] However, insofar as the processes of human burial and retention prove to be, even in Harrison's own analysis, the function of world building, which means, I argue, prosthetic and technological activity; insofar, that is, as the human mind is essentially self-externalizing, and insofar as through burial human mind always retains and transmits, in fact, more than it can ever actualize in the presence of conscious memory, the basic

---

36. Robert P. Harrison, *Dominion of the Dead* (Chicago: University of Chicago Press, 2003), 35.

operation of burial—retention—could be read to exceed us and dislocate us in much the way that the networks of posthuman existence exceed and dislocate us. In that direction, I aim to show that the conditions of tradition and inheritance themselves, which are in fact fundamentally technological, entail also an essential indetermination of the creative human. The implications of this take on inheritance for our place in the world will occupy me in the conclusion, where the question of world and its possibility appears as a question of love.

～∞～

The appearance of the creative human's indetermination in posthuman thought recalls the depths of mystical tradition even as it extends more recent human-scientific theorizations (sociological, anthropological and psychoanalytic) of the technological and world-building human as "neotenic," which is to say, as born essentially premature and thus destined to an eternal infancy or incompletion. Such an understanding of human "neoteny," or "pedomorphosis," as fundamental to human creativity was first advanced systematically as scientific theory by Dutch anatomist Louis Bolk in the 1920s and developed later by anthropologists like Georges Lapassade, sociologists like Peter Berger, psychoanalytic thinkers like Jacques Lacan, and the post-Heideggerian philosopher Giorgio Agamben—and it offers a wonderfully suggestive means to think together the indetermination of the creative human in mystical tradition and the indetermination of the creative human in our own emerging technological culture. The modern figure of the neotenic human, in its indetermination and lack of definition, indeed looks much like that traditional mystical figure of the human as image of an incomprehensible God—but the mirror in which modern thought first finds the image of such indetermination is not God but an intriguing species of salamander, the axolotl. As Agamben points out in his brief meditation "The Idea of Infancy" (1985), it was this species of albino salamander living in the freshwater lakes of Mexico whose "stubborn infantilism . . . offered a new key to the understanding of human evolution," by suggesting the possibility that the human constitutes, like the axolotl, a pedomorphic or neotenic creature—one that while retaining the physical traits of the infant becomes capable of sexual reproduction. According to this theory of evolution, "man did not evolve from individual adults but from the young of a primate which, like the axolotl, had prematurely acquired the capacity for reproduction." Thanks to such premature reproduction, the human would, like the axolotl, pass from one generation to the next the morphological traits of the fetus, such that "characteristics which in primates are transitory become final in man, thereby in some way giving rise, in flesh and blood, to a kind of eternal child."[37] Relatively unspecialized or indeterminate, a creature incompletely formed and thus in need of formation, and information, the neotenic human stands, like a child, in lifelong dependence on sociality and all it entails—starting with language and education and all the various other technological extensions and information systems that enable, even as they require, something like the transmission or tradition of sociality over time. As the indeterminate—and hence totipotent—ground of the distinctively human capacity for tradition, the neotenic human, an eternal child, carries the distinction of an indistinction, the property of an impropriety thanks to which alone the human might ever create those traditions in which the human so often aims to define and secure itself. Thinking human evolution on the basis of the neotenic, "this hypothesis makes for a new approach to language and to the entire sphere of the exosomatic tradition, which, more than any genetic imprint, characterizes *homo sapiens*"—which is to say, that being who, as Agamben points out elsewhere, has for "definition" the never fulfilled imperative to know itself.[38]

Theorized first in the work of Bolk in the 1920s and upheld more recently, on the basis of a revised argument, by Stephen Jay Gould (who also points out that one of our more familiar neotenic images is surely that of Mickey Mouse) and Oxford zoologist Clive Bromhall, the neotenic human finds expression also in literature—and in its unsettling mirror image with the axolotl.[39] In his wonderful short story "Axolotl," Argentine writer Julio Cortázar creates a narrator who, happening one day upon the axolotls in

37. Giorgio Agamben, "The Idea of Infancy," in *Idea of Prose*, trans. Michael Sullivan and Sam Whitsitt (Albany: State University of New York Press, 1995), 95, 96.

38. Ibid., 96. See also Giorgio Agamben, *The Open: Man and Animal*, trans. Kevin Attell (Stanford: Stanford University Press, 2004), 25: "In truth, Linnaeus's genius consists not so much in the resoluteness with which he places man among the primates as in the irony with which he does not record . . . any specific identifying characteristic next to the generic name *Homo*, only the old philosophical adage: *nosce te ipsum* (know yourself). Even in the tenth edition [of his *Systema naturae*], when the complete denomination becomes *Homo sapiens*, all evidence suggests that the new epithet does not represent a description, but that it is only a simplification of that adage, which, moreover, maintains its position next to the term *Homo*. It is worth reflecting on this taxonomic anomaly, which assigns not a given, but rather an imperative, as a specific difference."

39. See "A Biological Homage to Mickey Mouse," chapter 9 in Stephen Jay Gould, *The Panda's Thumb: More Reflections in Natural History* (New York: W.W. Norton, 1980); and Clive Bromhall, *The Eternal Child: An Explosive New Theory of Human Origins and Behavior* (London: Ebury Press, 2003).

an aquarium at the Jardin des Plantes in Paris, becomes obsessed with the creatures. Returning every day thereafter to stare at the axolotls, the narrator finds in his obsessive return "nothing strange . . . because after the first minute I knew that we were linked, that something infinitely lost and distant kept pulling us together [*que algo infinitamente perdido y distante seguía sin embargo uniéndos*]." In this infinitely lost and distant "something," there is finally nothing to mark securely the distinction between the narrator and the image he finds in the axolotl—an image that proves indeterminate to the point that the narrative voice slips from the ostensibly human "I," to an "I" seemingly spoken by the salamander, to a blurring between the two that seems to end, though rather ambiguously, "with my human mind intact, buried alive in an axolotl."[40] In his illuminating, largely Lacanian, reading of Cortázar's story, the first chapter of his *Lettres sur la nature humaine à l'usage des survivants* (Letters on Human Nature for the Use of Survivors), Dany-Robert Dufour, a professor of philosophy and education, sees in this relation between the human and the salamander "an absolute mirror stage, formative of an archaically abyssal 'I' where the axolotls reveal themselves to be infinitely 'close to us'"—close, that is, according to an extreme proximity wherein they and we alike "sense the particularity of being not finished [or non-finite, *non finis*] in-finite [*in-finis*]. In this unrealized part [*cette part non advenue*] that characterizes them consists their mysterious humanity."[41]

In a related and more extensive work that traces understandings of the human as neotenic from the Epimethean and Promethean myths, through Giovanni Pico della Mirandola's writing on the dignity of man, to Jacques Lacan's mirror stage, and on into the body art of Stelarc and the bio-bunks of San Francisco, Dufour aims also to give what he calls an "atheistic proof for the existence of God," positing that God, the *grand Sujet* and *grand d'hommesticateur*, serves as a figure of fullness and stability in subjection to whom the neotenic human evades or masks its own incompletion and instability.[42] This means for Dufour that "so long as men have no sense of

40. Julio Cortázar, "Axolotl," in *End of the Game and Other Stories*, trans. Paul Blackburn (New York: Harper and Row, 1967), 4, 8. A Spanish edition of this collection is also available: *Final del juego* (Madrid: Punto de Lectura, 2003).

41. Dany-Robert Dufour, *Lettres sur la nature humaine à l'usage des survivants* (Paris: Calmann-Lévy, 1999), 28, 29.

42. Dany-Robert Dufour, *On achève bien les hommes: De quelques conséquences actuelles et futures de la mort de Dieu* (Paris: Denoël, 2005), 90ff. In this Dufour's analysis recalls the kind of argument that Mark C. Taylor has often made, if with more complexity, that religion (figure of

their state of incompletion, they remain tightly subjected to God, but as soon as they manage to reach some form of consciousness of that state, they tend to gain in free will."[43] Total submission to God, from this perspective, entails flight from human incompletion, while the acknowledgment and affirmation of human incompletion means a daring, and for Dufour distinctively modern, liberation from God.

Dufour's intuition that the neoteny discovered in our relation to the axolotl might be reflected also in our relation to God is a significant one, but he takes that intuition in a direction opposite to that I will take here. Indeed, on my reading of mystical theological tradition, it can well be that, in the God of whom the human is an image (or vice versa), the human finds not, in fact, the fulfillment or masking of its lack or indetermination but the abyssal ground and image of that indetermination itself. The mystical traditions where this God appears, then, can lead one to question in fundamental ways the security with which Dufour asserts that "it is certainly not easy to prove God and to remain an atheist."[44] On the contrary, as mystical theology may suggest, the God who can be proved is the very support of atheism, and atheism requires just the kind of definition and conception on which proof depends. While Dufour largely neglects traditions that might have yielded a different reading of the theological than the one he gives, he does point in their direction, implicitly, through the role he assigns Pico della Mirandola within a rich and informative history of inchoate neotenic theory.[45]

Within Pico's revision of theological traditions treating the human as the creative and indefinite image of an incomprehensible Creator God, the human has to be seen in all of its activity and artistry, as creative process rather than as achieved or accomplished product—and hence as infinitely open. As Ernst Cassirer comments in his study "Giovanni Pico della Mirandola," which notes Pico's distinction of the human both from the animal and from the angel, who alike remain untroubled in a way the human cannot, "the freedom of man consists in the uninterrupted creativity he

---

plenitude and stability) is constructed to exclude the sacred (a nonabsent absence that can only unsettle and elude figure).

43. Ibid., 24.

44. Ibid., 89.

45. This is also suggested, but not appreciated, in a footnote where Dufour, informed by André Wénin, notes that "the theme of human incompletion is equally present in the patristic tradition" (ibid., 24 n. 2). Dufour's failure actually to take up that tradition weakens, I think, his subsequent reading of Pico, and his take on the theological overall.

exercises upon himself, which can at no point come to a complete cessation. Such a cessation is in a certain sense the lot of every other nature
except man."[46] Elaborating this contrast of the human, on one side, and the
animal and angel, on another, Cassirer highlights the insecurity and danger
of the human's free, creative movement, which lacks both the security of
uniform repetition (given the animal by instinct) and the untroubled happiness of the angel (whose beatitude cannot be undone). The human is a
creature shadowed always by that danger whose risk run is the only chance
for creation.[47]

46. Ernst Cassirer, "Giovanni Pico della Mirandola," *Journal of the History of Ideas* 3, no. 2
(1942): 330. The valuation of such creative freedom might be read to involve, Cassirer elaborates,
a distinctively modern departure from the metaphysical traditions—and values—of Plato and Aristotle as these extend through the Christian Middle Ages. Cassirer first notes that what Pico sets
up "as the distinctive privilege of man is the almost unlimited *power of self-transformation* at
his disposal. Man is that being to whom no particular form has been prescribed and assigned. He
possesses the power of entering into any form whatever." He then goes on to posit—along lines
that may call for slight modification in light of our own engagement with the medieval mystical thinkers—that "what is novel in the idea lies not in its content, but rather in the *value* Pico
places on this content. For it is an extraordinarily bold step of Pico's to reverse at this point the
conventional metaphysical and theological estimate. The latter proceeds from the basic notion
that the highest and indeed in the end the only value belongs to what is immutable and eternal.
This notion pervades Plato's theory of knowledge and Aristotle's metaphysics and cosmology.
With them is joined the medieval religious world-view, which sets the goal of all human activity
in eternity, and which sees in the multiplicity, in the mutability, in the inconstancy of human
action but a sign of its vanity" (331).
    Taking the Platonic idea of man as created without faculties or equipment, Pico modifies
that idea significantly by insisting that it is God, or the "Supreme Architect," who wills such
nudity or indetermination, precisely to encourage the freedom of technological innovation and
self-transformation. Departing thus from Platonic and Aristotelian valuations of unity, immuta-
bility, and eternity, Pico would bring to expression the divine affirmation of multiform, variable,
and temporal-historical existence. If the technological supplement to human indetermination in
Plato is thought in terms of struggle and transgression against the gods, in Pico it is thought as
sponsored or willed by the divine, such that the indeterminate and creative human mirrors in
its freedom the freedom of divine creativity itself. As I will argue below, such an affirmation of
human freedom, even in its technological forms, is in fact not foreign to much earlier Christian
thought. Following Cassirer in this view of the distinctively modern accents in Pico, Dufour
writes that "this Platonic graft effected by Pico within monotheism entails nothing less than a
revolution: the free will [*libre arbitre*] is henceforth established within Christianity" (*On achève
bien les hommes*, 27). While Dufour's account does very productively highlight the significance
of the neotenic figure in modern thought from Pico through Charles de Bovelles, Montaigne,
Charron and Erasmus, to Kant and the Romantics, its emphasis on the revolutionary character
of Pico could lead one to overlook, as Dufour does, the important precursors to Pico within theological tradition, an oversight worth noting, I think, because it seems to shape Dufour's position
on the theological and religious significance of the neotenic.
    47. Looking ahead to chapter 5, I note that Samuel Beckett sees a similar logic in the "purga-
torial" character of Joyce's *Wake*, whose flow and vitality are a function, precisely, of the work's

The turn to Pico is notable in recent thinkers such as Agamben and, as I'll note below, Marion, for whom the issues at stake in Pico's Renaissance humanism achieve new significance in relation to current worries over the indetermination or instability of the human—or over its slippage into the posthuman. As Agamben puts it, aiming to counter common misconceptions, what Pico's humanism brings to light is not the security but in fact the "precariousness of the human," its lack of clear place and hence secure definition within the order of the world: "The humanist discovery of man is the discovery that he lacks himself, the discovery of his irremediable lack of *dignitas*."[48] Agamben's argument that Pico's humanism is actually about man's lack of *dignitas*, which means not dignity so much as rank or place, is made, of course, in light of Pico's famous "manifesto of humanism," his oration known (incorrectly) as *De hominis dignitate*, "On the Dignity of Man"—a title not given by Pico to what he wrote as an introductory speech for the public disputation of his 900 theses, which were published in December of 1486 but never publicly debated thanks to the findings of a papal commission that some were heretical.[49]

Recounting the story of man's creation by God, the "Oration" traces man's universality (often associated with the theme of man as a microcosm joining the spiritual and the material) to his originary lack of proper place or nature, a lack that actually grounds the human freedom of decision and self-fashioning:

> When the work was finished, the Craftsman kept wishing that there were someone to ponder the plan of so great a work, to love its beauty, to wonder at its vastness. Therefore, when everything was done (as Moses and Timaeus bear witness), He finally took thought concerning the creation of man. But there was not among His archetypes that from which

---

lacking both the security of heaven and the stasis of hell. As Cassirer puts it with respect to Pico: "The heavenly intelligences are blessed in contemplating divinity—and this beatitude is a possession accorded them forever: for them it can never be troubled or diminished. Mere natural creatures, plants and animals, lead their lives within a narrowly limited circle and within a uniform and ever-repeated rhythm of existence. Their instinct impels them to follow certain paths, and within the channels of this instinct they move with unconscious security. But to man this security is denied. He must be forever seeking and choosing his own path: and this choice carries with it for him a perpetual danger" (Cassirer, "Giovanni Pico della Mirandola," 330).

48. Agamben, *The Open*, 30.

49. See Paul Oskar Kristeller's introduction to the oration in *The Renaissance Philosophy of Man*, ed. Ernst Cassirer, Paul Oskar Kristeller, and John Herman Randall, Jr. (Chicago: University of Chicago Press, 1948), 217.

he could fashion a new offspring, nor was there in His treasure-house anything which He might bestow on His new son as an inheritance, nor was there in the seats of all the world a place where the latter might sit to contemplate the universe. . . . At last the best of the artisans ordained that that creature to whom He had been able to give nothing proper to himself should have joint possession of whatever had been peculiar to each of the different kinds of being. He therefore took man as a creature of indeterminate nature [*indiscretae opus imaginis*] and, assigning him a place in the middle of the world addressed him thus: "Neither a fixed abode nor a form that is thine alone nor any function peculiar to thyself have we given thee, Adam, to the end that according to thy longing and according to thy judgment thou mayest have and possess what abode, what form, and what functions thou thyself shalt desire. The nature of all other beings is limited and constrained within the bounds of laws prescribed by Us. Thou, constrained by no limits, in accordance with thine own free will, in whose hand We have placed thee, shall ordain for thyself the limits of thy nature. . . . We have made thee neither of heaven nor of earth, neither mortal nor immortal, so that with freedom of choice and with honor, as though the maker and molder of thyself, thou mayest fashion thyself in whatever shape thou shalt prefer."[50]

As suggested by this crucial passage from the Oration, what is distinctive about man, as a poetic work, or as a creature who creates even himself, is his lack of limit or definition, his lack of distinction, or more precisely his

---

50. Giovanni Pico della Mirandola, "Oration on the Dignity of Man," trans. Elizabeth Livermore Forbes, in Cassirer, Kristeller, and Randall, *The Renaissance Philosophy of Man*, 224–25. The Latin, available in Pier Cesare Bori, *Plualità delle vie: Alle origini del "Discorso" sulla dignità umana di Pico della Mirandola* (Milan: Feltrinelli, 2000), 102–3, reads as follows:

Sed, opere consumato, desiderabat artifex esse aliquem qui tanti operis rationem perpenderet, pulchritudinem amaret, magnitudinem admiraretur. Idcirco iam rebus omnibus (ut moses Timeusque testantur) absolutis, de producendo homine postremo cogitavit. Verum nec erat in archetipis unde novam sobolem effingeret, nec in thesauris quod novo filio hereditarium largiretur, nec in subsellis totius orbis, ubi universi contemplator iste sederet. . . . Statuit tandem optimus opifex, ut cui dari nihil proprium poterat commune esset quicquid privatum singulis fuerat. Igitur hominem accepit indiscretae opus imaginis atque in mundi positum meditullio sic est alloquutus: "Nec certam sedem, nec propriam faciem, nec munus ullum peculiare tibi dedimus, o Adam, ut quam sedem, quam faciem, quae munera tute optaveris, ea, pro voto, pro tua sententia, habeas et possideas. Definita caeteris natura intra praescriptus a nobis leges cohercetur. Tu, nullis angustiis cohercitus, pro tuo arbitrio, in cuius manu te posui, tibi illam prefinies. . . . Nec te celestem neque terrenum, neque mortalem neque immortalem fecimus, ut tui ipsius quasi arbitrarius honorariusque plastes et fictor, in quam malueris tute formam effingas."

lack, as a work, of distinctive resemblance to any definite model or archetype: his being, in short, the open and ongoing work of an "indiscrete image." This is perhaps the most straightforward, if the least common, or even
until now nonexistent, translation of the key phrase from the lines where
God takes man as *indiscretae opus imaginis*, the work of an indiscrete image, and it suggests well the theological version of my central hypothesis
here: that the worklike or poetic character of the human creature, as image
of God, is bound inextricably with that image's lack of secure definition, its
lack of clear and distinct model or form, its being a nature without determination.[51] As in the deeper traditions of mystical thought I will explore,
where the creative human creature is created as such in the image of an
unimaginable Creator, so here in Pico, who is an important early modern
heir to those traditions, the human is like an active work of art, a living image whose vitality is a function of that image's very lack of fixed or distinct
type, form, model, or structure.[52]

᛫᭡᭡᭡᭡᛫

This poetic human and its indefinite divine image find one another also
at the center of a two-page text by Jorge Luis Borges. Indeed, Borges's "Everything and Nothing" might be taken as offering an alternate subtitle for
the book at hand, and as articulating another version of its thesis. Imagin-

---

51. Other renderings out of the Latin of this *indiscretae opus imaginis*, both through their
individual meanings and perhaps especially through their necessary multiplicity, suggest much—
but necessarily not all—of what is at stake in such an image. Elisabeth Livermore Forbes gives
two different versions: the "creature of indeterminate nature" in her translation cited above and,
in an earlier version, "the function of a form not set apart" (*Journal of the History of Ideas* 3
[1942]: 348.). Other English versions give "a work of indeterminate form" and "this creature
of indeterminate image" (see, respectively, On the Dignity of Man, trans. Charles Glenn Wal-
lis [New York: Bobbs-Merrill, 1965], 4; and Oration On the Dignity of Man [Chicago: Henry
Regnery, 1956], 6). The English translator of Agamben's text gives "created without a definite
model" (*The Open*, 29). Similar clusters of meaning are operative in the Italian renderings *opera di tipo indefinito, opera dall'immagine non definita*, and *opera di natura indefinita*, in the
French *cette oeuvre de type indéfini*, and in the German *Geschöpf von Unbestimmter Gestalt*—
in, respectively, Bruno Cicognani, *Dignità dell'uomo [De Hominis dignitate]*, 3rd ed. (Florence:
Le Monnier, 1943); Saverio Marchignoli, in Bori, *Plualità delle vie*, 103; Fabio Sante Pignagnoli,
La Dignità dell'uomo (Bologna, 1960), 75; Pierre-Marie Cordier, *Jean Pic de la Mirandole, ou
"La plus pure figure de l'humanisme chrétien"* (Paris: Nouvelles Éditions Debresse, 1957), 125;
and *De hominis dignitate, Über die Würde des Menschen: Lateinisch-deutsch* (Hamburg: Felix
Meiner Verlag, 1990), 5.

52. In rendering *imago* by *natura*, Pignagnoli notes that he does not intend the
Aristotelian-Thomistic *species* or *physis* but something like *struttura* (*La Dignità dell'uomo*,
75–76).

ing a meeting between Shakespeare, figure for the modern poetic genius, and his Creator God, who speaks from the whirlwind, Borges understands the image relation between the two not in terms of secure foundation and lucid comprehension, such that in finding his God Shakespeare would find and know himself, but rather in terms of darkness and abyss, which themselves prove to be the ground of an infinite creation that entails infinite self-creation. "History adds that before or after dying [Shakespeare] found himself in the presence of God and said to him: 'I, who have been so many men in vain, want to be one and myself.' The voice of God answered him from a whirlwind: 'I, too, am not I; I have dreamed the world as you dreamed your work, my Shakespeare, and among the forms in my dream are you, who like I are many and no one.'"[53] Well acquainted with the traditions of apophatic and mystical theology from Dionysius and Eriugena onward, up to and including Joyce, Borges appeals here indirectly to those traditions and to the anthropological insight they yield.[54] God, indetermi-

53. Jorge Luis Borges, "Everything and Nothing" (English title and Spanish text), from *El Hacedor* (1960), in Jorge Luis Borges, *Obras Completas II: 1952–1972* (Barcelona Emecé Editores, 1996), 182. I have followed exactly here neither the translation of James Irby, in Jorge Luis Borges, *Everything and Nothing* (New York: New Directions, 1999), 77–78, nor that of Andrew Hurley, in Jorge Luis Borges, *Collected Fictions* (New York: Penguin Books, 1999), 320. The Spanish reads as follows: "La historia agrega que, antes o después de morir, se supo frente a Dio y le dijo: 'Yo, que tantos hombres he sido en vano, quiero ser uno y yo.' La voz de Dios le contestó desde un torbellino: 'Yo tampoco soy; yo soñé el mundo como tú soñaste to obra, mi Shakespeare, y entre las formas de mi suño estabas tú, que como yo eres muchos y nadie.'" This scenario can be read as indebted to William Hazlitt and other interpreters of Shakespeare. The fuller context of the Hazlitt essay Borges evokes, "Shakespeare's Genius," is worth quoting more fully:

> The striking peculiarity of Shakespeare's mind was its generic quality, its power of communication with all other minds—so that it contained a universe of thought and feeling within itself, and had no one peculiar bias or exclusive excellence more than another. He was just like any other man, but that he was like all other men. He was the least of an egotist that it was possible to be. He was nothing in himself, but he was all that others were, or that they could become. He not only had in himself the germs of every faculty and feeling, but he could follow them by anticipation, intuitively, into all their conceivable ramifications, through every change of fortune or conflict of passion, or turn of thought. He had "a mind reflecting ages past" and present: all the people that ever lived are there. There was no respect of persons with him. His genius shone equally on the evil and on the good, on the wise and the foolish, the monarch and the beggar. "All corners of the earth, kings, queens, and states, maids, matrons, nay, the secrets of the grave," are hardly hid from his searching glance. He was like the genius of humanity, changing places with all of us at pleasure, and playing with our purposes as with his own.

54. The linkage between Shakespeare and the theological lineage of Dionysius and Eriugena, or more generally between poetic genius and the *nihil* of theological creation, is made more explicitly in Borges's piece "From Someone to Nobody," in *Selected Non-Fictions*, ed. Eliot Weinberger (New York: Penguin Books, 1999). Here Borges traces, both within the history of God's

nate and unknowable, creates himself and is reflected in the human, who is likewise indeterminate or unknowable, and likewise creative—in such a way that the human, again like God, can, or must, be virtually anyone because at bottom it remains no one, virtually anything because at bottom no thing. If our technological humanity today seems to exercise a creative capacity that threatens human definition, in ways that recall the mystical, perhaps with the mystics we can rethink such indefinition as the ground of creation itself; and perhaps we can see in the technopoetic human, as the mystics saw in God, what Victor Hugo saw in Shakespeare when, as Borges reminds us, "he compared him to the ocean, which is the seedbed of all possible forms."

---

naming and within in the interpretation of Shakespeare, what he calls "a magnification to noth-ingness." In the biblical context, Borges notes, locutions concerning Jehovah, who walks in the garden in the cool of the day, who feels grief and jealousy and wrath, "is indisputably Someone, a corporal Someone whom the centuries will magnify and blur" (341), and the process of that magnification finds an exemplary instance in the theologies of Pseudo-Dionysius and Eriugena. If the former writes a theology about which Schopenhauer can say that it "is the only true one, but it has no content" (quoted at 342), the latter, the "Irish Irish," will read that theology to yield "a doctrine of a pantheistic nature: particular things are theophanies (revelations or appearances of the divine) and behind them there is God, who is the only reality, 'but who does not know what He is, because He is not a what, and is incomprehensible to Himself and to all intelligence.'" Borges continues: "He is not sapient, He is more than sapient; He is not good, He is more than good; He inscrutably exceeds and repels all attributes. John the Irishman, to define Him, uses the word nihilum, which is nothingness; God is the primordial nothingness of the creatio ex nihilo, the abyss where first the archetypes and then concrete beings were engendered. He is Nothing and Nobody; those who imagined him in this way did so in the belief that this was more than being a What or a Who. Similarly, Shankara teaches that all mankind, in a deep sleep, is the uni-verse, is God" (342).

The magnification to nothingness within the cult of God proves operative also within the cult of Shakespeare, Borges notes, while omitting that he too, in writing "Everything and Noth-ing," participates in that cult. He highlights those interpreters, from Johnson, Dryden, and Mau-rice Morgann to Coleridge, Hazlitt, and Hugo, who see Shakespeare in quasi-theological terms echoing or imaging terms operative in the apophatic mystics just noted. Hazlitt—"corroborating" Coleridge's likening of Shakespeare to a literary version of Spinoza's infinite God, "the universal which is potentially in each particular opened out to him . . . the substance capable of endless modifications" (Coleridge, quoted by Borges at 342)—could well be writing, with a slight change in terms, of Eriguena's God when he writes of Shakespeare: "He was just like any other man, but that he was like all other men. He was nothing in himself, but he was all that others were, or that they could become" (quoted by Borges at, 342; translation modified). For Borges, the "confused intuition" of the truth that "to be something is inexorably not to be all the other things" yields "this fallacy" wherein mankind imagines "that being nothing is more than being something and is, in some way, to be everything" (342). Perhaps a clarification of the intuition would hold that to be no one thing is to inhabit an inexhaustible potential.

⚶

"I am":
Technological Modernity, Theological Tradition,
and the Human in Question

Anxious response to the proliferation of new technologies often high-lights the apparent threat posed by such technologies, or by techno-science, to our "authentic" humanity, to our very life or nature, whose in-herent dignity and value would be ignored and violated by technological interference that subjects "human nature" or the "natural life" of human-ity to various forms of artificial manipulation, replication, or simulation. Technologies and techniques associated with genetic engineering, cloning, artificial life, and the like, feed an anxious reaction that aims to resecure, by delimiting and defending, the nature of the real and the reality of nature as these pertain to the human. Similar threats are perceived, and similar anxieties prove operative, in the proliferation of media culture and its tech-nologies, whose apparently infinite capacity for reproduction and simula-tion seem to call into question any unique reality at all, human or other-wise. The "authentic" human, both in terms of species being and in terms of the individual existence true to that being, appears threatened by the technological ability to copy, simulate, or fundamentally alter the human in both natural and cultural registers.[1] Furthermore, the perception of these threats to the properly human, or to human properties, and the reactive

1. Literary critic and theorist Geoffrey Hartman, e.g., highlights well the proximity of bio-logical and mediatic forms of reproduction in the generation of anxieties over authenticity, in his *Scars of the Spirit: The Struggle against Inauthenticity* (New York: Palgrave, 2002), x: "The ques-tion that arises, beyond whether realism as a style has reached its term, concerns interpersonal relations as well as the future of sensibility. Those equivocal simulacra, so real and yet unreal, can be playful as long as they leave the normative world untouched. If that world is not in ques-tion, the anxiety I have talked about remains manageable. Yet our present, immense, pixelish capacity for technological reproduction, including biological cloning, opens an alarming vista that extends Freud's discovery of the psyche as terra incognita with uncanny mechanisms and drives."

defense often go hand-in-hand with a perceived destruction or degradation of some tradition in which one imagines the human and its nature once to have been kept safe and sound—or sacred—in their proper value and dignity. Technological existence, the worry goes, threatens to "dehumanize" us individually and as a species, to dispossess or defeat the human itself. Hence, resistance to the technological, along with the "return" to tradition, intends to rescue the human, to resanctify and shore up the boundaries of its life and nature, to save its value and dignity. As Martin Heidegger suggests in his 1947 "Letter on Humanism," which treats the relation of human ethics to the fundamental ontology he attempts to develop in his 1927 masterwork *Being and Time*, such appeals to the values of tradition, or to the traditions of value, can be read as signs that the human, in the nature and ways of its life, finds itself fundamentally in question—and at a fundamental loss before such question. "The desire for an ethics presses ever more ardently for fulfillment," Heidegger notes, "as the obvious no less than the hidden perplexity [*Ratlosigkeit*] of man soars to immeasurable heights. The greatest care must be fostered upon the ethical bond at a time when technological man, delivered over to mass society, can be kept reliably on call only by gathering and ordering all his plans and activities in a way that corresponds to technology."[2]

Many voices in our current context, wanting or promising to save the human, seek to do so by removing it from just such perplexity or helplessness, by finding or at least positing in it something given or natural, and thus beyond question—a clear and definite "value." This is consistent with the possibility that the human's falling into question, prompted in especially acute ways by recent technological innovation, cannot but yield anxiety—and thus that the appeal to a definite human nature with inherent value or dignity serves a flight from that anxiety, by reducing the indefinite ground of a mood that is by definition without object to the delimited object or definite field of fear.[3] An indetermination of the human, in other words, brought to light by the technological and answered by anxiety, is often evaded or denied by a definition of the human whose potential loss

---

2. Martin Heidegger, "Letter on Humanism," in Heidegger, *Basic Writings*, rev. ed., ed. David Farrell Krell (San Francisco: Harper Collins, 1993), 255; for the German see "Brief Über den Humanismus," in *Wegmarken* (1967; rev. ed., Frankfurt am Main: Vittorio Klostermann, 1996), 353. Hereafter cited parenthetically as LH, with English pagination followed by German.

3. On such a definition of anxiety in contrast to fear, see *Being and Time* §40, as well as the indispensable ground for Heidegger's analysis in Kierkegaard's *The Concept of Anxiety*, trans. Reider Thomte (Princeton: Princeton university Press, 1980), which I treat in my essay "Possibility and Passivity in Kierkegaard: The Anxieties of Don Giovanni and Abraham," in *Journal of the American Academy of Religion* 62, no. 2 (1994).

can thus be made the object of fear, which by contrast to anxiety and its indeterminate ground, one can take hold of or manage so as to defend against it. One conjures a definite figure of the human, whose loss might be feared as object, in order to avoid the more unsettling anxiety that conditions the human as indefinite structure of possibility. The rhetoric of danger today, bound with the appeal to a value and tradition that would clearly define the human so as to save it, can thus lead one to suspect an unquestioned certainty, masking anxiety, that the human has a definition, as well as an assumption that knowledge of that definition is essential to saving the human we value.

Overlooked or underplayed within a good part of the discourse on the dangers posed by technology to the human is the distinctive capacity of the human, implicitly acknowledged by the anxious response itself, to "lose" itself—to pass or slip by its "own" means from its authentic or proper mode of existence, its true self-possession, toward an inauthentic or dispossessed mode of existence, which is taken to "dehumanize." After all, who other than the human being runs the risk of invention or activity that threatens to alter so fundamentally the being at stake? Also overlooked are the senses in which tradition, and indeed, most prominently here, Christian tradition, not only may not yield a stable conception of the human but may well suggest that the human has in the end no single or stable conception. "Tradition" is more complex and more fluid than the anxious appeals to (or, for that matter, smug dismissals of) tradition usually grant, just as the "human" may be defined by the lack or instability of its definition—and hence by its irreducibility to "value," at least if value is a function of the modern subject's objectification of being.

One can well argue, as Heidegger does, that "through the characterization of something as 'a value' what is so valued is robbed of its worth. That is to say, by the assessment of something as a value what is valued is admitted only as an object for man's estimation. But what a thing is in its Being is not exhausted by its being an object, particularly when objectivity takes the form of value. Every valuing, even where it values positively, is a subjectivizing. It does not let beings: be. Rather, valuing lets beings: be valid—solely as the objects of its doing. The bizarre effort to prove the objectivity of values does not know what it is doing" (LH, 251 [349]). What Heidegger objects to here in the logic of value—namely, the reduction of all being to the status of object for an estimating or willing human subjectivity—he argues to be operative also in a technological modernity likewise grounded in the metaphysics of subjectivity. To the degree that such an argument holds, those who resist the technological today in the name of human value may well deceive themselves and, indeed, recapitulate the very logic they seek to escape. At the same time, if Heidegger's critique of humanism offers ground for a productive response to the discourse of human value, his thinking on technology may itself call for revision, insofar as it imagines the technological primarily according to the metaphysics that undergirds humanism. In what follows, then, we might ask, both with Heidegger and in resistance to him, whether—and how—the ostensible threat of technology to the human might not prove to be less an extension of modern metaphysics and its humanism than an instance where thinking could in fact "risk a shock that could for the first time cause perplexity concerning the *humanitas* of *homo humanus* and its basis. . . . In this way, it could awaken a reflection . . . that thinks not only about man but also about the 'nature' of man, not only about the nature but even more primordially about the dimension in which the essence of man, determined by Being itself, is at home [*heimisch ist*]" (LH, 248 [346]; translation modified). If, as much recent thought associated with the posthuman suggests, our technological existence can be seen to unsettle more than to extend the modern metaphysics of subjectivity, it can also be seen to diverge from those diverse metaphysical humanisms for which "the *humanitas* of *homo humanus* is determined with regard to an already established interpretation of nature, history, world, and the ground of world, that is, of beings as a whole" (LH, 225 [321]). While for Heidegger the humanism of *homo faber*, as operative in Marxism, for example, remains no less metaphysical and thus no less subject to critique than the humanism of Christianity's *imago Dei*, I would ask whether both technological humanity and the traditions of the *imago Dei* do not lend themselves also to alternative readings. Before turning to those readings in chapters 3 and 4, respectively, I will sketch out my take on Heidegger's understanding of the interplay between the metaphysics of technological modernity and the metaphysics of Christian theological tradition.

⟨∽⟩

Heidegger's critique of technoscientific culture, like his thought more broadly, can be read to involve an unresolved tension between, on the one hand, a longing for some human authenticity that would stand at odds with the main currents of technological culture (as uprooting, dislocating, deindividuating) and, on the other hand, an acknowledgment of the distinctively human capacity for just the kind of inauthenticity that technological culture itself threatens—an inauthenticity that may be, from Heidegger's own perspective as well as from the perspective of more recent theorizations, inherent to creative possibility itself. Such ambivalence and tension shape likewise Heidegger's assessment of the relation between modernity's technological culture and the heritage of Christian theology in the West. Thus, his account of the modern metaphysics grounding technological culture traces it back to the ontotheology of Christian tradition even as his critique of that same metaphysics and culture draws deeply on a line of Christian thinking that one can trace from Augustine through Luther to Kierkegaard.

First, then, we should consider the relation of modern metaphysics and its technological culture to Christian ontotheology in Heidegger's thought. As he argues, with immeasurable influence, the metaphysics of the modern age, which would ground a scientific thinking and a technological existence that threaten to become all-consuming, interprets being in terms of objectivity and defines truth in terms of the certainty achieved by the thinking human subject. The human subject secures such certainty in and through the representation of objective being as constant presence and calculability—to the point of reducing the world itself to a view or picture, a "worldview," produced by that subject alone, who thus becomes the ground and measure, if not already the maker, of all that is. If such a reduction of world to picture has roots running deep within idealist traditions going back to Plato, it reaches its extreme in a modernity that grows from even as it extends medieval Christian thought. Through this reduction of being to objective presence, the subject frames or produces a world that appears, in every part and as a whole, to remain comprehensible and calculable to scientific knowing and therefore subject to the control and exploitation of humanity's technological machinations.

If Heidegger's best-known writings on technology and science—above all "The Question concerning Technology"—date from the postwar period, his earlier writings seem to me indispensable for understanding his thought on technoscientific modernity, especially insofar as they cast important light on that modernity's relation to Christian theological tradition. In his *Contributions to Philosophy (from Enowning)*, a second major work written in 1936–38 about a decade after *Being and Time* but published only posthumously, Heidegger traces the technological subject of scientific modernity to a Christian theology that interprets all being as made, as *ens creatum*, and God the Creator as maker and hence as "highest being," a certain and extant cause, which, according to the logic of efficient causality or sufficient reason, provides a first principle on which one counts to make all other being intelligible. As modern man frees himself from that God and comes increasingly to rely on himself, he becomes indeed the very measure of being's intelligibility and thus the maker whose calculative think-ing yields technological power.[4]

In this respect, the ostensibly post- or anti-Christian thinking of mod-ern science, modern technology, and their shared founding metaphysics actually extends and perpetuates the domination of Christianity's on-totheological concept of God as "highest 'being,'" or the "most 'being'" (ὄντως ὄν)—the "source of 'being'" and the "manufacturing cause of all beings" (B, 172 [243]). By taking over the creative or productive function, modernity's technoscientific humanity can thus remain in line with "the Christian-biblical interpretation of beings as ens creatum" (B, 92 [132]). Just as the Creator God represents in his mind that which he creates, such that the truth of creation consists in its correspondence to the divine ar-chetype, so the modern subject, by means of its representational activity, turns productive in a technological sense, within a metaphysics counting truth as correspondence. If modern metaphysics takes truth as "correctness of representing (intellectus)," Heidegger insists, it repeats and extends that relationship to beings operative in the Christian understanding of all beings as represented in the intellectus divinus, "a relationship that continues to be correct only under the presupposition that omne ens (Deus creator ex-cepted) is ens creatum—whereby, seen 'ontologically,' Deus too is grasped in terms of creatio, which proves how crucial the story of creation in the Old Testament is for this kind of 'philosophy'" (B, 244–45 [349–50]; trans-lation modified). This line of argument from 1936–38 stands out likewise in Heidegger's important lectures from the same period (1935), appearing in 1953 under the title An Introduction to Metaphysics, which elucidate this sense in which modern metaphysics—in and through mathematics, calculation, and the technology these sustain—extends a Christianity that "reinterprets the Being of beings as Being-created": "Because beings have been created by God—that is, have been thought rationally in advance—then as soon as the relation of creature to creator is dissolved, while at the same time human reason attains predominance, and even posits itself as absolute, the Being of beings must become thinkable in the pure thinking of mathematics. Being as calculable in this way, Being as set into calculation,

4. Along these two lines, one can see the two forms of ontotheology that Jean-Luc Marion identifies and elucidates so carefully in the thought of Descartes: the ontotheology of God as causa, which grounds all beings as causata, and the ontotheology of the ego cogitans, which represents all beings as cogitata. On this double ontotheology in the father of modern philosophy, see Marion's major study Sur le prisme métaphysique de Descartes (Paris: Presses Universitaires de France, 1986), translated into English by Jeffrey L. Kosky as On Descartes' Metaphysical Prism (Chicago: University of Chicago Press, 1999).

makes beings into something that can be ruled in modern, mathematically structured technology."⁵

Along these lines, Heidegger argues that the linkage between rational conception and creation in theological contexts, where all created being preexists in the mind of God, carries over into modernity through the linkage between a representational, mathematical, and calculative thought and the "making" or "producing" of a technological culture. Centered no longer in God but in the rational and willful human subject of representation, who frames being in mathematical terms by projecting the ground plan according to which alone beings might appear, modern metaphysics thinks the presence of beings in terms of their calculability and disposability for what Heidegger names the "machination" of technological humanity. The mathematical character of such metaphysics, one should note, consists not primarily in its use of number but in this setting-ahead-of-time the secure ground plan that establishes the conditions of possibility for the appearance of beings as they appear.⁶

"Machination" (*Machenschaft*), then, which concerns the human comportment of making, refers more fundamentally in Heidegger to an interpretation of beings—in terms of making and being made—that derives from a Christian, medieval theology of God as *actus* and *causa*. In that theology, on Heidegger's account, the self-giving or self-manifesting of Being that would have been thought by the Greeks in terms of *physis*, is replaced and obscured by a reduction of appearances to their first cause (in what Jean-Luc Marion names an alienation of the phenomenon):⁷

> The medieval concept of *actus* already covers over what is ownmost to the inceptual Greek interpretation of beingness. It is in this connection that what belongs to machination now presses forward more clearly and that *ens* becomes *ens creatum* in the Judaeo-Christian notion of

---

5. Martin Heidegger, *Introduction to Metaphysics*, trans. Gregory Fried and Richard Polk (New Haven: Yale University Press, 2000), 207; *Einführung in die Metaphysik*, 6th ed. (Tübingen: Max Niemeyer, 1998), 147–48. Hereafter cited parenthetically as *IM*, with English followed by German pagination.

6. "*Ta mathēmata* means for the Greeks that which man knows in advance in his observation of whatever is and in his intercourse with things: the corporeality of bodies, the vegetable character of plants, the animality of animals, the humanness of man" (Heidegger, "Age of the World Picture," 118 [78]).

7. For a treatment of this alienation in Marion's analysis of modern metaphysics, see my "Blindness and the Decision to See: On Revelation and Reception in Jean-Luc Marion," in *Counter-Experiences: Reading Jean-Luc Marion*, ed. Kevin Hart (Notre Dame: University of Notre Dame Press, 2007).

creation, when the corresponding idea of god enters into the picture. Even if one refuses crudely to interpret the idea of creator, what is still essential is beings' being-caused. The cause-effect connection becomes the all-dominating (god as *causa sui*). That is an essential distancing from φύσις and at the same time the crossing toward the emergence of machination as what is ownmost to beingness in modern thinking. The mechanistic *and* biological ways of thinking are always merely consequences of the hidden interpretation of beings in terms of machination. (*B*, 88 [126–27])

For Heidegger, then, modern metaphysics and its technological machination, derived from and preserving a Christian ontotheology of the *ens creatum*, reduce Being—and hence, I'll emphasize, possibility—to the scope of what actually is or can be determined in a presence that stands at the disposal of a rational (now human) subject who, in thus reducing Being to the actual or extant through the activity of representational thought, exercises a will to mastery and subjects all that is or could be to the calculation and control of the rational-technological. The real failure of modern metaphysics and its technological culture, from this perspective, is its overly restricted sense of possibility—which excludes any possibility not reducible to actuality or, in other words, which renders impossible the thought or representation of "the impossible." An essential correlate of machination, the ideal of "unconditional controllability" suggests that "the single thing that is impossible is the word and representation of 'impossible'"; it involves "the utmost intensification of the power of calculation" and hence "the most indifferent and most blind denial of the incalculable" (*B*, 311, 314 [442, 446]). This distinctive attitude of modern thought and culture assumes that

everything "is made" and "can be made" if one only musters the "will" for it. But that this "will" is precisely what has already placed and in advance reduced what might be possible and above all necessary—this is already not appreciated [*Verkannt*] and left outside any questioning. For this will, which makes everything, has already subscribed to machination, that interpretation of beings as re-presentable and re-presented. In one respect re-presentable means "accessible to intention and calculation"; in another respect it means "advanceable through pro-duction and execution." But thought in a fundamental manner, all of this means that beings as such are re-presentable and that only the re-presentable *is*. For machination, what apparently offers resistance and a limit to machination is only the material for further elaboration and the impulse for progress and an occasion for extension and enlargement. (*B*, 76 [108–9]; translation modified)

In this notion of machination, furthermore, Heidegger appeals not only to modern man's preoccupation with technological making—as a production that excludes the Greek notion of *physis* as self-presencing—but also to the restless distraction of modern Western culture, the ceaseless "business" of a thinking and living that prove forgetful of Being and preoccupied with beings, a thinking and living in which such technological making reigns over a humanity and world that themselves, under such reign, grow smaller and emptier—and precisely because they are no longer open to real question. Along these lines, the machination of modern culture marks a technological and natural-scientific tendency that finds also a cultural and social-scientific correlate in what Heidegger names "newspaper science," which he understands as that pervasive public thinking and discourse in which "all" is assumed to be universally and immediately accessible and understandable, a thinking and discourse that enact the "total lack of questioning" characteristic of modernity. "'Newspaper' and 'machine' are meant essentially as the dominant ways of ultimate objectification, which forges ahead (in modernity, the objectification that advances to completion) by sucking up all concreteness [*Sachhaltigkeit*] of beings and taking these [beings] only as occasions for live-experience [*als Anlaß des Erlebens*]" (*B*, 109 [158]). Both newspaper and machine, as ways of objectification, are ways also for the reduction of possibility to actuality. They are forms, then, of the "leveling" that is effected in and through the subjection of everything whatsoever to the logic of technological control—and of everybody to the assumption that the project of such control is the only possible project. This assumption, whose hidden goal (or ground) may well be a "total boredom" (*B*, 109 [157]) whose significance today should not be underestimated, is promoted and sustained by the kind of bewitching spell that machination and newspaper science cast over a modern humanity that might otherwise seem "disenchanted."

Much like the "disenchantment of the world" (*die Entzauberung der Welt*) famously defined and analyzed by Max Weber in his 1918 lecture "Science as a Vocation," which assumes that the world is comprehensible in objective terms and thereby controllable on the basis of rational calculation, and which thus views the unknown only as the not-yet-known and never as unknowable, machination and newspaper science disallow the possibility that anything could remain beyond actualization in some present being, resistant to intention and calculation, or inaccessible to production or execution.[8] As Heidegger notes, however, such "disenchantment" tends toward yet another "enchantment," one bound up with a "bewitchment" by technicity that proves operative under the all-encompassing sway of machination, which signals already what Heidegger later names and understands as the "framework" or "enframing" of technology (*das Gestell*).[9]

> One is accustomed to calling the epoch of "civilization" one of *disenchantment* [Ent-*zauberung*], and this seems for its part exclusively to be the same as the total lack of questioning. However, it is exactly the opposite. One has only to know from where the enchantment comes. The answer: from the unrestrained domination of machination. When machination finally dominates and permeates everything, then there are no longer any conditions by which still actually to detect the enchantment [*Verzauberung*] and to protect oneself from it. The bewitchment by technicity [*die Behexung durch die Technik*] and its constantly self-surpassing progress are only *one* sign of this enchantment by vir-

8. Weber's classic lecture "Science as a Vocation" (Wissenschaft als Beruf) argues that the "intellectualist rationalization" characteristic of modernity, "created by science and by scientifically oriented technology," means "the knowledge or belief that if one but wished one *could* learn it [i.e., knowledge of the conditions under which one lives] at any time. Hence, it means that principally there are no mysterious incalculable [*unberechenbaren*] forces that come into play, but rather that one can, in principle, master all things by calculation [*durch Berechnen beherrschen könne*]. This means: the disenchantment of the world [*die Entzauberung der Welt*]." See "Science as a Vocation," in *From Max Weber: Essays in Sociology*, ed. H. H. Gerth and C. Wright Mills (New York: Oxford University Press, 946), 139; translation modified. For the German see Weber, *Gesammelte Aufsätze zur Wissenschaftslehre*, ed. Johannes Winckelmann (1922; Tübingen: J. C. B. Mohr, 1988), 594. See also, along with Weber's "disenchantment of the world," the "decay of the aura" in Walter Benjamin's influential analysis "The Work of Art in the Age of Mechanical Reproduction," in *Illuminations*, ed. Hannah Arendt (New York: Schocken Books, 1968). For an illuminating discussion of Benjamin and the Heidegger of "Age of the World Picture," see Samuel Weber, "Mass Mediauras, or Art, Aura, and Media in the Work of Walter Benjamin," in *Mass Mediauras: Form, Technics, Media* (Stanford: Stanford University Press, 1996).

9. "Man stands so decisively in subservience to the challenging-forth of enframing that he does not grasp enframing as a claim, that he fails to see himself as the one spoken to, and hence also fails in every way to hear in what respect he ek-sists, in terms of his essence, in a realm where he is addressed, so that he *can never* encounter only himself. / But enframing does not simply endanger man in his relationship to himself and to everything that is. As a destining, it banishes man into the kind of revealing that is an ordering. Where this ordering holds sway, it drives out every other possibility of revealing. Above all, enframing conceals that revealing which, in the sense of *poiêsis*, lets what presences come forth into appearance" (Heidegger, "The Question concerning Technology," in *Basic Writings*, ed. Krell, 332; for the German see "Die Frage nach der Technik," in *Vorträge und Aufsätze* [Stuttgart: Neske, 1954], 31).

tue of which everything presses forth into calculation, usage, breeding, manageability, and regulation. Even "taste" now becomes a matter for this regulation, and everything depends on a "good ambiance." The average becomes better and better, and by virtue of this bettering it secures its dominion always more irresistibly and more inconspicuously. (B, 86–87 [124])

Like the givenness and pervasiveness of "mood" in *Being and Time*, where one always inhabits mood but most often without its being made at all conspicuous—or like the enframing of technology as defined in Heidegger's later work, where the dominant mode of revealing not only excludes all other modes but also, at the same time, hides itself—so here machination's disenchantment is tied intimately to a bewitchment that is all the more thoroughgoing insofar as it remains inconspicuous. The spell of disenchantment, under the reign of regulation, is precisely that which cannot be regulated.

Through its inconspicuous pervasiveness, the bewitching assumption that everything can or should be pressed forth "into calculation, usage, breeding, manageability, and regulation," the subjection of all being to machination, or the exclusion from appearance *tout court* of any being not subject to machination, yields what Heidegger names "the gigantic": a pervasive, all-consuming frame whose enormity effects a "diminution" of being and a "hollowing" of man. The "gigantic" is to be understood here less in terms of quantity and more in terms of quality, less in terms of large numbers and more in terms of the predominance of the mathematical—which itself, again, concerns not so much the reduction of the real to number but more the unquestioned presupposition of a ground plan for the appearance of any and all being in terms of representation and production. "The gigantic [*das Riesenhafte*] unfolds in the calculative and thus always manifests the 'quantitative,' but is itself—as the unconditioned domination of representing and producing—a denial of the truth of be-ing in favor of 'what belongs to reason' and what is 'given,' a denial that is not in control of itself and, in heightened self-certainty, is simply never aware of itself" (B, 313 [442]). Within the gigantic, the objectification of all being, its reduction through machination to a representation and production grounded in the subject who becomes midpoint of all that is, is itself always already given, and so never the matter of a true questioning or decision. "The gigantic is grounded upon the decidedness and invariability of 'calculation' and is rooted in a prolongation of subjective re-presentation [*Vor-stellens*] unto the whole of beings. . . . The gigantic shows the magnitude of the self-certain *subjectum* which builds everything on its own representing and producing" (*B*, 310–11 [441]).

This modern extreme of the human subject's self-assertion, which exceeds the control or even awareness of those who find themselves operating within it, paradoxically entails a hollowing of man and a diminution of the world he encounters. The world now becomes a vast, boring emptiness that offers no possibility that truly grips one's existence, an emptiness or withholding of possibility that tends to yield the obsessive, compensatory, but necessarily self-defeating longing for "lived experience."[10] The diminishing of the world, as a function of the world's being reduced to controllability, is a metaphysical and not a quantitative matter; that is, even if the world is indeed growing "smaller" in terms of objectively measurable distances (spatial, temporal), the smallness that really matters is more fundamentally a consequence of the fact that "the being-character of beings," which entails the incalculable openness of their possibility, is dissolved or effaced as all beings are subjected to the logic of actuality that founds control (*B*, 348 [495]). When experience itself falls under the imperative of such control, the search for "lived experience," whose authentic form requires the incalculable, can only be self-defeating.

Just as Max Weber notes, within his sober discussion of disenchantment, the misdirected yearning among his day's youth for an "experience" that would refuse the cold demands of a rationalized world,[11] so Heidegger highlights, in the world of machination and newspaper science, the experiential emptiness that spreads when all, including experience, is subjected to a project of calculation and control so boundless that we do not even see it—even as it threatens to deprive us of any genuine, which is to say unprogrammed or veritably decisive experience.

The metaphysical diminishing of the "world" produces a hollowing-out of man. The relation to a being as such loses, in and with this being, all

---

10. On such withholding of possibility and its relation to boredom, see Heidegger's brilliant analyses in *The Fundamental Concepts of Metaphysics* (*FC*).

11. See "Science as a Vocation," 149 [605]; translation modified: "What is hard for modern man, and especially for the younger generation, is to measure up to the everyday [*einem solchen Alltag gewachsen zu sein*]. The ubiquitous chase for 'experience' [*Alles Jagen nach dem 'Erlebnis'*] stems from this weakness; for it is weakness not to be able to countenance the stern seriousness of our fateful times. . . . Those of our youth are in error who react to all this by saying, 'Yes, but we happen to come to lectures in order to experience something more than [*um etwas anderes zu erleben als*] mere analyses and statements of fact.' The error is that they seek in the professor something different than the one who stands before them. They crave a leader and not a teacher."

purpose; the relation as comportment of man extends itself only to itself and to its methodical [*plannmässig*] enactment. The feeling of feeling feels only feeling, feeling itself becomes the object of enjoyment. The "live-experience" attains the utmost of what is ownmost, lived experiences are lived. The lostness into beings is lived as capability of transforming "life" into the calculable whirlwind of empty circling around itself and of making this capability believable as something "true to life." (*B,* 348–49 [495])

As if already diagnosing the cultural and metaphysical conditions that yield "reality TV," Heidegger explicates the relation of modern technological culture—a culture not only of anxiety but of profound boredom—to an obsession with experience that cannot but involve "the most insipid 'sentimentality'" (*B,* 86 [123]).

The compensatory hunt for lived experience, within a world that risks the loss of genuine experience precisely insofar as all being is subjected to the logic of calculation, is woven together with several related phenomena typical of modern culture in Heidegger's day—and surely still in our own. "Acceleration" spreads and means not only "the mechanical increase of technical 'speeds'" but even more our "not-being-able-to-bear the stillness of hidden growth and awaiting; the mania for what is surprising, for what immediately sweeps [us] away and impresses [us], again and again in different ways." Related to the "anxiety of boredom," this culture of acceleration requires (or allows) that one "forget rapidly and . . . lose oneself in what comes next" (*B,* 84–85; [121]). Hence, in and through the spread of acceleration, aided and abetted by forgetting and self-loss, operates the "empty 'and-so-forth'" whose logic in turn supports "the outbreak of massiveness," where the masses "mount up only because numbers and the calculable already count as what is equally accessible to everyone" (*B,* 85 [121]). In the logic of that universal access, one should note the related development, likewise typical of mass culture, of the "divesting, publicizing, and vulgarizing of all attunement," which yield "the growing artificiality of every attitude and together with that the disempowering of the word" (*B,* 86 [123]). These interwoven phenomena constitute and express the "total lack of questioning" (*B,* 86 [123]) that Heidegger associates with the mass technological culture of machination and newspaper science—and he makes that association along lines I want to highlight that demonstrate his debt to Kierkegaard, and to the deeper lineage of Christian-Augustinian tradition.

In his critical analysis of the phenomena associated with machination and newspaper science, Heidegger extends and elaborates a position and a sensibility advanced already by Kierkegaard, notably in his 1846 work *The Present Age*, which can be read as both a deeply religious text and one of the modern West's first major critiques of media culture.[12] Kierkegaard argues there that our "age of advertisement and publicity" (*PA*, 35)—whose talkativeness "jabbers on incessantly about everything and nothing" and does away with the "vital" distinctions between "concealment and manifestation," "what is private and what is public" (*PA*, 69, 75, 72)—is distinguished by "the process of leveling" and "the victory of abstraction over the individual" (*PA*, 51, 52), the eclipse of any individual someone, or any concrete something, by an everyone or everything who can be only "no one" or "nothing": what Kierkegaard, foreshadowing Heidegger's figure of *das Man*, the "one" or the "they," names "the public." "In order that everything should be reduced to the same level," Kierkegaard writes, "it is first of all necessary to procure a phantom, its spirit, a monstrous abstraction, an all-embracing something which is nothing, a mirage—and that phantom is the public" (*PA*, 58). Setting the terms for Heidegger's analysis of the inauthentic "they" who comes to dominate through idle talk and curiosity the culture of machination and newspaper science, themselves correlative with "the gigantic," Kierkegaard's conception of the public traces its emergence to a press that, in a society where the individual is no longer "personally present," is "able to create that abstraction 'the public,' consisting of unreal individuals who never are and never can be united in an actual situation or organization—and yet are held together as a whole" (*PA*, 60). Like Heidegger's "they-self," which dwells anonymously as placeless medium of machination and newspaper science, Kierkegaard's "public" is an "everyone" whose abstraction amounts to no one; it contains or consumes all of us without appearing distinctly in any one of us who might answer for it. It is "everything and nothing, the most dangerous of all powers and the most insignificant: one can speak to a whole nation in the name of the public, and still the public will be less than a single real man" (*PA*, 63). When the concrete individual is supplanted or effaced by the abstract universality of humanity in general, or by the "numerical equality of man and man," or, in short, by the "monstrous nothing" that is "the public," then I am—or

---

12. Søren Kierkegaard, *The Present Age and Of the Difference between a Genius and an Apostle*, trans. Alexander Dru (New York: Harper Torchbooks, 1962); this edition hereafter cited parenthetically as *PA*. Published on its own in English, *The Present Age* first appeared in the final section of Kierkagaard's *A Literary Review*, available in an English translation by Alistair Hannay (New York: Penguin Classics, 2002).

we are—lost in "the unlimited panorama of abstract identity," which Kierkegaard understands to be "a sea of desert" that stands at odds with the
"reality of religion" (*PA*, 81).

Heidegger's critical analysis of the leveling effected by modernity's
technological and media culture should be understood both in relation to
the Kierkegaardian lineage and against the background of his own analyses,
in *Being and Time*, of Dasein's inevitable and constant "falling" into "idle
talk" and into the anonymous social being of the "they."[13] The deracinating and dehumanizing threat operative in technological and media culture
follows a logic already discernable in that fallen form of discourse, idle talk
(*das Gerede*), whose collective, anonymous subject is everyone and no one,
a subject that moves everywhere and nowhere, "curious" about everything
and nothing. Curiosity, indeed, is the key mode of being whose analysis
yields insight into the character of idle talk and of *das Man*, and its distin-
guishing traits might be understood along spatial and temporal coordinates,
according to which curiosity wants to move everywhere at once. Always
on the move to the next novelty or entertainment, and thus neither leaving the time nor finding the place to dwell and reflect, to remember and
understand, curiosity is defined by the same logic that defines newspaper
science and its demand that all be always immediately "accessible" and
"understandable"—a demand that befits the total lack of questioning that
comes increasingly to define the modern age.

That total lack of questioning, one should note, like the thoughtlessness that Heidegger later sees at the heart of a modernity consumed by
research,[14] manifests itself in a mode of thought that is all too understanding and hence that excludes the possibility of any amazement in which *not*
understanding would, in fact, be the precondition of genuine—that is, truly
questioning or truly philosophical—thought: curiosity "does not seek the
leisure of tarrying observantly [*des betrachtenden Verweiliens*], but rather
seeks restlessness and excitement of continual novelty and changing encounters [*Unruhe und Aufregung durch das immer Neue und den Wechsel
des Begegnenden*]. In not tarrying [*In ihrem Unverweilen*] curiosity is concerned with the constant possibilities of *distraction* [*die ständige Möglich-
keit der Zerstreuung*]. Curiosity has nothing to do with observing entities
and marveling at them [*dem bewundernden Betrachten des Seienden*]—
θαυμάζειν. To be amazed to the point of not understanding is something in

---

13. See also the role of the "public" in a later text like "Letter on Humanism."
14. For a brief and relatively accessible discussion of research and thoughtlessness, see Heidegger's "Memorial Address" in *Discourse on Thinking* (New York: Harper and Row, 1966).

which it has no interest."[15] From this perspective, the "enchantment" of a culture dominated by machination and newspaper science appears wholly to lack genuine amazement. Having little capacity for the kind of reflection that might occur in a place and time of not understanding, or unknowing, the technological culture of curiosity, operative as much in the media as in scientific research, is at bottom a culture of distraction and dispersion.

> To be amazed to the point of not understanding is something in which [curiosity] has no interest. Rather it concerns itself with a kind of knowing, but just in order to have known. Both this *not tarrying* in the environment with which one concerns oneself, and this *distraction* by new possibilities, are constitutive items for curiosity; and upon these is founded the third essential characteristic of this phenomenon, which we call the character of *"never dwelling anywhere."* Curiosity is everywhere and nowhere. This mode of Being-in-the-world reveals a new kind of Being of everyday Dasein—a kind in which Dasein is constantly uprooting itself.[16]

Insofar as it thus targets the mode of being operative in curiosity, even as it suggests an intimate linkage and ambiguity between distracted, uprooted, and thus inauthentic curiosity and attentive, grounded, and hence authentic care (*Sorge*) or *cura*, Heidegger's critique of technological and media culture, against the deeper background of the critique of ontotheology, might be seen to derive in significant ways from an Augustinian thought of alienation. As in Augustine, where one's pretension to freedom is itself the sign and the enactment of one's bondage, so the knowing exercised by curiosity in Heidegger ignores the more fundamental not knowing of amazement and genuine questioning.

Taken as the unrestrained desire to look and to see, as a restless greed for inquiry and knowing without determined, productive, and hence justifiable end or purpose, curiosity has been met with deep suspicion, if not dread, and often prohibition and condemnation, throughout a Christian tradition shaped decisively by Augustine and subsequent heirs, such as Bernard of Clairvaux and Thomas Aquinas in the Middle Ages, Blaise Pascal in the early modern context, and on the later end, Kierkegaard and Heidegger themselves. In the pivotal book 10 of his *Confessions*, Augustine highlights

15. Martin Heidegger, *Being and Time*, trans. John Macquarrie and Edward Robinson (Oxford: Basil Blackwell), 216; for the German see *Sein und Zeit* (Tübingen: Max Niemeyer Verlag, 1986), 172 (in subsequent cites, English pagination is followed by the German).

16. Ibid., 217 [172–73].

the dangers of curiosity—the temptations and gratifications of the eye—
and its linkage to science, technology, art, and entertainment. "This fu-
tile curiosity masquerades under the name of science and learning [*nomine
cognitionis et scientiae*]," Augustine warns, "and since it derives from our
thirst for knowledge and sight is the principal sense by which knowledge
is acquired, in the Scriptures it is called *lust of the eyes* [*concupiscentia
oculorum*] [1 John 2:16]."[17] This concupiscence of the eye, an eagerness to
see or know simply for the sake of seeing or knowing, also proves operative
in relation to the technological and artistic creations and manipulations
of man, whose value is found not solely or primarily in their use to meet
basic needs or, still less, in the demands of religious devotion, but in the
gratuitous satisfaction they bring to an eye tempted by—and absorbed excessively in—the worldly:

> By every kind of art and the skill of their hands [*innumerabilia variis
> artibus et opificiis*] men make innumerable things—clothes, shoes, pot-
> tery, and other useful objects [*et cuiuscemodi fabricationibus*], besides
> pictures and various works which are the fruit of their imagination.
> They make them on a far more lavish scale than is required to satisfy
> their own modest needs or to express their devotion [*atque his usum
> necessarium atque moderatum et piam significationem longe transgre-
> dientibus*], and all these things are additional temptations to the eye,
> made by men who love the worldly things they make themselves but
> forget their own Maker and destroy what he made in them.[18]

Insofar as they exceed need and devotion, technological and artistic creation, for Augustine, threaten human being with distraction and forgetting,
for they draw astray the curious eyes that can mistake the world's beauty
and pleasures for God's. Perhaps the ultimate form of such distraction is
seen, for Augustine, in the sphere of entertainments, whose vanity is the
same as that of inquiry into nature:

> It is to satisfy this unhealthy curiosity that freaks and prodigies are put
> on show in the theater, and for the same reason men are led to inves-

---

17. Augustine *Confessions* 10.35. I cite the edition translated by. R. S. Pine-Coffin (New York:
Penguin Books, 1961); translation modified. The Latin text, edited by James J. O'Donnell and
published along with his extensive commentary by Oxford University Press (1992), is available in
a very useful electronic version on a Stoa Consortium/Perseus Project site accessible through the
following two URLs: http://www.stoa.org/hippo/ and http://ccat.sas.upenn.edu/jod/conf/.

18. Augustine, *Confessions* 10.35.

tigate the secrets of nature, which are irrelevant to our lives, although such knowledge is of no value to them and they wish to gain it merely for the sake of knowing [*ex hoc morbo cupiditatis in spectaculis exhibentur quaeque miracula, hinc ad perscrutanda naturae, quae praeter nos non est, operata proceditur, quae scire nihil prodest aliud quam scire scire homines cupiunt*]. It is curiosity, too, which causes men to turn to sorcery [*per artes magicas*] in the effort to obtain knowledge for the same perverted purpose. And it even invades our religion, for we put God to the test when we demand signs and wonders from him, not in the hope of salvation, but simply for the love of the experience [*hinc etiam in ipsa religione deus temtatur, cum signa et prodigia flagitantur, non ad aliquam salutem, sed ad solam experiantiam disiderata*].[19]

Thus understanding curiosity to constitute a morbid disease, operative in the human fascination with scientific inquiry, technological innovation, and autotelic entertainment and experience, and thus articulating for theological reasons a moral sensibility that condemns the "concupiscence of the eyes" for its sinful gratuitousness and self-involvement, Augustine sets the stage for much of subsequent thought and culture in the West while drawing decisively on selected elements of biblical tradition.[20]

Just as the story of the Fall in Genesis suggests the mortal dangers of seeking knowledge where it is forbidden, beyond God's dictated boundaries, and just as Proverbs likens the insatiability of eyes to the abysses of hell,[21] so in 1 John, Augustine and his heirs find a condemnation of the eyes for their lustful, self-involved attachment to a transient world—and thus for their neglect of an everlasting Father: "Do not love the world or the things in the world. If anyone loves the world, love for the Father is not in him. For all that is in the world, the lust of the flesh and the lust of the eyes and the pride of life [ὅτι πᾶν τὸ ἐν τῷ κόσμῳ, ἡ ἐπιθυμία τῆς σαρκὸς καὶ ἡ ἐπιθυμία τῶν

19. Augustine, *Confessions* 10.35.

20. For an important account of the role played by the Augustinian condemnation of curiosity in the West, especially in relation to the emergence of a modern science in which the self-assertion of reason will require the triumph of theoretical curiosity over that condemnation, see Hans Blumenberg's major study *The Legitimacy of the Modern Age*, trans. Robert Wallace (Cambridge: MIT Press, 1983), esp. pt. 3, "The 'Trial' of Theoretical Curiosity." An illuminating discussion, especially on differences between morbid curiosity and healthy wonder, can be found also in Lorraine Daston and Katherine Park's engaging work *Wonders and the Order of Nature* (New York: Zone Books, 2001), esp. 120–26 ("Curiosity and the Preternatural") and all of chapter 8, "The Passions of Enquiry."

21. See Proverbs 27:20, "Insatiable are Sheol and the abyss, insatiable also the eyes of men," and commentary in André Cabassut, "Curiosité," in *Dictionnaire de spiritualité ascétique et mystique*, bk. 2, pt. 2 (Paris: Beauschesne, 1953), 2655.

ὀφθαλμῶν καὶ ἡ ἀλαζονεία τοῦ βίου], is not the Father but is of the world. And the world passes away, and the lust of it; but he who does the will of God abides forever" (1 John 2:15–17).[22] The condemnation of lustful eyes, whose attachments parallel those of the flesh more broadly, is written here against the crucial horizon of a time that is ending, a time in which the decisions of life and death are to be made. The condemnation signals a need for vigilance against threats of deception and distraction, for "it is the last hour; and as you have heard that antichrist is coming, so now many antichrists have come; therefore we know it is the last hour" (1 John 2:18). In this last hour, where the decisions of love will be decisions of life and death, there is no time for the multiple and ever multiplying vanities of a distracted and distracting curiosity—and Augustine frames the condemnation of curiosity (like everything else) in terms of love and its right order. This matter of life and death he works out by means of his influential distinctions between use (uti) and enjoyment (frui) and between caritas (which enjoys God and uses all else) and cupiditas (which enjoys what is meant only to be used)—and in terms of the role played by pride (or humility) in ordering our loves toward proper use and enjoyment. Enjoyment of what is meant only to be used—in the end, all save God—constitutes cupiditas and the mortal danger of curiosity.[23] Vain is the curiosity that revels in a multiplicity of transient, worldly phenomena rather than seeking, along the path of eternal salvation, the authentic self-knowledge and the knowledge of God that imply one another. The seriousness of salvation stands at odds with the amusements of this world.

This Augustinian seriousness decisively shapes subsequent Christian thought concerning curiosity and the empty, distracted forms of life that it is feared to engender—those, indeed, that amount to death. Along these lines, Bernard condemns curiosity for being grounded in pride and thus

22. See also Augustine's second tractate on 1 John (2:12–17), §13: "'And the desire of the eyes.' He calls all curiosity the desire of the eyes. Now how widely does curiosity extend? This in shows, in theaters, in the rites of the devil, in magical arts, in sorceries, this is curiosity. Sometimes it tempts even the servants of God so that they wish, as it were, to work a miracle, to test whether God listens to them in regard to miracles." I cite here John W. Rettig's edition, *The Fathers of the Church: St. Augustine, Tractates on the Gospel of John 112–24, Tractates on the First Epistle of John* (Washington, D.C.: Catholic University of America Press, 1995), 155–56. A version appears also in John Burnaby, ed., *Augustine: Later Works* (Philadelphia: Westminster Press, 1980), 276–77.

23. See Augustine's *On Christian Doctrine* 3.10: "I call 'charity' the motion of the soul toward the enjoyment of God for His own sake, and the enjoyment of one's self and one's neighbor for the sake of God; but 'cupidity' is a motion of the soul toward the enjoyment of one's self, one's neighbor, or any corporeal thing for the sake of something other than God" I cite the edition translated by D. W. Robertson (New York: Macmillan, 1958), 88.

contrary to the end of salvation. Contrasted with "prudence," curiosity amounts to "any knowledge other than that of self-knowledge aiming at salvation,"[24] that is, the self-knowledge that grows only from compunction. Indeed, Bernard posits compunction as the necessary starting point of the humility that alone pierces through the blindness and self-deception of sin; for the pride of sin, exercised in curiosity, wants to know everything but the self—the truth of all except the self's own relation to that truth.[25]

A first sign of distraction from the self and from its true relation with the truth, a fundamental correlate of vain curiosity, is the empty talk or chatter toward which curiosity always tends. Heidegger's debt to Augustinian tradition is perhaps nowhere more evident than in his elucidation of the link between curiosity and idle talk, which he develops along lines that recapitulate quite directly the Augustinian contention that the "first effect" of *curiositas* is empty chatter, or *bavardage*, which poses a constant obstacle to silent retreat and to the attentive prayer retreat supports. Just as the distractions of curiosity are "the cause of interruption and distraction from our prayers,"[26] so are its social-discursive expression and exercise. "So tight is the union of this effect with its cause," writes André Cabassut in his article on curiosity in the *Dictionnaire de spiritualité ascétique et mystique*, "that one can almost make *bavardage* a part of the definition of curiosity. 'Curiositas. Proprie cupiditas sciendi noscendi; interdum subest notio loquacitatis' (*Thesaurus linguae latinae*, s.v. *Curiositas*)."[27] According to Augustine's early modern heir Pascal, "Curiosity is but vanity. Most often one wants to know only in order to talk about it. One would not travel the sea in order never to talk about it and for the sole pleasure of seeing, without any hope of ever talking about it with someone."[28]

24. See Cabassut, "Curiosité," 2656.

25. See also Marion's recent essay "The Banality of Saturation," in Hart, *Counter-Experiences*, in light of which we might also read his earlier condemnations of the audiovisual epoch for its voyeurism. In that direction, see, e.g., "L'aveugle à Siloé" in *La croisée du visible* (1991; Paris: Presses Universitaires de France, 1996), 97: "The televisual image, structurally idolatrous, obeys the voyeur and produces only prostituted images. This onanism of the gaze completes the metaphysical figure of the monad: every supposedly extraverted perception of the world is reduced to an expression of the monad itself, deploying its essence alone in images that take the place of a world." For my own discussion of that earlier work, see "Consuming Desire's Deferral," in *Practices of Procrastination*, ed. Paul Bowman, Joanne Crawford, and Alison Rowley, *Parallax* 10 (January–March 1999): 39–55.

26. Augustine *Confessions* 10.35.

27. Cabassut, "Curiosité," 2657.

28. Pascal, *Pensées*, no. 146; likewise, La Fontaine, *Fables* 10.3: "Imprudence, babbling and idiotic vanity—And vain curiosity,—Have together the same lineage" (both quoted in Cabassut, "Curiosité," 2657).

Enemy of silence and withdrawal, enemy, then, of authentic inward-
ness and composure, curiosity feeds and feeds on the chatter in which I
can be distracted endlessly and painlessly from myself and my only true
end—and thus I remain both deceived about that self, which assumes in
its distraction and chatter a posture of security or complacency, and at the
same time dispossessed of self, incontinent. This torn condition in which
the self is ignorant of itself, blind to its own alienation, or lost in its own
dispersion, typifies the Augustinian predicament of sin, where the illusion
of self-control or self-possession, the illusion of "life," coincides with an
utter loss of self, indeed a "death," that ensues from just that illusion. The
Augustinian analysis of sin as alienation thus articulates the logic of what
later in Kierkegaard and Heidegger becomes the despair of not knowing I'm
in despair, or the distress of not knowing I'm in distress—despair or distress
that entails an inauthenticity whose first sign is to ignore itself and that
takes the form of smug contentment (itself perhaps the mask of profound
boredom).[29] Against the life that is in fact death, against the self-possession
that is in fact dispossession, the Augustinian thinking that proves crucial to
Heidegger will set the possibility of death as a condition of life, a dispossession of self as that which gives the self to itself. While thoroughly indebted
to Augustine here, however, Heidegger also modifies the Augustinian position significantly, by understanding as originary the condition that Augustine counts as fallen and hence secondary.

The Augustinian ground and character of Heidegger's thinking along
these lines are illuminated in striking ways by his 1921 summer seminar
"Augustine and Neoplatonism," in which his analysis of curiosity, working out already many of the concerns that become widely known through
Being and Time, is framed in terms of the possibility that would (or would
not) sustain "life."[30] In and through a reading of book 10 of the *Confessions*,
the 1921 seminar treats the topics of falling and dispersion, bustling activity and flight from self in relation to the eagerness and greed of a curiosity

---

29. See Kierkegaard's *The Sickness unto Death*, trans. Edna Hong and Howard Hong (Princeton: Princeton University Press, 1983), and on the question of boredom, Heidegger's *Fundamental Concepts of Metaphysics*, where he writes, e.g., that "the absence of oppressiveness is what
fundamentally oppresses and leaves us most profoundly empty, i.e., the *fundamental emptiness
that bored us*" (FC, 164 [245]; emphasis in original).

30. In Martin Heidegger, *The Phenomenology of Religious Life*, trans. Matthias Fritsch and
Jennifer Anna Gosetti-Ferenci (Bloomington: Indiana University Press, 2004); for the German
see *Phänomenologie des religiösen Lebens*, vol. 60 of Heidegger's *Gesamtausgabe* (Frankfurt am
Main: Vittorio Klostermann, 1995). Hereafter cited parenthetically as *PRL*, with English pagina-
tion followed by the German. Heidegger's abbreviation *PL* refers to J. P. Migne, ed., *Patrologiae
Cursus Completus, Series Latina*, vol. 32 (Paris: Migne, 1853).

that wants to see and to know all except the self, who like a voyeur seeks to place all in the light of truth while wanting itself to remain hidden and protected in darkness (to the point, indeed, of hating the truth when its light turns toward it).[31]

Those "many people" who "intend to deceive others" but "do not want to be deceived themselves," Augustine argues and Heidegger highlights, are "absorbed" in "bustling activity" (Geschäftigkeit), but "the cheap tricks to which they abandon themselves" (die Lumpereien, an die sie sich wegwerfen) render them only more miserable, making them "more and more lose the beata vita" (PRL, 146, 147 [198, 199]). Such loss of life through absorption in bustling activity is tied intimately to the "dispersion of life" (die Zerstreuung des Lebens) in multiplicity and flux, and the struggle of genuine life would be the struggle for a re-collection into self-possession and unity, a continent self-presence or self-proximity, which would stand the test of such dispersion and multiplicity: "For 'in multa defluximus' [we are scattered into the many],[32] we are dissolving into the manifold and are absorbed in the dispersion. You [God] demand counter-movement against the dispersion, against the falling apart of life. 'Per continentiam quippe colligimur et redigimur in unum [necessarium—Deum?] [By continence we are gathered together and brought into the One (the necessary One—God?)]"[33] (PRL, 151–52 [205]). If the re-collection of self into unity is demanded and thus effected in Augustine by God, it operates much like the anxiety of Being-toward-death in Heidegger's Being and Time and the boredom of his Fundamental Concepts of Metaphysics. In both cases I am thrown back upon myself, unable to escape my singularity, insofar as my anxiety or my boredom renders indifferent or insignificant any and all beings and relations that might otherwise distract me from myself or serve as supports for my flight—as in the exercise of curiosity and in the idle chatter with which I busy myself so as to lose myself, in flight from the possibility of a death that is unavoidably and distinctively my own or in avoidance of

31. See Augustine Confessions 10.23: "But why does truth engender hatred? Why does your servant meet with hostility when he preaches the truth, although men love happiness, which is simply the enjoyment of truth? It can only be that man's love of truth is such that when he loves something which is not the truth, he pretends to himself that what he loves is the truth, and because he hates to be proved wrong, he will not allow himself to be convinced that he is deceiving himself. So he hates the real truth for the sake of what he takes to his heart in its place. Men love the truth when it bathes them in its light: they hate it when it proves them wrong." For a phenomenological reading of this Augustinian position, see Marion's "Banality of Saturation," in Hart, Counter-Experiences.

32. Augustine Confessions 10.29, 40; PL 32, p. 796.

33. Augustine Confessions 10.29, 40; PL 32, p. 796.

the boredom that remains profound. If *Being and Time* leaves the question of life notably underdeveloped, its analyses, from the perspective I am suggesting here, can be seen to derive in decisive ways from the question of life in its Augustinian version.

The securing of life against the threat of dispersion, however, must also be understood not only to allow but indeed to require the potential for self-difference and the risk of self-loss. In Heidegger's distinctive reading of Augustine, as in his subsequent thought, life, taken in terms of possibility, implies an openness in which I can be both myself and not myself, or in which "my" life includes not only "my own" but also what exceeds the clear bounds of ownership or authenticity. Authentic life, along these lines, implies an insurmountable inauthenticity; my own or my "ownmost" property thus entails that which I can, in fact, never possess.

In a crucial section of his Augustine seminar, titled "The Problem of the 'I am'" (§13b), Heidegger treats this question of self-difference as it appears in Augustine's reflections on the ego-logical significance of the transition between a dreaming consciousness, where "I" may be absent to or at odds with "myself," and a waking consciousness, where I can seem to regain my composed self-presence. Augustine understands this transition in terms of my relative capacity or incapacity to regulate images that occur to me and affect me not only in my mind but also in my body (insofar as the images most troubling to Augustine are those deriving from the life of sexual drives and copulation, *concubitus*).[34] "And yet there is so much difference between myself and myself," Augustine writes, "in that moment wherein I pass from waking to sleeping, or return from sleeping to waking!" [Et tamen tantum interest inter meipsum et meipsum, intra momentum quo hinc ad soporem transeo, vel huc inde restranseo!] (*Confessions* 10.30, 41; *PL* 32, p. 796; quoted in *PRL*, 157 [213]). Heidegger's commentary, seeking to elucidate the issue "not in a biological-psychological and theoretical attitude, but according to the characteristics of how [Augustine] has factically experienced it and still experiences it" (*PRL*, 157 [212]), which is to say along the lines of an existential phenomenology, emphasizes that "this difference is not only the difference that 'I' behave differently in different situations, but precisely through this difference *I experience that I* — in dreams for example — behaved in such and such a way, that *I myself was not really there [daß ich nicht eigentlich selbst dabei war]*" (*PRL*, 158 [213]; my emphasis).

---

34. See *PRL*, 157 [212].

According to this Augustinian concept of *molestia,* or trouble, the self can experience, as present to itself, its own absence from itself. It can and inevitably does undergo its own "having been" absent—as in the transition from dream to wakefulness, a transition experienced by Augustine as one of regret *(dolor).*[35] The suffering of such regret is significant in Heidegger's analysis less for the moral compunction it entails than for what it discloses phenomenologically: "Especially in the 'transition' we have a noteworthy *experience with ourselves* [my emphasis], namely, that there is something *quod nos non fecimus* [that we have not made], which is not enacted *by us, quod in nobis factus est* [(but) which is made in us], but which nonetheless occurs and proceeds with us and in us, so that we are somehow sad about it, something that is in us, something that we 'are' ourselves and yet, that we are not" *(PRL,* 158 [213]). If Augustine's discussion focuses on dreams and seems to suggest an important distinction between the dream state and the waking state, what is at stake phenomenologically (and theologically too) is the more general fact that the self can and does trouble itself. The phenomenological point concerns not the exact boundaries or character of dreaming or of waking consciousness but a fundamental condition of self-experience, according to which selfhood "itself" implies an inevitable and recurring passage through its own self-difference or self-absence—the experience of being traversed or inhabited or carried along by what works "in" me "without" me, such that I can be "away" from myself, or even such that I am in some fundamental sense "the away." As Heidegger puts it in his commentary, *"me ipsum,* my being myself [*mein Selbstsein*], is determined in its full facticity" in just such cases of self-difference *(PRL,* 158 [213]), which is to say, in the self's ownmost exposure and indebtedness to what it does not ground or own. The human self here inhabits a quite distinctive, uncanny, possibility—namely, one of self-loss or self-difference, which is a possibility neither avoidable nor fully realizable.

The *molestia* with which Augustine struggles "can pull life down" indeed. But this possibility, the "can" that suggests a dispossession of self or an inauthenticity, is at the same time from Heidegger's (ambivalent) perspective what belongs most distinctively to the living self. The possibility of self-loss is, from this perspective, the condition of the living self's vital-

---

35. "[E]vigilantes ad conscientiae requiem redeamus; ipsaque distantia reperiamus nos non fecisse, quod tamen in nobis quoquo modo factum esse doleamus" [(W)hen we wake up we return to peace of conscience; by the distance discovering that we did not do what, however, we regret that it has somehow been done in us] *(Confessions* 10.30, 41; *PL* 32, p. 796f., quoted in *PRL,* 158 [213]).

ity, an irreducible possibility whose threat and danger only grow as life itself grows. If "what is peculiar to the burden [of *molestia*] lies precisely in the fact that *molestia* can pull down," Heidegger insists, "the 'can' is formed by the enactment that belongs to each experience itself. Thus: this possibility 'grows' *the more life lives*; this possibility grows, *the more life comes to itself*" (*PRL*, 181). The more life "comes to itself" as life, the more life lives, the more it opens itself to the possibility of loss. As Heidegger concludes in his 1929–30 lecture course, *The Fundamental Concepts of Metaphysics*, such an overlapping between a going-out of self and the coming-to-oneself can be understood as distinctive to the human as existent or projective being: "What is *most proper* to such activity and occurrence [i.e., projection] is what is expressed in the prefix 'pro-' [*Ent*], namely, that in projecting [*Entwerfen*], this occurrence of projection *carries* whoever is projecting *out and away from themselves* in a certain way. It indeed removes them into whatever has been projected, but it does not as it were deposit and abandon them there—on the contrary: in this being removed by the projection, what occurs is precisely a peculiar *turning toward themselves on the part of whoever is projecting*" (*FC*, 363 [527]).[36] The "turning toward that is a removal" (*fortnehmende Zukehr*), the human Dasein's existence (or ek-sistence) as "an exiting from itself in the essence of its being, and yet without abandoning itself" (*FC*, 365 [531]), which is central to Heidegger's analysis of the existent human as Dasein in *Being and Time*, is being worked out already through the analysis of Augustinian life. In and through that analysis of life, Heidegger comes to highlight the sense in which human Dasein, or there-being, is in fact never simply "there" in the discrete presence of a present. Existent life implies the openness of a possibility that is, so long as life lives, never yet determinate or actually present—and hence an ongoing departure and irreducible danger that inhere in all existent life still to be lived.

As living existence, the self is given to itself only insofar as given over also to the irreducible possibility of risk, which means likewise the risk of irreducible possibility—and from this perspective one might see that the possible loss of life or dispossession of self signaled in the Heideggerian

---

36. One might note here an early Heideggerian marker in the direction of Marion's phenomenological and also theological (especially Dionysian) analyses of generosity, according to which reception means always already giving: I am given to myself, or receive myself, insofar as I am turned away from myself, or given over to another. On this dynamic in the theology of Pseudo-Dionysius, see my analysis in "Transcending Negation," and on Marion's phenomenological appropriation of Dionysius, "The Naming of God and the Possibility of Impossibility," chapters 5 and 6 of *Indiscretion*.

"falling" would actually consist not in running such risk or in living such possibility but in fleeing risk through a restriction of possibility's indeterminate character, through an attempted reduction of all possibility to an actuality simply waiting to become present in its disposability and manageability. This understanding of falling as the restriction of possibility's scope through its reduction to the logic of actuality and presence, disposability and manageability—an understanding central both to the analysis of Being-toward-death in *Being Time* and, as we've seen, to the analysis of machination and newspaper science subsequently—is worked out first in the engagement with Augustine's understanding of selfhood and life, an engagement wherein, significantly, the question of creativity and self-formation also emerges.

The analysis of falling that Heidegger finds in Augustine plays an important role in Augustine's critique of the "operatores et sectatores pulchritudinum exteriorum" (the artists and followers of external beauty), whose "creativity" involves only a falling into that "possibility" which they can actualize: "Homines: 'foras sequentes quod faciunt' (cadunt in ea quod valent) [Humans: 'outwardly they follow what they make' (they fall into that which they are able to)], they settle themselves and follow that which they can accomplish" (*PRL*, 163 [219–20]). Within the creative process, falling involves the all-too-secure and all-too-settled reliance on what one already knows or believes to be possible—which is to say, what one already knows or believes to be realizable, or reducible to present actuality, by means of production or execution, organization and management. The human subject here falls and hence loses itself by resting overly secure with what it is able to make or accomplish. Consistent with his critique of curiosity, Augustine sees this falling form of creativity operative in the fabrication of things enticing to the eyes—things that produce a kind of beauty and pleasure that would, like the vain entertainments and distractions of curiosity, serve no higher purpose: "Quam innumerabilia . . . addiderunt homines as illecebas oculorum" (Innumerable things . . . have men made to entice their eyes).[37]

For Heidegger, following a certain line in Augustine,[38] the loss of self or life, operative in falling and its inauthenticity, ensues from the refusal to risk loss of self or life, a refusal enacted in the tenacious reliance on what we already (think we) know to belong within the scope of the humanly pos-

---

37. Augustine *Confessions* 10.34, 53; *PL* 32, p. 801, quoted in *PRL*, 163.

38. Augustine does not, however, finally see *molestia* as originary to the human in the way Heidegger seems to; he sees it rather as the disorder—eventually to be repaired—that results from sin.

sible, precisely because it has already been made actual and thus remains present (or presentable) and hence available for secure management—providing, thus, the necessary support for the ongoing "bustling activity" in which we "secure" the self by fleeing and hence losing the self. As Heidegger makes clear in subsequent works, this flight evades such fundamental moods as anxiety and boredom at the cost of closing the existent human off to the indeterminate, irreducible possibility actually disclosed by the kind of refusals operative in anxiety and boredom: "Whoever makes no demand upon himself can never know of a refusal or of being refused [ein Versagen und Versagtsein], but sways in a contentment that has what it wants and wants only what it can have" (FC, 164 [246]).[39] An authentic and living engagement with self-experience, by contrast, would run the risk of anxiety and boredom alike, which means the risk of an existential possibility that exceeds and unsettles the secure boundaries of the actual or the actualizable—a possibility that would condition existence without being exhausted in or by any given possibility for a determinate, actual this or that. To run such risk would be to rupture the "lack of distress" (Not-losigkeit) that, like Kierkegaard's despair of not knowing one is in despair, proves "greatest where self-certainty has become unsurpassable, where everything is held to be calculable and, above all, where it is decided, without a preceding question, who we are and what we are to do" (B, 87 [125]).

⚬

If Heidegger can see in the essence of technology the modern expression of unsurpassable self-certainty, we may nonetheless ask whether the technological does not harbor also an opening of the self-certain human beyond itself, in a creation that is genuine insofar as it proceeds without knowing who we are and what we are to do, thus opening the human again as question to itself. The technological, from this perspective, insofar as it may well unsettle the boundaries of the human self or of its life and nature "themselves," may also open the space of authentic possibility—genuine amazement and truly reflective questioning—as much as closing in around the already secure. Along these lines, we need to ask how and in what ways the technological can sustain the kind of genuine creativity in which the

---

39. One might note here the Heideggerian-Augustinian ground of the "courage to be" for which Paul Tillich calls in an age of anxiety. See Tillich's classic work by that title, The Courage to Be (New Haven: Yale University Press, 1952).

human proves to be "the strangest" or "most uncanny" of all—and finds the ground or condition of creation in that strangeness.

To understand the technological as opening possibility—rather than closing it through the reduction of Being to actuality—requires that one disengage its creative potential from the modern metaphysics defined by the "conquest of the world as picture," an essential correlate of newspaper science and machination, which involves the reduction of world to world picture (*Weltbild*) or to worldview (*Weltanschauung*). Worldview, according to Heidegger, is always machination (*Machenschaft*) and "like domination of 'world-pictures' is an outgrowth of modernity, a *consequence* of modern metaphysics" (*B*, 27 [38]). Tending toward totality and its closure, aiming to secure its own ground and to determine already its future, worldview is opposed to any "creating-beyond-itself" (*B*, 29 [40]) insofar as it excludes genuine questioning and decision—precisely by conceiving possibility always already according to the assumed logic of actuality. "*The total worldview must close itself off from the opening of its ground and from engrounding the domain of its 'creating'; that is, its creating can never arrive at what is its ownmost way of being and become creating-beyond-itself, because thereby the total worldview would have to put itself into question.* The consequence is that creating is replaced by endless operations [*Betrieb*]" (*B*, 29 [41]). The total worldview—whether "total political belief" or "total Christian faith," the worldview of scientific "research," or any other—in every case entails renunciation of "essential decisions" (*B*, 29 [41]), the forsaking of any genuine future, any projection in which the self can come to itself only in departing from itself, or find its authenticity in the risk of its dispossession.

The total worldview and its founding metaphysics might give the appearance, then, of "life" and "creation," but this appearance remains, thanks to its exclusion of decision and questioning—or of any "decidedness-to-question" (*B*, 29 [41])—only artifice and deception. In place of authentic creation—which means the questioning and decision that can exceed or resist the "endless operations" of planning and calculating within an already established ground plan whose grounding is itself unquestioned—stands only the appearance or the artifice of life. "The consequence is that creating is replaced in advance by *endless operations*. The ways and risks that belong to what was once creating are arranged according to the machination's gigantic character, and the machinational gives the appearance of the liveliness of creating" (*B*, 29 [40–41]). Just as life in Heidegger's Augustine is *molestia* and so never quite settled with or in itself, just as life implies the unsettling and indeterminate "can" that involves irreducible risk or danger, so the critique of a modern machination that only appears to yield "life" and "creating" targets that machination's inordinate assumption of secu- rity or control, at odds with a truly lively creating. In other words, the au- thentic creativity and life suggested both in Heidegger's early engagement with Augustine and in his later critique of technological culture and its founding metaphysics implies the human capacity for dispossession or in- authenticity, such that the human's "ownmost" determination might rest in its distinctive indetermination.

This paradox, on Giorgio Agamben's illuminating interpretation, is the very center of Heidegger's engagement with and debt to Augustine, who more than Husserl was the deep source of Heidegger's conception of "fac- ticity." According to that conception, authenticity presupposes inauthen- ticity, and inauthenticity is tied to essentially creative potential. "If one wants to understand the development of the concept of facticity in Heideg- ger's thought," Agamben writes, "one should not forget this origin of the word, which ties it to the sphere of non-originarity and making."[40] If Augus- tine asserts that "factitia est anima," this is to highlight the indebtedness of the soul to another. As Agamben explains, the Latin "facticius is opposed to nativus; it means qui non sponte fit, what is not natural, what did not come into Being by itself." Along these lines emphasizing the factical or made in its contrast to the naturally self-generated or spontaneous, Augus- tine uses the term also "to designate pagan idols, in a sense that seems to correspond perfectly to our term 'fetish': genus facticiorum deorum, the nature of factical gods."[41] In its facticity, Heidegger's Dasein brings together these two senses of the factical from Augustine. Dasein is not native but thrown, always already out of place within its place; and it becomes maker precisely insofar as it is not native, creative insofar as strange, or not quite at home—uncanny—in its own dwelling.[42]

40. Giorgio Agamben, "The Passion of Facticity," in Potentialities: Collected Essays in Phi- losophy, trans. Daniel Heller-Roazen (Stanford: Stanford University Press, 1999), 189.

41. Ibid.

42. In his important study of technology from deconstructive and phenomenological per- spectives, La technique et le temps, vol. 1, La faute d'Épiméthée (Paris: Éditions Galilée, 1994), Bernard Stiegler also captures well the sense in which my facticity signals precisely what is not mine. Citing "one of the most important passages from Sein und Zeit," where Heidegger asserts that "expressly or not, Dasein is its past," Stiegler comments that "Dasein is a past that is not its own, or that is its own only if it is (only if the Dasein is its past—after the fact)" (246–47). Stiegler's analysis shows well, furthermore, the necessary, irreducible technological condition of access to pastness and hence to the facticity—and inheritance—of Dasein. I'll return to this matter in chapter 6.

The conjunction of essence and existence, of what-being and that-being, in the human as Dasein, whose "essence lies in its existence," involves not simply the reversal but the subversion of the metaphysical distinction between essence (as potential) and existence (as actuality). Heidegger himself highlights this reading of *Being and Time* in the later "Letter on Humanism," where, in thinking human ethics as dwelling and dwelling as openness to the unfamiliar, he writes that "what man is—or, as it is called in the traditional language of metaphysics, the 'essence' of man—lies in his ek-sistence. But ek-sistence thought in this way is not identical with the traditional concept of *existentia*, which means actuality in contrast to the meaning of *essentia* as possibility" (LH, 229 [325]). This "ontological contraction," where ek-sistence is the actuality of possibility as such and not actuality contrasted with unrealized essence, can be read, as Agamben points out, not only in terms of Augustinian facticity but also in terms of Nicholas of Cusa's conception of God as possibility (to which I will return in the next chapter):

> If Heidegger can simultaneously pose the question of the meaning of Being anew and distance himself from ontology, it is because the Being at issue in *Being and Time* has the character of facticity from the beginning. This is why for Dasein, quality, *Sosein*, is not a "property" but solely a "possible guise" (*mögliche Weise*) to be (a formula that must be heard in accordance with the same ontological contraction that is expressed in Nicholas of Cusa's *possest*). Original opening is produced in this factical movement, in which Dasein must be its *weise*, its fashion of Being, and in which Being and its guise are both distinguishable and the same. The term "fashion" must be heard here in its etymological sense (from *factio, facere*) and in the sense that the word has in Old French: "face," like the English "face." Dasein is factical, since it must be its face, its fashion, its manner—at once what reveals it and that into which it is irreparably thrown.[43]

This coimplication of the proper and the improper, my given being and my fashioning of being, within a thought of existence as possibility prior and irreducible to actuality, or as the actuality of possibility itself, opens ground from which to think the interplay of creativity and indetermination of the

---

43. Agamben, "Passion of Facticity," 194–95. One might also read productively, in light of this Augustinian-Heideggerian take on facticity and fashion, the stakes of Taylor's treatment of fashion and the superficial in *Hiding*.

human—as Heidegger highlights in his *Introduction to Metaphysics*, which more than other works seems explicitly to affirm the priority of Dasein's inauthenticity or impropriety over its authenticity.

Heidegger there posits a tie between indetermination and creative potential in his reading of Sophocles' famous lines from *Antigone*: "πολλὰ τὰ δεινὰ κοὐδὲν ἀνθρώπου δεινότερον πέλει." Heidegger translates Sophocles thus: "Manifold is the uncanny, yet nothing uncannier than man bestirs itself" [Vielfältig das Unheimliche, nichts doch über den Menschen hinaus Unheimlicheres ragend sich regt](*IM*, 156 [112]).[44] The view of man as *to deinotaton*—for Heidegger the "strangest" or "most uncanny"—troubles interpretations that would see in his thought the primacy or final privilege of authenticity and its correlates (self-possession, self-presence, autarchy, rootedness, dwelling, and the like). It also signals the degree to which Heidegger traces a genuine creativity to the necessary dispossession or inauthenticity, uprootedness or uncanniness, of the one who creates.[45] Along these lines, what is "proper" to man as decisive, creative, and capable of

44. Mannheim's translation (Yale, 1959) gives "there is much that is strange, but nothing surpasses man in strangeness" (146). Hereafter cited parenthetically in the text.

45. Recent interpreters and heirs of Heidegger take a range of positions on this question. While Marion reads and critiques Heidegger for privileging the autarchy of Dasein, Stiegler notes an ambivalence, where *Introduction to Metaphysics* proves especially important. Agamben, while noting a similar ambivalence, argues finally for the co-originary or even primary status of inauthenticity. See, in these directions, Marion's brief but important piece "L'Interloqué," in *Who Comes after the Subject?* ed. Eduardo Cadava, Peter Connor, and Jean-Luc Nancy (New York: Routledge, 1991); and Stiegler's *Technique et le temps*, e.g., 1:212 n. 1. Agamben summarizes the issue well and argues that the impropriety of human Dasein is co-originary:

> At times, Heidegger seems to retreat from the radicality of this thesis, fighting against himself to maintain a primacy of the proper and the true. But an attentive analysis shows not only that the co-originarity of the proper and the improper is never disavowed, but even that several passages could be said to imply a primacy of the improper. Whenever *Being and Time* seeks to seize hold of the experience of the proper (as, for example, in proper Being-toward-death), it does so solely by means of an analysis of impropriety (e.g., factical Being-toward-death). The factical link between these two dimensions of *Dasein* is so intimate and original that Heidegger writes, "*authentic* existence is not something which floats above falling everydayness; existentially it is only a modified way in which such everydayness is seized upon" ("*Die eigentliche Existenz ist nichts, was über der verfallenden Alltäglichkeit schwebt, sondern existentzial nur ein modifiziertes Ergreifen dieser*"). And on the subject of proper decision, he states, "[*Dasein*] authentically makes the untruth its own." ("[*das Dasein*] eignet sich die unwahrheiteigentlich"). . . . *Authentic existence has no content other than inauthentic existence; the proper is nothing other than a seizing-hold of the improper*. We must reflect on the inevitable character of the improper that is implied by these formulations. Even in Being-toward-death and in decision, *Dasein* seizes hold only of its impropriety, mastering only an alienation and becoming attentive only to a distraction. Such is the originary status of facticity. ("Passion of Facticity," 197; translation modified)

self-transcendence is man's impropriety, his refusal to be contained or constrained by fixed limits, to rest content in the familiar—which, while it can
seem to be the place where I find myself and dwell properly with myself, in
my self-presence, can at the same time, to the degree that it goes without
question or decision, constitute a form of rootlessness or inauthenticity:
"We understand the un-canny [das Un-heimliche] as that which throws one
out of the 'canny,' [aus dem 'Heimlichen'] that is, the homely, the accustomed, the familiar, the un-endangered. The unhomely does not allow us
to be at home. Therein lies the over-whelming. But human beings are the
uncanniest, not only because they spend their lives essentially in the midst
of the un-canny understood in this sense, but also because they step out,
move out of the limits that at first and for the most part are accustomed
and homely, precisely in the direction of the uncanny in the sense of the
overwhelming" (IM, 161 [115–16]; translation modified).

In its strangeness or uncanniness, the capacity of the human to create paths is bound inextricably to its profound lack of any one given path.
Heidegger makes this point in his gloss on man as the strangest or most
uncanny by drawing on that other famous line from Antigone (line 360),
"παντοπόρος ἄπορος ἐπ᾽οὐδὲν ἔρχεται"—"Everywhere trying out, underway;
untried, with no way out he comes to Nothing" [Überall hinausfahrend
unterwegs, erfahrungslos ohne Ausweg kommt er zum Nichts]—which he
explicates by noting that

> everywhere humanity makes routes for itself; in all the domains of be-
> ings, of the overwhelming sway, it ventures forth, and in this very way
> it is flung from every route. Thus the whole uncanniness of the human,
> the uncanniest, first opens itself up; it is not just that humans try what
> is, as a whole, in its un-canniness, not just that as violence-doing they
> drive themselves in this way beyond what is homely for them, but in
> all this they first become the uncanniest, because now, as those who
> on all ways have no way out, they are thrown out of all relations to
> the homely, and atê, ruin, calamity [der Verderb, das Unheil], overtakes
> them. (IM, 162 [116])

Strangest of all, uncanniest, without path insofar as open to all paths, or
vice versa, the human that Heidegger draws out in his reading of Antigone
is likewise thought to be placed insofar as placeless, or political insofar as
apolitical. Citing line 370—ὑψίπολις ἄπολις—which for him completes the
interpretation of man as strangest, Heidegger notes of the poets and priests
and rulers who are genuine creators: "Rising high in the site of history, they

also become *apolis*, without city and site, lonesome, un-canny, with no way out amidst beings as a whole, and at the same time without ordinance and limit, without structure and fittingness [*Fug*], because they *as* creators must first ground all this in each case [*als Schaffende dies alles je erst gründen müssen*]" (*IM*, 163 [117]). Along lines forecasting the Derridean analyses of aporetics, creative violence, and the mystical foundations of authority, Heidegger here binds creative capacity to an absence or abandonment of place, such as that of one who breaks forth "on the heaving groundlessness [of the waves], forsaking solid land [*das Ausbrechen auf das wogende Grundlose, das Aufgeben des festen Landes*]" (*IM*, 164 [118]; translation modified), one who "gives up the place, [who] heads out—and ventures to enter the superior power of the sea's placeless flood [*der ortlosen Meerflut*]" (*IM*, 164 [153]).

To remain at home with oneself, close to oneself, or in proximate possession of oneself and of what one takes to be one's own, to remain fixed in one's place, solidly rooted, can prove from this perspective to be one's fall into a tranquilizing inauthenticity, where one does not decisively own—or become—oneself by creating beyond oneself. This fall is as likely to be the risk of a technological modernity that bewitches as it is of a tradition that hands its categories and ways over to an ostensibly secure self-evidence. By contrast, to create beyond oneself, to risk the loss of oneself and one's own, to depart from the familiar and its defining limits, forsaking solid land and venturing into the placeless flood, can be the chance of an authentically living existence, whether technological or traditional (which themselves, I will argue, cannot finally be disentangled). In order to sustain the possibility of creation, the familiar abode or place of dwelling needs to be an "open region" for the unfamiliar, as Heidegger argues at the core of his reflections in the "Letter on Humanism." "The (familiar) abode for man," Heidegger writes in translating Heraclitus' ἦθος ἀνθρώπῳ δαίμον, "is the open region for the presencing of the god (the unfamiliar one)" [Der (geheure) Aufenthalt ist dem Menschen das Offene für die Anwesung des Gottes (des Un-geheuren)] (LH, 258 [356]; translation modified). If the familiar remains wholly closed, it excludes, in fact, the ethical dwelling that would be open to a coming of the unfamiliar (the god in the "Letter on Humanism," or the "last god" evoked already throughout the *Contributions to Philosophy*). Such closure is a risk run as much by tradition as by technological modernity, and one notable today in the reactive appeal to tradition in resistance to the technological—and it is a risk that tends, in fact, to foreclose the possibility of historical being.

If the ethical dwelling sketched out in Heidegger's treatment of humanism keeps open the space and time of historical creation, which means a space and time of decision, then the one who dwells is open to venture. Never guaranteed, always "tossed back and forth between structure and the structureless [zwischen Fug und Un-fug]" (IM, 172 [123]; Mannheim, 161), and for that reason truly open, creative-historical venture entails at all times the danger of loss or dispersion:

> The one who is violence-doing, the creative one, who sets out into the un-said, who breaks into the un-thought, who compels what has never happened and makes appear what is unseen, this violence-doing one stands at all times in daring (tolma, line 371). Insofar as he dares the sur-mounting of Being, he must risk the assault of un-beings, the mê kalon, dispersion, un-constancy, un-structure and unfittingness [das Un-gefüge und den Unfug]. The higher the peak of historical being-there, the more gaping the abyss for the sudden plunge into the unhistorical, which then only flails around in a confusion that has no way out and at the same time has no site. (IM, 172 [123]; translation modified)[46]

On this reading, to "be-there" in the manner of the strangest of all, which means to dwell in a human sense, is not, indeed, to be in the auto-matic manner of the everyday. It is not to find oneself in the "usual bustle and activity" in which I can distract, disperse, and lose myself, but it is nonetheless to abide with the familiar. The risk of distraction, dispersion, and loss, an exposure to the unfamiliar, are an essential condition of the creative openness that will do other than recreate or replicate the already known and understood, the already foreseen and programmed. Inauthentic-ity will not, then, be averted through genuine creativity; it will be required. And unshakeable authenticity, the autarchic self-possession for which Hei-degger is often critiqued, forecloses genuine creativity. As Heidegger notes, the dangers of technology and tradition alike, consisting in their tendency toward automatic repetition, or mechanicity, and hence foreclosure of the unforeseeable and genuinely true event of disclosure, find their basic logic in language itself, which gives both the chance of authentic, creative open-ing and the risk of inauthentic, deadening rote. Beginning already with Plato's logical interpretation of nature or physis, "the logos becomes the definitive and essential determination of discourse. Language, as what is

46. See likewise the interplay of decision and historicity in Contributions to Philosophy and Fundamental Concepts of Metaphysics. The obstacle to decisive historicity, which tradition can be, is elucidated in Being and Time in terms of the self-evidence to which this latter would hand things over.

spoken out and said, and as what can be said again, preserves in each case
the being that has been opened up. What has been said can be said again
and passed on. The truth that is preserved in this saying spreads in such a
way that the being that was originally opened up in gathering is not itself
properly experienced in each particular case. In what is passed on, truth
loosens itself, as it were, from beings. This can go so far that the repetition
[*Nachsagen*] becomes mere hearsay [*Hersagen*], *glôssa* (see *Being and Time*
§44b)" (*IM*, 198 [141–42]; translation modified). Both "authentic discourse"
or "correct saying" and "mere babbling" or "mere hearsay" have, then, the
same ground in the *logos* capable both of disclosing the unique truth of
possible being and of becoming a ready-made tool that flattens truth into
the repetition of correctness (*IM*, 198 [142]; Mannheim, 186). Such ambivalence, inherent to *logos*, likewise marks any tradition or any technology.⁴⁷

The technological age thus intensifies and spreads a tendency already
operative in language itself, and in doing so it yields the mass anonymity,
the threat of dehumanization, that so concerned Heidegger, and Kierkegaard
before him, in the technologies, especially media technologies, of reproduction—and that so worries many today not only in the forms of reproduction
operative throughout our media culture but also in the forms of reproduction, replication, or simply production operative in the biotechnological
and related fields. The "public realm" that results from the dominance of
subjectivity in modern metaphysics and culture "is the metaphysically
conditioned establishment and authorization of the openness of individual
beings in their unconditioned objectification. Language thereby falls into

47. See especially, in these directions the *Introduction to Metaphysics*: "In the form of assertion, logos itself has become just another thing that one comes across. This present-at-hand
thing is something handy, something that is handled in order to attain truth as correctness and
establish it securely. So this handle for attaining truth can easily be grasped as a tool, *organon*,
and the tool can easily be made handy in the proper way. This is all the more necessary the
more decisively the *originary* opening up of the Being of beings has been suspended, with the
transformation of *physis* into *eidos* and of *logos* into *katêgoria*. The true as the correct is now
merely spread about and spread afar by way of discussion, instruction, and prescriptions, thereby
becoming ever more leveled out. Logos must be made ready as a tool for this. The hour of the
birth of logic has arrived" (*IM*, 201 [143]). Heidegger continues: "Appearance [*der Schein*], doxa, is
not something external to Being and unconcealment but instead belongs to unconcealment. But
doxa is also ambiguous in itself. On the one hand, it means the view in which something prof-
fers itself, and on the other hand it means the view that human beings have. Dasein settles into
such views. They are asserted and passed on. Thus *doxa* is a type of logos. The dominant views
now obstruct our own view of beings. Beings are deprived of the possibility of turning themselves
toward apprehension, appearing on their own right. The view granted by beings [*Aussicht*], which
usually turns itself toward us, is distorted into a view upon beings [or an opinion, *Ansicht*]. The
dominance of views [or opinions] thus distorts beings and twists them" (*IM*, 205 [146]; translation modified).

the service of expediting communication along routes where objectification—the uniform accessibility of everything to everyone—branches out
and disregards all limits. In this way language comes under the dictatorship
of the public realm [*die Diktatur der Öffentlichkeit*], which decides in advance what is intelligible and what must be rejected as unintelligible" (LH,
221 [317]). For Heidegger, the possibility of genuine human creation, rooted
in language, always also holds the danger of falling into inauthenticity and
machinelike automaticity, the very condition of modern mass culture's
anonymous humanity as analyzed and illuminated by Kierkegaard. In that
culture, the emergence of an everyone who is no one, or an everything that
is nothing, is tied to the objectivizing, abstracting, and calculative thinking
of modern technoscience and its distinctive metaphysics, a thinking that
grounds the machinelike existence of utter anonymity. Under the sway of
objective and calculative thought, everyone comes to speak interchange-
ably and hence anonymously; everyone, then, is really no *one* to the degree
that "people's remarks are so objective, so all-inclusive, that it is a matter
of complete indifference who expresses them, and where human speech is
concerned that is the same thing as acting 'on principle.'"(*PA*, 77). Much as
the passive voice in social scientific writing, or what Heidegger calls "newspaper science," can hide the authorial voice in the anonymity of ostensible
objectivity and universality, so according to Kierkegaard a language of the
press renders indifferent the individuality of the speaker—and in this way
removes actual responsibility from any one speaker. Thus, just as the one
who acts constantly and solely "on principle" or "according to the rule"
never actually assumes the responsibility of a singular individual, because
she or he shifts "responsibility" from the self to a program in whose accounting the singular never counts, so an "objective" speech comes to reign
in which the speaker's idiosyncrasy or idiomaticity is rendered indifferent.[48]
It is this logic that grounds the assumption of immediate accessibility and
unlimited possibility in newspaper science and the correlative machination; there, a certainty about what or who the human is and the assumption that all is possible and knowable—a certainty and assumption that
can only spell a total lack of questioning—can prove profoundly *de*human-
izing. As Kierkegaard puts it, "there is no longer any one who knows how
to talk, and instead objective thought produces an atmosphere, an abstract

48. The Derridean analysis of responsibility marks one of the more significant among recent extensions of this Kierkegaardian (and later Heideggerian) insight concerning the abstraction
of the public. See especially the seminal analysis of responsibility in the first part of Derrida's
"Force of Law: The 'Mystical Foundation of Authority,'" in *Deconstruction and the Possibility of
Justice*, ed. Drucilla Cornell (New York: Routledge, 1992).

sound, which makes human speech superfluous, just as machinery makes man superfluous" (*PA*, 77). Or as Heidegger puts it in the closing line of his *Contributions to Philosophy*, echoing the critical voice of Kierkegaard, "*Language*, whether *spoken or held in silence*, [is] the primary and broadest humanization of beings. So it seems. But *it* [is] precisely the most originary non-humanization of man as *extant living-being* and 'subject' and all heretofore. And [it is] thereby the grounding of Da-sein and of the possibility of the non-humanization of beings" (*B*, 359 [510]; translation modified). If, as our analyses have been suggesting, *cura* cuts always two ways, opening the possibility both of a dissipating curiosity and of a genuine care, this duplicity can be understood in terms of the linguistic condition that both grounds or roots Dasein, keeping the open humanly open, and carries away, uproots, unearths, and so *de*humanizes. This condition, furthermore, mirrors that of all historical dwelling as tied to tradition, which both carries over or hands down so as to give place for dwelling and carries away, dispossesses, and displaces by depriving one of genuine decision.[49]

Being too much "at home," dwelling too closely with "oneself" and one's "own," for example, in the smug contentment of one's tradition, or in the similar arrogance of a self-assured technoscientific culture—again, the two not always so distant as each might be inclined to think—can itself become a form of uprooting or dispersion, in which the authentically human and its creative potential are threatened or lost. At the same time, that unsettling dispersion in which the human can seem to be lost may well open the possibility of genuine creation. Poetic potential, then, can find its condition in the unavoidable coimplication and ambiguity between authenticity and inauthenticity.

Some clearly think that modernity's scientific and technological "assault" on the human, on its very life and nature, signals the danger of losing what we somehow know to be the human, what we securely understand to be its true or authentic life and nature—and they would ground such security through appeal to tradition. What may in fact need to be thought, however, and with the philosopher perhaps most noted for hoping to secure authenticity in the face of technological culture and its metaphysics, is the sense in which the real assault on human life and nature might consist in the security or seeming self-evidence of a thinking that believes that we indeed know and understand that life and nature, or that we can or that we

---

49. On the relation of historicality and decisive creation—and on the effacement of such creation by too much knowing and too secure a knowing of historical and cultural forms in all their diversity, see already Heidegger's 1920–21 course "Introduction to the Phenomenology of Religion," esp. §7, in *The Phenomenology of Religious Life*.

will know and understand them—and in such a way that we do not only comprehend but prove able to manage and control them. Tradition that seeks to save us from the technological can itself become automatic and inauthentic, just as a technology seeming to threaten the life of tradition can save us from its security and keep open the risk of life. A function of the total worldview operative in machination and newspaper science, and a danger of all tradition and technology alike, the assault of management and control, which threatens not by unsettling the bounds of the human but by closing them all too securely, is grounded in a thinking that restricts the unsettling potential or possibility according to which the authentically human may never be established—unless to say that the distinction of the human is its capacity for indistinction, that the authentically human is its openness to inauthenticity.

As I want now to show, this take on the human may be developed further both through postmodern or posthuman analyses of technological culture, which in this regard deviates from the modern metaphysics with which Heidegger associates it, and through a rereading of theological tradition, which especially in its mystical currents already imagines the human—as creative and incomprehensible—beyond the ontotheology of Christian tradition.

CHAPTER THREE

The Living Image:
Infinitude, Unknowing, and Creative Capacity
in Mystical Anthropology

Heidegger's influential reading of the relation between Christian theology and the metaphysics of technoscientific culture suggests that the divine vision within theological tradition, where God rules over all creation through his conception and making of it, is carried over into the representational subject of modern metaphysics, who, as ground and measure of all that is, likewise reigns in a technoscientific culture that is driven, through a relentless will to mastery, by the logic of total organization—which itself yields the anonymous humanity of a public or mass already attacked by Kierkegaard in the name of real religion, or religious reality. As I've suggested, this critique of modern metaphysics in Heidegger, and of the Christian ontotheology it extends, turns on their reduction of all possibility to the logic of actuality and presence. This reduction operates at the heart of "machination" and "newspaper science," as well as in their later form, "enframing," and thus within the defining attitude of mass culture's "they," the anonymous and deindividuated self for whom nothing remains inaccessible or impossible. Machination, newspaper science, the pervasive but anonymous "they" of a technologized and mediated culture that is dominated by endless production and reproduction—all depend on their blindness to that form of possibility that can never be reduced to the possibility for this or that eventual actuality. They fail to think, in other words, what Heidegger understands by the ontological difference between the possibility of Being, never actualized as such in a present presence, and the actuality of any given thing that is, or eventually could be, present in some such presence—a difference figured already by Heidegger in the mortal being, Dasein, whose Being-toward-death marks the possibility of an absolute impossibility, the being who in its Being-toward-death is determined by the indeterminate and knows an unknowing.[1]

A good deal of work in recent decades suggests that this Heideggerian reading of the relation between modern metaphysics and its culture, on the one hand, and the history of Christian theology, on the other, if surely correct in demonstrable and far-reaching ways, is not exhaustive.[2] It leaves open alternative paths not only for rereading theological tradition but also, as I aim to show here, for reimagining the logic of technological culture. These two paths can, I believe, inform one another in significant ways. The first, the history of a mystical theology not exhausted by the logic of ontotheology, may well offer both theoretical resources and historical linkages to the second, a technological culture likewise not exhausted by the Heideggerian analysis and critique. The traditions of mystical theology that resist the logic of ontotheology may well resist also the logic of machination that Heidegger discerns in the modern extensions of ontotheology— and they do so while understanding the human, as *imago Dei*, in terms of a creative capacity in and through which that image is most to be seen. As I'll show in what follows, all of this entails, within the mystical tradition of Dionysian lineage, a notion of world as infinite and incomprehensible (and hence irreducible to world picture) and a related definition of the human as indefinable (and thus resistant to the aspirations of self-knowledge and self-determination characteristic of modernity's representational subject). Both this notion of world and this definition of the human entail a theological thinking that foregrounds the incomprehensible immanence of a God who, like the world where he embodies himself, proves infinite, and who, like the human created in his image, proves creative, or even self-creative, in and through that world and on the ground of darkness or unknowing.

If modernity can rightly be understood to highlight the creative or poetic capacities of the human subject, to the point that humanity aspires to its own self-creation, it can also rightly be understood, in that very empha-

---

1. For my reading of Being-toward-death and the difference between ontological and ontic senses of possibility, and of the resonance of these in the logic of Being-toward-God in mystical theology, see chapter 4, "The Mortal Difference," in *Indiscretion*.

2. See especially the work of Jacques Derrida and Jean-Luc Marion (both of whom I take up in chapter 6 of *Indiscretion*, "The Naming of God and the Possibility of Impossibility"), as well as the numerous engagements with these figures and the traditions they explore, including Kevin Hart, *Trespass of the Sign: Deconstruction, Philosophy and Theology* (Cambridge: Cambridge University Press, 1989); John D. Caputo, *The Prayers and Tears of Jacques Derrida: Religion without Religion* (Bloomington: Indiana University Press, 1997); and Hent de Vries, *Philosophy and the Turn to Religion* (Baltimore: Johns Hopkins University Press, 1999).

sis, to inherit these deeper traditions of theological reflection on the nature of the human. These traditions prove, in their mystical bent, to deviate significantly from the logic of an ontotheology in which man, modeled on an omniscient and omnipotent God, achieves, through rational comprehension and its practical extensions, mastery of world and self. The late medieval and Renaissance conceptions of man as poetic, which do shape the emergence of a distinctively modern thought and culture, can be seen to transmit at the same time a tradition of speculative mystical theology, rooted in both the biblical and Greek worlds, according to which the creative capacities of man are grounded not simply, or even at all, in a rational comprehension yielding mastery and totality, but indeed in man's incomprehension both of world and of self. From the patristic writings of Origen (d. c. 254) and Gregory of Nyssa (c. 332–95), through the early medieval vision of John Scotus Eriugena (d. c. 877), to the late medieval and early modern achievements of Nicholas of Cusa (1401–64) and Giordano Bruno (1548–1600), Christian tradition includes a speculative-mystical lineage of deeply Neoplatonic influence, for which creative—and indeed technological—capacity is linked intimately both to a definition of the human as indefinable, which means without secure location, and to a conception of the universe as inconceivable, because without circumference or center. To reread this lineage both in light of Heidegger's analysis of ontotheology and technological modernity, on the one hand, and, on the other, in light of recent theorizations of the posthuman is to glimpse a technological humanity for which the world is not, and cannot be, conquered as picture by the self-certain, representing subject of modernity.

Strikingly, if perhaps unexpectedly, one can see shadows of this mystical universe and humanity in the very mass culture that Kierkegaard and Heidegger, both following a particular line in Augustine, attack in the name of real religion or of authentic existence. The object of the attack—our anonymous humanity adrift in its technological "sea of desert"[3]—appears to bear distinctive traits of the mystical God just evoked. Everywhere and nowhere, everything and nothing, Kierkegaard's leveled humanity or "public," recurring in Heidegger's anonymous "they," is likened to an "all-embracing something which is nothing," a "body" that "cannot even be represented,"[4] recalling the infinite God whose center is everywhere and circumference nowhere, the God who bears all names and none, within an

3. Søren Kierkegaard, *The Present Age*, trans. Alexander Dru (New York: Harper and Row), 81.

4. Ibid., 59, 60.

incomprehensible but all-comprehending *coincidentia oppositorum*. The unlikely likeness between a mass technological humanity and the mystical logic of theological tradition is rightly noted, then, more recently by contemporary thinkers such as Michel Serres, who in his book *Angels* speaks of an "invisible city that has its center everywhere and its circumference nowhere," a global humanity networked by transportational, communicational, and informational technologies that comprise "an unimaginable mediator, invisible and all-embracing."[5]

The delocalizing effect of this technologically networked culture, which seems to yield a collective humanity that resists placement and hence definition, may well signal a trace of the mystical in modern and contemporary culture. This mystical notion of God as infinite sphere has a history dating back to the late-twelfth-century pseudo-Hermetic *Book of the Twenty-Four Philosophers*, and it plays a significant role also in the pivotal thought of Nicholas of Cusa, who inherits and extends the medieval traditions of mystical speculation even as he initiates a distinctively modern sense of the world as infinite and of human knowing, in turn, not only as relative, conjectural, and immersed in unknowing, but also as fundamentally creative or poetic. The intersection between human unknowing and human creative capacity has a rich history within the mystical traditions that flow through Cusa, and it marks an especially suggestive inflection of the negative or apophatic anthropology that answers, within those traditions, to the logic of their negative or apophatic theology. In the Cusan version of such anthropology, whose lineage and significance this chapter explores, the creative or poetic human may be understood as a theological simulacrum: an image effectively without original insofar as its archetype, the God in whose image the human is created, remains himself unimaginable. It is, furthermore, an active or living image, which resembles its archetype not in any fixed form or content so much as in creative capacity and movement. Deviating significantly from the metaphysics of mimesis so influential throughout the history of Christian-Platonic thought and culture, the *imago Dei* in Cusa and related thinkers proves creative, and self-creative, in the measure that it imitates a Creator who—unlike the Platonic demiurge and its Christian variants, who create through the reproduction of pregiven, eternal archetypes[6]—creates in imitation of nothing. Moving somewhere between a nominalist constructivism whose implications he cannot wholly affirm and

5. Michel Serres, *Angels*, 59, 71.
6. See, e.g., Plato's treatment of the demiurgic creator in *Timaeus* 28–29.

a Platonic realism whose traditional version he no longer accepts, Cusa attempts to think poetic activity and its freedom as themselves participant in the real. Free human creativity, or indeed "the cultural" broadly construed, on the one hand, and a given or natural reality, on the other, are in fact for Cusa interwoven in such a way that the real contains, as integral to itself, the indeterminate freedom of creative humanity. The deeper history out of which Cusa develops this notion of the human as creative in its infinite lack of definition grounds that notion in a doctrine of the *imago Dei* that is inflected by the apophatic insistence on God's own incomprehensibility. Through a reading of Cusa in relation to his key precursors and heirs, I want to highlight within Christian tradition a line that resists Heidegger's reading of Christian tradition as ontotheological even as it resonates, in ways at odds with Heidegger's account of technological modernity, with more recent theorizations of the human as technological.

In writing Christian tradition's first systematically apophatic theology, according to which God is inconceivable and ineffable, Gregory of Nyssa writes also the tradition's first apophatic anthropology, according to which man, created in God's image, proves likewise inconceivable and ineffable. While this linkage between negative theology and negative anthropology is often noted in the scholarship on Gregory, very rarely noted and often simply ignored is the related connection he posits between the human's lack of definition and its freely creative, indeed technological, capacity. As if already theorizing the human as neotenic, Gregory's account of the apophatic likeness between God and the human traces man's creative capacity to an original deficiency at the organic or natural level. That lack, in turn, becomes the spur to inventiveness on the part of a creature who never fully attains its divine end but rather inhabits, even in the afterlife, an infinitely open-ended movement of desirous expectation, or epektasis, in relation to that end.

In his contention that the human who cannot comprehend itself is a human born into organic or natural poverty, which itself becomes the condition of creative, technological potential, Gregory extends and develops a linkage that Origen posited in the third Christian century between man's indigence and intelligence—itself a theme inherited from the Stoics and developed previously by Plato, who himself inherits and elaborates the Greek myth of Prometheus and Epimetheus. As recounted in Plato's *Protagoras*, the myth of Prometheus links man's need to his inventiveness while explicitly marking the creature of need and invention as a believer in the gods whose portion that creature shares.[7] After the gods form mortal creatures out "of a mixture made of earth and fire," they assign to Epimetheus and Prometheus the task of distributing "to each the equipment of his proper faculty" (προσέταξαν Προμηθεῖ καὶ Ἐπιμηθεῖ κοσμῆσαί τε καὶ νεῖμαι δυνάμεις ἑκάστοις ὡς πρέπει) (320d), a task Epimetheus takes upon himself for Prometheus' subsequent review. Following the principle of "compensation" (321a) that allots to some animals speed without strength and to others strength without speed, to all animals suitable protection against cold and heat, and to the various kinds their appropriate food, Epimetheus exhausts all available powers on the brute beasts and thus leaves the human race "unequipped" (ἀκόσμητον). Discovering man naked, unshod, unbedded, and unarmed on the very day when man "should emerge from earth to light," Prometheus finds himself at a loss concerning "what preservation [σωτηρίαν] he could devise for man" (321c). He is hence compelled to steal from Hephaestus and Athena "wisdom in the arts together with fire" (τὴν ἔντεχνον σοφίαν σὺν πυρί), which he then bestows on man (321d). A founding offense against the gods, this bestowal gives man, at one and the same time, kinship to the gods, whom man alone worships, and the artful capacities of language, technological invention, and agricultural know-how. From this mythic perspective, technological man, at one with religious man, is the creature of a need that yields just the artful capacity that likens man to the gods.[8] That need, a function of the "fault of Epimetheus," as Bernard

---

7. Plato, *Protagoras*, trans. Benjamin Jowett, revised by M. Ostwald, in *Plato II*, ed. G. P. Goold, Loeb Classical Library (Cambridge: Harvard University Press, 1999); hereafter cited parenthetically.

8. "And now that man was partaker of a divine portion, he, in the first place, by his nearness of kin to deity, was the only creature that worshipped gods, and set himself to establish altars and holy images; and secondly, he soon was enabled by his skills to articulate speech and words, and to invent dwellings, clothes, sandals, beds, and the foods that are of the earth" (*Protagoras* 322a). It is worth noting that Plato imagines the invention of technology to precede the art of war; lacking that art and hence the protections it would yield, man stands in need of politics, which is figured as a gift from Zeus:

> Thus far provided [with technology and language], men dwelt separately in the beginning, and cities there were none; so that they were being destroyed by the wild beasts, since these were in all ways stronger than they; and although their skill in handiwork was a sufficient aid in respect of food, in their warfare with the beasts it was defective; for as yet they had no civic art, which includes the art of war. So they sought to band themselves together and secure their lives by founding cities. Now as often as they were banded together they did wrong to one another through the lack of civic art, and thus they began to be scattered again and to perish. So Zeus, fearing that our race was in danger of utter destruction, sent Hermes to bring respect and right among

Stiegler highlights, suggests the insurmountable delay and forgetting upon which technological capacity is founded as constitutive of the human.[9] A similar treatment of the interplay between need and invention is worked out within the Stoic celebration of man's rational and technological capacities as these are signaled, notably, by the power of the hands. Cicero, following Posidonius in this Stoic optimism, sees in the multivalent capacity of our hands the power that makes of man a world builder and shaper of nature. "In fine," he writes—concluding a celebration of the hands' capacity to shelter, clothe, and protect, to gather and cultivate, breed and collect, delegate and cooperate, to "confine the rivers and straighten or divert their courses"—"by means of our hands we essay to create as it were a second nature within the world of nature" (*nostris denique manibus in rerum natura quasi alteram naturam efficere conamur*). That capacity of the hand to shape or to create "another nature," the literally manipulative ground of culture as "second nature," corresponds with the rational capacity to structure and manipulate the world even in its temporality—a work Cicero explicitly relates to the work of piety: for "we alone of living creatures know the risings and settings and the courses of the stars, the human race has set limits to the day, the month and the year, and has learnt the eclipses of the sun and moon and foretold for all future time their occurrence, their extent and their dates. And contemplating the heavenly bodies the mind arrives at a knowledge of the gods, from which arises piety."[10]

Assuming a similar view of that thanks to which "man's nature surpasses all other living creatures,"[11] Origen links this rational and technological capacity of the human, which operates to shape a distinctively human—and religious—nature and temporality, to the indigence, need, or lack of the human, which distinguishes the human from the animal. In significant contrast to the Greek myth, however, Origen understands the interplay between need and invention not in terms of an offense against God, and hence in terms of fault or guilt, but as something willed by God himself: "From a desire that human understanding should be exercised

---

man, to the end that there should be regulation of cities and friendly ties to draw them together. (322b–c)

9. In *La faute d'Épiméthée*, the first volume of *La technique et le temps*, his study concerning the question of technology and Heideggerian thought, Stiegler highlights the significance of the Promethean and, especially, the Epimethean myths so commonly overlooked by philosophy—and notably that of Heidegger. Stiegler's own illuminating investigations nevertheless overlook the resonance of those myths in the mystical lineage I am tracing here.

10. Cicero *De natura deorum* 2.152, 153.

11. Cicero *De natura deorum* 2.153

everywhere, in order that it might not remain idle and ignorant of the arts, God made man a needy being, so that by his very need he has been compelled to discover arts, some for food and others for protection." Going on to note that need gives birth not only to agriculture and related arts but also to a range of inventions from wool-carding, spinning, and weaving, through building and architecture, to the technologies of transportation, Origen argues that human lack is intended for the human's benefit as a uniquely rational creature. "For the irrational animals," he writes, "have their food ready for them because they have nothing to urge them to practice arts; and they also have natural protection, for they are covered with hair or with wings or with scales or with a shell."[12] By contrast to the animal, which by nature does not lack and so does not know itself as lacking, the human is defined as a being who not only lacks but *knows* such lack and finds in it the spur to invention. It is this lack of "natural" endowment that prompts inventiveness and self-awareness, yielding the world-building, or cultural, creature—the one whose reason needs and finds "another nature."

⟨oͽͼ⟩

In Gregory's seminal treatise from 379, *De hominis opificio* (On the Creation of Man, περὶ κατασκευῆς ἀνθρώπου), the apophatic anthropology that unfolds in concert with Christianity's first systematically apophatic theology takes its starting point in this Origenist understanding of the interplay between human lack and the human capacity tied to that lack, thanks to which man is likened to the God who himself wills that likeness—thus making of it something other than the transgression of Promethean tradition. In *De hominis opificio*, Gregory insists that a technological humanity, endowed, in the image of its creator and for the purpose of dominion over world, with the comprehension of sight and the rational power of language, cannot in the end comprehend itself. The incomprehensibility of the human, Gregory argues, is in fact the point of highest resemblance between the human and the divine. It is also, as the history of its development suggests, a potential point of resistance to the language and logic of domination that also shapes Gregory's vision of human freedom.

This key anthropological insight appears in chapter 11 of Gregory's treatise, where he argues that "since one of the properties of the divine essence is its incomprehensible character [τὸ ἀκατάληπτον τῆς οὐσίας], in that also the image must resemble its model [ἀνάγκη πᾶσα καὶ ἐν τούτῳ τὴν εἰκόνα πρὸς τὸ

12. Origen *Contra Celsum* 4.76

αρχέτυπον ἔχειν τὴν μίμησιν]" (*DO*, 156b).[13] The God whose essence (οὐσία) is incomprehensible (ἀκατάληπτον) is a God not to be grasped, seized, or conquered by thought,[14] and the human mind that sees God to be incomprehensible is itself the image of that God—and hence likewise incomprehensible, unable to grasp, seize, or conquer itself. In the very degree, then, that "we do not manage to know the nature of our own mind" (*DO*, 156b), we constitute the perfect image of our Creator—just as that image of God would fall short of perfection in the measure it were to prove comprehensible.

For Gregory, the human subject who cannot know the nature of its own mind—who cannot fix or place itself because it has no fixed place or definition—relates to creation through an openness of vision whose potential remains unlimited. Emphasizing the resemblance between Creator and creature, or between archetype and icon, Gregory notes that "the Divinity sees all, hears all, scrutinizes all. You also, through sight and hearing, you possess a hold over things [ἔχεις καὶ σὺ τὴν δι' ὄψεως καὶ ἀχοῆς τῶν ὄντῶν ἀντίληψιν][15] and you possess a thinking [or intellect] that examines and scrutinizes the universe [καὶ τὴν ζητικήν τε καὶ διερευνητικὴν τῶν ὄντων διάνοιαν]" (*DO*, 137c). As if the indetermination of the human mind were a condition of its potentiality and receptivity, openness to the universe, according to Gregory, intersects with the incapacity for human self-comprehension.

If the comprehension that Gregory signals here seems to suggest a will to mastery like that of modernity's representing subject, one should keep in mind both the agent of vision (a mind incapable of comprehending itself) and its goal (the incomprehensible God in whose image that mind stands). While Gregory argues that God made man "appear in this world" precisely "in order to be both the contemplator [θεατὴν] and the master [κύριον] of the marvels [θαυμάτων] of the universe," he goes on to state that the enjoyment of those marvels "should give to man the understanding [τὴν σύνεσιν] of the one who provides them, while the grandiose beauty of what he sees places

---

13. I follow here the pagination of *De hominis opificio* (cited parenthetically as *DO*) in the J.-P. Migne edition, *Patrologiae Cursus Completus, Series Graeca*, vol. 44 (Turnhout: Brepols Editores Pontificii). For translations, I have worked among the original Greek, the French translation, *La création de l'homme*, trans. Jean Laplace (Paris: Éditions du Cerf, 1944), and the English translation in *Nicene and Post-Nicene Fathers*, ser. 2, vol. 5, *Gregory of Nyssa: Dogmatic Treatises, etc.*, ed. Philip Schaff and Henry Wace (Peabody, Mass.: Hendrickson, 1994).

14. All possible meanings of ἀκατάληπτον—from the α-privative and καταλαμβάνω, "to seize upon, lay hold of, take possession of; to hold in, keep down or under check; to catch, overtake, hence to discover, detect, find." See H. G. Liddell and R. A. Scott, *A Greek-English Lexicon*, 9th ed. (Oxford: Oxford University Press, 1995).

15. The sense of possession is indicated twice here, in the verb ἔχεὶς and in the noun ἀντίληψις, which, though often rightly translated as "perception" can mean also a laying hold of something, a seizure, or an attack.

him on the tracks of the ineffable and inexpressible power of the Creator [τὴν ἄρρητον τε καὶ ὑπερ λόγον τοῦ πεποιηκότος δύναμιν]" (*DO*, 133a). Along those tracks, the one seeking God never reaches the closure of comprehension but inhabits the infinite dynamic of expectant movement toward God, according to Gregory's doctrine of epektasis, tied to both Pauline and Neoplatonic thought.[16] A virtually all-knowing, all-seeing subject in Gregory, open and receptive to all, is one for whom the ground of knowing, or the God who gives that which is to be known, remains, like the human mind created in that God's image, itself incomprehensible. The one who, as κύριος, possesses the universe through the contemplation of a spectator (θεατής) at the same time finds, through that contemplation, a trace of the incomprehensible and ineffable (that which is beyond reason and speech, ὑπερ λόγον and ἄρρητος). The freedom and dominion that can seem to foreshadow already the will to mastery of modernity's technological subject are in fact a function of humanity's status as "living icon" of the incomprehensible— because infinite—archetype: "Creation in the image [εἰκόνα] of the nature that governs all [τῆς δυναστευούσης τῶν πάντων φύσεως] shows precisely that it has from the start a royal nature [βασιλίδα . . . τὴν φύσιν]. . . . Thus, human nature [ἡ ἀνθρωπίνη φύσις], created to dominate the world [πρὸς τὴν ἀρχὴν ἄλλων], because of its resemblance with the Universal King [διὰ τῆς πρὸς τὸν βασιλέα τοῦ παντὸς ὁμοιότητος], was made as a living image [ἔμψυχος εἰκὼν] who participates in the archetype both in dignity and in name" (*DO*, 136c). As I will point out below, the reception and development of Gregory's apophatic anthropology, taking the human as living image of an infinite and incomprehensible Creator, will in later medieval and early modern contexts yield a thought of the human as participant in the ongoing, indeed infinite, creativity of a nature that, by virtue of such infinity, ultimately resists the logic of any mastery.

The freedom, then, or life, that marks our resemblance to God does imply for Gregory a level of control or possession, both of self and of world, but it remains grounded, at the same time, in that which cannot be comprehended or possessed. This is the condition of technological humanity as Gregory theorizes it: having asserted that man is created for the purpose of comprehending the universe both in sight and in thought, in order there also to find a trace of the incomprehensible God, Gregory goes on to explain and celebrate humanity's technological ingenuity and the domina-

---

16. On this, see Kevin Corrigan's fine article "Ecstasy and Ectasy in Some Early Pagan and Christian Mystical Writings," in *Greek and Medieval Studies in Honor of Leo Sweeney, S.J.*, ed. William J. Carrol and John J. Furlong (New York: P. Lang, 1994).

tion it enables. Echoing Origen and the Epimethean tradition, his explanation begins by noting a physical poverty that forces rational innovation, for
man "comes into the world stripped of any natural protections, without
arms [ἄοπλος][17] and in poverty [πένης], lacking everything needed to satisfy
the needs of life" (DO, 140d). Lacking most notably the natural arms or
instruments of war that one can see in the animal's horn or hoof, claw or
stinger, man is forced to innovate technologically—but in such a way that
his power eventually exceeds that of other creatures. "What appears to be a
deficiency of our nature," Gregory can thus argue, "is in fact an encouragement to dominate [πρὸς τὸ κρατεῖν] that which is near us" (DO, 141b).

Man therefore "works the iron that he uses for war" (πρὸς τὸν πόλεμον),
and through "the ingenuity of his *techne* [ἡ τέχνη δι᾽ ἐπινοίας ποιησαμένη]
gives wings to arrows and, by means of the bow, turns to our use the speed
of the bird" (DO, 141d, 144a).[18] As these key passages attest, man's mastery over creation is realized for Gregory through the ingenuity of a thinking that assumes control over space and time by technological means[19]—
which becomes possible thanks to the physical poverty or deficiency that
forces rational, technological innovation. While emphasizing that poverty,
Gregory will note, following the Stoics, that the physical makeup of man
includes also both the sign and the means of man's dominion—the hands,
which most directly embody man's rational capacity. "Anyone who would
see in the use of hands that which is proper to a rational [λογικῆς] nature
would not be mistaken" (DO, 144b–c), Gregory reasons, not only because
the hands make possible the rational self-expression or self-embodiment
exemplified in writing but even more fundamentally because the hands free
the mouth for language.

The linguistic subject in Gregory is made possible only through the endowment of hands, and thus the linguistic subject is at the same time a
subject endowed with the capacity to manipulate and rule the world technologically. As much as technological manipulation, the hands signal for
Gregory language or logic itself (λόγος) and thus the dignity and power of
the linguistic or rational subject who alone exercises a technological rule:
"One can undoubtedly list by the thousands the needs of life for which the
finesse of these instruments, which suffice for everything [πρὸς πᾶσαν τέχνην
καὶ πᾶσαν ἐνέργειαν], has served man in peace as in war; however, it is above

17. From τό ὅπλον, any tool or instrument, which in the plural, τὰ ὅπλα, refers especially to
implements of war, arms.

18. Man also "bends to his use the wing of the birds, so that by his ingenuity he has at his
disposal the speed of flight" (DO, 141d).

19. ἐπίνοια, the power of thought, inventiveness, design, is tied closely here to τέχνη.

all else for language [τοῦ λόγου] that nature added the hands to our body" (*DO*, 148c–d). While Gregory does not quite see it this way, the condition that grounds rational and technological power—the totipotence signaled by the hands, which prove fit for all and free up an equally open-ended linguistic capacity—can likewise be thought as a condition that resists the impulse of mastery because, thanks to it, man and his world cannot be delimited or fixed. It is this apophatic anthropology, along with its theological ground, that Eriugena inherits from and extends beyond the thought of Gregory.

࿇

For the development of mystical thought in the West, the most important heir of Gregory, as of Dionysius, is John Scotus Eriugena, who translates the writing and the thinking of both these figures into the language and conceptuality of the Latin world. Eriugena develops in a strikingly original and systematic fashion, on the ground of his apophatic theology, the intimate interplay between the anthropology and cosmology answering to such a theology—insisting that the divine, the human, and the cosmos alike are included under the heading of nature. In Eriugena's thought and writing, an infinite and incomprehensible world proves to be not only the self-embodiment but the self-creation of a creative subject, God, who remains incomprehensible to himself. As image of that God, and cocreator, the human for Eriugena will likewise prove incomprehensible. The incomprehensibility both of creative humanity and of its world stand at the center of Eriugena's theological vision, which thinks human and divine creativity alike in terms of their inextricable interplay and their shared incomprehensible ground.

The core dialectic of Eriugena's masterwork, the *Periphyseon*, or *The Division of Nature*, stands in line with Pseudo-Dionysius' Christian version of the Proclean scheme of divine procession, return, and remaining (πρόοδος, ἐπιστροφή, μονή).[20] According to that dialectic, the superessential cause of all

20. I cite here *Periphyseon (The Division of Nature)*, trans. I. P. Sheldon Williams, rev. John J. O'Meara (Montreal: Editions Bellarmin, 1987). All citations are given parenthetically as *P*, according to the Migne pagination, as follows: book number, with Migne page number and column letter. Citations of the Latin original for books 2, 3, and 4 are from I. P. Sheldon Williams, ed., *Periphyseon (De Divisione Naturae)* (Dublin: Dublin Institute for Advanced Studies, 1968, 1972, 1995), and otherwise from J. P. Migne, ed., *Patrologiae Cursus Completus, Series Latina*, vol. 122 (Paris: Migne, 1853). For my treatment of Pseudo-Dionysius' theology, see chapter 5 of *Indiscretion*, "Transcending Negation."

things moves through all things as immanent to them and stands beyond all things as transcendent of them. As cause, the divine is all in all—and so addressed, metaphorically, by affirmative theology (*P* 1, 458B); and as superessential, the divine is nothing in anything—and so most properly addressed by negative theology (*P* 1, 458A–B; see also *P* 3, 682D).[21]

In his treatment of this dialectic, Eriugena argues not only that the divine cause shows itself in all created things, but indeed that it *creates* itself in and through that which it creates. Self-showing is self-creation, and self-creation is self-showing:[22] "Whoever looks into the meaning of these words will find that they teach, indeed proclaim, nothing else but that God is the maker of all things and is made in all things" (*P* 3, 682D). For Eriugena, this self-creation of the divine—and it alone—gives the subsistence of creatures.[23] Thus the whole of the intelligible and sensible world can be seen as divine self-creation and self-manifestation, a creative theophany that issues from and returns to the divine nothingness or simplicity that always remains:

> And thus going forth into all things in order He makes all things and is made in all things, and returns into Himself, calling all things back into Himself, and while He is made in all things, He does not cease to be above all things and thus makes all things from nothing, that is, He produces from His Superessentiality essences, from His Supervitality lives, from His Superintellectuality intellects, from the negation of all things which are and are not the affirmations of all things which are and are not. (*P* 3, 683A–B)[24]

21. The resonance here of the Neoplatonic One, of course, is rather strong, insofar as "it is absent from nothing and yet absent from everything, such that present, it is not present, unless for those who are able to receive it" (Plotinus *Enneads* 4.9 [9].4.24–26). This passage is quoted, and likened to Heidegger's thought of Being, in Pierre Hadot's brilliant study *Le voile d'Isis: Essai sur l'histoire de l'idée de Nature* (Paris: Gallimard, 2004), 306.

22. Eriugena explicitly attributes the teaching that God both makes and is made in creation to Pseudo-Dionysius: "Therefore God *is* everything that truly is because He Himself makes all things and is made in all things, as St. Dionysius the Areopagite says" (*P* 3, 633A).

23. "For when it is said that it creates itself, the true meaning is nothing else but that it is establishing the natures of things [*nisi naturas rerum condere*]. For the creation [*creatio*] of itself, that is, the manifestation [*manifestatio*] of itself in something, is surely that by which all things subsist [*omnium existentium profecto est substitutio*]" (*P* 1, 455A–B).

24. Eriugena will elaborate this scheme in both Christocentric terms (which I address below) and, correlatively, in Trinitarian terms (which nevertheless insist on the utter incomprehensibility and mystery of divine Unity and Trinity). See, e.g., *P* 1, 456B and *P* 2, 570B. Signaling God in himself, in his causes, and in the effects of those causes, the three persons of the Trinity are an-

Thus interpreting the cosmic dialectic of divine immanence and transcendence as divine self-creation, Eriugena, like Dionysius, can see all of the cosmos as an infinitely varied showing or appearance of God. Just as the scripture in which God reveals himself opens the way to an endless variety of possible readings, where one meaning leads to the next within an endless exegetical *transitus* toward the absolutely simple and inaccessible ground of all meaning, so the cosmos offers an endless multiplicity of theophanies that can be read (*P*3, 679A) to show the invisible God from as many different angles as there are holy souls to desire God's appearance.[25]

Within this theophanic play of the cosmos, where God's self-manifestation is actually self-creation, Eriugena emphasizes, further, the fundamentally *co*creative interplay between Creator and creature: "We ought not to understand God and the creature as two things distinct from one another," Eriugena insists, "but as one and the same. For both the creature, by subsisting, is in God; and God, by manifesting Himself, in a marvelous and ineffable manner creates Himself in the creature" (*P*3, 678C). Much like the dialectical thought of Hegel, though with an apophatic intention that is notably absent in Hegel, Eriugena insists that God realizes himself in and through the creature, just as the creature finds its subsistence in God; God achieves self-consciousness in and through the creature's consciousness of God.[26] It

---

swered in turn by three motions of the soul, as sketched out in *P*2, 572C–573B. The soul answers in this way to God precisely because it constitutes the image of that God—and as Eriugena will insist, there is no difference here between the image and its exemplar "except in respect of subject. For the most high Trinity subsists substantially through itself and is created out of no cause, while the trinity of our nature is made by it, Which through Itself is eternal, out of nothing, in Its image and likeness" (*P*2, 598B).

25. See, e.g., *P*1, 448C–D: "For as great as is the number of the elect, so great will be the number of the mansions; as much as shall be the multiplication of holy souls, so much will be the possession of divine theophanies." McGinn points out, "John stressed that creation and scripture were two parallel manifestations of the hidden God", and he "often used the term *transitus* ('dynamic passage from one state to another' would be a possible translation) to describe the process of how the exegete moves through the infinity of textual meanings to the hidden divine unitary source" (*Growth of Mysticism*, 93, 94). For an extended discussion of spiritual exegesis in Eriugena, see McGinn, "The Originality of Eriugena's Spiritual Exegesis," in *Iohannes Scottus Eriugena: The Bible and Hermeneutics*, ed. Gerd Van Riel, Carlos Steel, and James McEvoy (Leuven: University Press, 1996). Werner Beierwaltes emphasizes that this movement of human *transitus*, wherein the believer passes through the infinity of God's scriptural and cosmic showings to return into God himself, answers to the divine *transitus* that is the very nature of both divine and created being: "Transition expresses an essential feature of divine being: the movement in which it develops itself and creates the world" ("Language and its Object," in *Jean-Scot Ecrivain*, ed. G.-H. Allard [Montreal: Editions Bellarmin, 1986], 224).

26. For a clear instance of this in Hegel, see, e.g., *Lectures on the Philosophy of Religion: The Lectures of 1827*, one-volume edition, ed. Peter C. Hodgson (Berkeley and Los Angeles: Univer

is in these dynamic, cocreative terms that "the Creator of all things" is "created in all things," and it is in these terms that all of creation can offer a field of luminous appearance that makes manifest the inaccessible darkness of the superessential (see, e.g., P3, 681B).[27]

Operating according to the paradox of God's brilliant darkness, wherein the invisible becomes visible as invisible, the theophanic in Eriugena follows the Dionysian logic of "dissimilar similarity," and thus it proves equally theocryptic:

> For everything that is understood and sensed is nothing else but the apparition of what is not apparent, the manifestation of the hidden, the affirmation of the negated, the comprehension of the incomprehensible, the utterance of the unutterable, the access to the inaccessible, the understanding of the unintelligible, the body of the bodiless, the essence of the superessential, the form of the formless, the measure of the measureless, the number of the unnumbered, the weight of the weightless, the materialization of the spiritual, the visibility of the invisible, the place of that which is in no place, the time of the timeless, the defini-

sity of California Press, 1988), 392 n. 3: "Finite consciousness knows God only to the extent that God knows himself in it" (1831). On the "apophatic erasure" that Hegel effects in his reading of the speculative mystics, see Cyril O'Regan's *The Heterodox Hegel* (Albany: State University of New York Press, 1994). On Eriugena and German Idealism, see especially the fine study by Dermot Moran, *The Philosophy of John Scotus Eriugena* (Cambridge: Cambridge University Press, 1989); for a brief treatment, Werner Beierwaltes, "The Revaluation of John Scottus Eriugena in German Idealism," in *The Mind of Eriugena*, ed. John J. O'Meara and Ludwig Bieler (Dublin: Irish University Press, 1973), 190–99. For a major account concerning the influence, via Jacob Boehme, of the Neoplatonic mystical traditions in German Idealism and modern thought more broadly, see Cyril O'Regan's multivolume project, beginning with *Gnostic Return in Modernity* (Albany: State University of New York Press, 2001) and *Gnostic Apocalypse: Jacob Boehme's Haunted Narrative* (Albany: State University of New York Press, 2002).

27. Divine self-manifestation, then, signals not simply the Incarnation but indeed more broadly "the ineffable descent of the Supreme Goodness, which is Unity and Trinity, into the things that are so as to make them be, indeed so as itself to be, in all things from the highest to the lowest, ever eternal, ever made, by itself in itself eternal, by itself in itself made" (*P*3, 678D). Several commentators have made this point with some force. See, e.g., Don Duclow: "Conceived as theophany, the entire created order becomes a field of translucent symbols which yield knowledge of the divine nature, even thought this position knowledge [sic] remains metaphorical and partial throughout," from "Divine Nothingness and Self-Creation in John Scotus Eriugena," *Journal of Religion* 57, no. 2 (April 1977): 118. On Eriugena's significance to medieval aesthetics and art, see Werner Beierwaltes, "Negati Affirmatio: Welt als Metapher/ Zur Grundlegung einer mittelalterlichen Ästhetik durch Johannes Scotus Eriugena," in *Jean Scot Erigène et l'histoire de la philosophie* (Paris: Éditions du Centre National de la Recherche Scientifique, 1977); and Yves Christie, "Influences et retentissement de l'oeuvre de Jean Scot sur l'art médiéval: Bilan et perspectives," in *Eriugena Redivivus*, ed. Werner Beierwaltes (Heidelberg: Carl Winter-Universitätsverlag, 1987).

tion of the infinite, the circumscription of the uncircumscribed. (*P* 3, 633A–B)²⁸

In sum, the theophanic self-creation of God constitutes a movement from the transcendence of superessential nothingness, which is absolutely simple and incomprehensible, into the manifold immanence of all created things, which can be known. That immanence, however, is always an immanence of the transcendent, and it can therefore ultimately signal only the impossible appearance of the inapparent—the limited and knowable determinacy of God's absolutely unlimited and unknowable indeterminacy.²⁹ Thought in terms of creativity and creation, the divine creativity—in which we participate—is the incomprehensible and invisible ground, or life, of all visible and comprehended creation.

⟨∽⟩

Eriugena seeks to elucidate the logic of theophanic self-creation, where the something of creation, which we can know, issues from the self-negation of the divine nothingness, which we cannot know, through the "example" of our own human nature—and at this point, the rich anthropological dimension of Eriugena's theological project becomes quite clear:³⁰

> For our own intellect [*intellectus*] too, although in itself it is invisible and incomprehensible [*invisibilis et incomprehensibilis*], yet becomes both manifest and comprehensible [*et manifestatur et comprehenditur*] by certain signs [*signis*] when it is materialized in sounds and letters and also indications as though in sorts of bodies; and while it becomes externally apparent in this way [*et dum sic extrinsecus apparet*] it still remains internally invisible [*semper intrinsicus invisibilis permanet*],

28. See also *P* 3, 678C: "And God, by manifesting Himself, in a marvelous and ineffable manner creates Himself in the creature, the invisible making Himself visible and the incomprehensible comprehensible and the hidden revealed and the unknown known and being without form and species formed and specific and the superessential essential and the supernatural natural and the simple composite and the accident-free subject to accident and the infinite finite, and the uncircumscribed circumscribed and the supratemporal temporal and the Creator of all things created in all things and the Maker of all things made in all things, and Eternal he begins to be, and immobile He moves into all things and becomes in all things all things."

29. As Don Duclow puts it, "The divine *nihil* constitutes the ground for theophanic self-creation, which in turn cannot be thought apart from the transcendence which it manifests in the otherness of created essence and being" ("Divine Nothingness and Self-Creation," 119).

30. For a fine full-length study of Eriugena's anthropology, see Willemien Otten, *The Anthropology of Johannes Scottus Eriugena* (Leiden: Brill, 1991).

and while it breaks out into various figures comprehensible to the
senses it never abandons the incomprehensible state of its nature; and
before it becomes outwardly apparent it moves itself within itself; and
thus it is both silent and cries out, and while it is silent it cries out and
while it is crying out it is silent; and invisible it is seen and while it
is being seen it is invisible; and uncircumscribed it is circumscribed,
and while it is being circumscribed it continues to be uncircumscribed.
(*P* 3, 633B–C)

The theophanic God, who through self-creation makes manifest his uncre-
ated invisibility, is mirrored by the human intellect, which, in itself indefinite and invisible, defines and shows itself through its self-expression, all
the while remaining indefinite and invisible. In both cases, Eriugena is finally pointing to the incomprehensible ground of creativity itself, the mystery of creation *ex nihilo*.

This human example, of course, is not really just an example, since it
is based in Eriugena's understanding of the human subject as incomprehensible image of the incomprehensible God. While every creature in Eriugena
constitutes an appearance of God (a theophany), the human creature alone
constitutes an image (*imago*) of God. Moreover, it constitutes an image of
God not simply to the degree that the human intellect, like the divine,
becomes self-conscious through its own self-expression but, even more,
insofar as the human intellect, again like the divine, ultimately proves
through that very self-consciousness—or in the deepest ground of that self-
consciousness—to be incomprehensible to itself.[31] The human image of the
divine is distinctive in that it is both self-conscious and incomprehensible to itself, indeed incomprehensible to itself *in* its self-consciousness. In
knowing the deepest incomprehensibility of the human, we come in fact to
know the true incomprehensibility of God. In both cases, the divine and the
human, such incomprehensibility is the ground of self-consciousness; it is

---

31. McGinn puts all of this quite well: "If all things are God manifested, then humanity is
God manifested in the most special way. It is the true and only *imago Dei*, because, like its divine
source, it does not know *what* it is (it is not a *what* at all), but it does know *that* it is—namely,
it possesses self-consciousness. Thus, the primacy of negative theology in Eriugena is comple-
mented by his negative anthropology: Humanity does not know God, but God does not know
God either (in the sense of knowing or defining a *what*); and humanity does not know itself, nor
does God know humanity insofar as it is one with the divine mind that is the cause of itself. This
brilliant anthropological turn, hinted at in Gregory's *The Image*, was brought to full and daring
systematic expression in the Irishman's writings. It is the ground for a remarkable elevation of
humanity (at least the idea of humanity) to a divine and co-creative status" (*Growth of Mysticism*, 105).

the incomprehensibility of a nothingness that is the ground of the creation in and through which alone self-consciousness is realized.

Here, Eriugena's apophatic anthropology complements his apophatic theology: neither God nor the human subject created in his image can comprehend *what* they themselves are—even as they achieve, through their own self-creative self-expression, an awareness *that* they are:

> For the human mind [*mens*] does know itself [*et seipsam novit*], and again does not know itself [*et seipsam non novit*]. For it knows that it is [*quia est*], but does not know what it is [*quid est*]. And, as we have taught in earlier books, it is this which reveals most clearly the Image of God to be in man [*maxime imago Dei esse in homine docetur*]. For just as God is comprehensible in the sense that it can be deduced from His creation that he is, and incomprehensible because it cannot be comprehended by any intellect whether human or angelic nor even by Himself [*nec a seipso*] what He is, seeing that He is not a what but superessential [*quia non est quid, quippe superessentialis*]: so to the human mind it is given to know only one thing, that it is—but as to what it is no sort of notion is permitted it. (*P*4, 771B)[32]

As becomes clear in this passage, Eriugena wants to insist not only that the human cannot comprehend God, nor even simply that the human created in the image of the incomprehensible God is itself incomprehensible, but also, in full consistency with these first two principles, that even God finally cannot comprehend himself.[33] In light of such thoroughgoing divine ignorance, Eriugena can insist that "the human mind is more honored in its

32. To elucidate more fully this interplay between the human creature's self-consciousness and its ultimate incomprehensibility to itself, one has to note that Eriugena distinguishes two aspects of the human substance. As created among the intelligible Causes in God, that substance is utterly simple and thus incomprehensible; as generated among the effects of those Causes, however, the human substance takes on the kind of determination that renders it comprehensible (*P*4, 771A). Having made this distinction, however, Eriugena finally insists, apophatically, on the ultimate incomprehensibility of the human substance—at the level *both* of generated effect *and* of created cause: "So it is that what is one and the same [substance] can be thought of as twofold because there are two ways of looking at it, yet everywhere it preserves its incomprehensibility [*ubique tamen suam incomprehensibilitem custodit*], in the effects as in the causes [*in causis dico et in effectibus*], and whether it is endowed with accidents or abides in its naked simplicity: under neither set of circumstances is it subject to created sense or intellect nor even the knowledge of itself as to what it is [*nec a seipsa intelligitur quid sit*] (*P*4, 771A).

33. For a concise and rigorous analysis of these three theses—with an insistence on their essential interconnection, see McGinn, "The Negative Element in the Anthropology of John the Scot," in *Jean Scot Erigène et l'histoire de la philosophie*, 315–25.

ignorance than in its knowledge" (*P* 4, 771C), for in that ignorance above all the image of the divine in the human achieves its perfection.[34]

Eriugena's apophatic celebration of ignorance—both theological and anthropological—is intended to mark the manner in which both the divine and human substance ultimately exceed or transcend all ten of the categories, or "predicables," delimited by that "shrewdest of the Greeks," Aristotle (*P* 1, 463A). One of those categories, however, assumes a particular importance: that of place, *locus*, or τόπος (along with its twin, time). In seeking to articulate the excess of the divine and its image over the categories, Eriugena emphasizes the impossibility of locating either the divine or the human substance, and he does so because it is above all *locus* that marks the kind of limitation, circumscription, or definition that alone makes knowledge (or discourse) possible: "The Divine Likeness in the human mind is most clearly discerned," Eriugena insists, when it is "not known what it is"—precisely because "if it were known to be something, then at once it would be limited by some definition, and thereby would cease to be a complete expression of the Image of its Creator, who is absolutely unlimited and contained within no definition [*qui omnino incircumscriptus est, et in nullo intelligitur*], because He is infinite, beyond all that may be said or comprehended, superessential [*quia infinitus est, super omne, quod dicitur et intelligitur, superessentialis*]" (*P* 4, 771C–D). The superessential God who remains beyond all that can be spoken or understood is a God beyond the definition or circumscription of any place (or time); indeed, he is the placeless place of all places, "present to all things by his immeasurable circumambience of them" (*P* 1, 523B)—and thus in that very presence to all things beyond those things.[35] Since knowledge for Eriugena, as for medieval thought more broadly, implies the definition or location of the object

34. And so it is that "the ignorance in it of what it is is more praiseworthy than the knowledge that it is, just as the negation of God accords better with the praise of His nature than the affirmation" (*P* 4, 771C).

35. On the placelessness of God's causal presence, see also, e.g., *P* 1, 468D–469A. The inextricable tie between definition and location runs throughout Eriugena's thinking, as throughout medieval thought more broadly, for "place is definition and definition is place" (*P* 1, 485B). Place, indeed, "is simply the natural definition of each creature, within which it is wholly contained and beyond which it by no means extends: and from this it is given to understand that whether one call it place or limit or term or definition or circumscription, one and the same thing is denoted, namely the confine of a finite creature" (*P* 1, 483C); and place is tied, in turn, to time, the two together marking the conditions of existence and knowledge: "For it is impossible to conceive place if time *is withdrawn*, as it is impossible for time to be defined without *understanding it in connexion* with place. . . . Therefore the essence of all existing things is local and temporal, and thus it can in no way be known except in place and time and under place and time" (*P* 1, 481C).

known, the unknowable God and its human image alike stand beyond all location.

At the same time, such definition or location, such circumscription, is the condition of created being. Thus, insofar as self-creation implies definition, which means location, even as it issues from and returns to a nothingness that cannot be defined or located, we can see in the movement of self-creation an intersection between self-awareness and ignorance of self.[36] That is, the creative intellect (human or divine) must define or locate what it only thereby comes to know, and in what it comes to know it achieves its own self-consciousness or self-awareness, its very subsistence At the same time, however, the same creative intellect necessarily exceeds or stands beyond that which it creates, and to that degree it remains beyond all location and thus incomprehensible—even to itself. The ground of definition and knowledge here proves indefinable and unknowable.

This interplay between the self-consciousness and self-ignorance of creative intellect, between knowable creation in all its multiplicity and the unknowable simplicity of creation's ground, comes to light most forcefully in Eriugena where the divine and the human are most essentially united— in the Word of God as reason or cause of the universe (see P 3, 642C–D). As the self-expression of God, that Word—which, according to the Psalm, "runs swiftly" through all things "in order that all things may be" (P 3, 642D)—creates all things and is created *in* all things (P 3, 646C). It proceeds out into all things even as it calls all things back into itself, such that the creative Word is also the salvific. In this understanding of the Word as that which "runs" through all things so as to make them be and bring them back into God, Eriugena, while evoking the Psalms, is alluding also to one of two etymologies that he signals elsewhere to articulate the meaning of the Greek name for God. If θεός derives from the verb θέω (I run), he reasons, then it articulates the sense in which God "runs *throughout all things* and . . . by His running fills out all things, as it is written: 'His Word runneth swiftly'" (P 1, 452C). If θεός derives from the verb θεωρῶ (I see), then it articulates the sense in which God "sees in Himself all things that are [while] He looks upon nothing that is outside Himself because outside Him there is nothing" (P 1, 452C). The God who runs through all things to

36. As Marta Cristiani nicely puts it, one can see throughout Eriugena "the clearest affirmation that *place* is identified with the activity of the human, angelic or divine intellect that localizes and circumscribes beings, that knows reality thanks to that very act, thanks to that power of definition, which is considered at the same time as the power of *creation*" (in O'Meara and Bieler, *The Mind of Eriugena*, 47).

make them be is also the God who creates and sustains all things by seeing all things in himself—and himself in all things—according to the dialectic of immanence and transcendence. As seer and seen, maker and made ($P\,3$, 677C), the God who expresses himself through his creative Word is at once most present and most hidden, all things in all and nothing in nothing ($P\,3$, 668C). The ineffable intellectual light present to all but contained by none, seen in all things visible while remaining itself invisible, he is the placeless "place of all places" that can be defined neither by itself nor by any other intellect, the placeless place from which all things proceed and to which all things return.[37]

Along these lines, Eriugena appropriates and develops a deeper tradition that links or even equates divine creation with vision, such that vision is not simply passive reception but is actively involved in producing—by seeing—that which it sees. As the German scholar of Neoplatonism and modern Idealism Werner Beierwaltes explains, the vision that is creation "does not therefore mean receiving, passively becoming aware of, grasping, discovering, observing or also seeing into (*speculari*, er-*spähen*), but is to be understood as an act which constitutes, which grounds and produces being: vision [*Sehen*] as an active intuition (Er-*sehen*) of being."[38] The created world, then, is the vision of God— in both senses of the genitive, for the world is theophany, or self-showing of God, created in and through God's seeing of it and of himself in it. And the created human, in its relation to the theophanic creation, sees itself as seen by the God who creates by seeing—in a coincidence of seeing and being seen that has a very rich history in the traditions of mystical speculation, the most famous expression of which would perhaps be Meister Eckhart's assertion that "the eye in which I see God is the same eye in which God sees me: my eye and God's eye are one eye, one knowing, and one loving."[39]

37. See especially those passages such as $P\,2$, 592C–D: "The Divine Nature is without any place, although it provides place within itself for all things which are from it, and for that reason is called the Place of all things; but it is unable to provide place for itself because it is infinite and uncircumscribed and does not allow itself to be located, that is, defined and circumscribed, by any intellect nor by itself. For from it, being infinite and more than infinite, all finites and infinites proceed, and to it, being infinite and more than infinite, they return." Similarly, $P\,3$, 643C: "For who, taking thought for the truth, would believe or think that God had prepared for Himself places through which he might diffuse Himself, He who is contained in no place since He is the common place of all things and therefore, as Place of places, is held by no place?"

38. Werner Beierwaltes, "Cusanus and Eriugena," in *Dionysius* (Halifax, N.S.: Dalhousie University Press, 1989), 126.

39. Meister Eckhart, Sermon 12, quoted in Werner Beierwaltes, *Identität und Differenz* (Frankfurt am Main: Vittorio Klostermann, 1980), 146 n. 2: "Das ouge, dâ inne ich got sihe, daz ist daz selbe ouge, dâ inne mich got sihet; mîn ouge und gotes ouge daz ist éin ouge und éin gesiht

God sees himself, then, in being seen by the human, just as the human, insofar as it sees God, sees that it is seen by God. In the human image especially, we can glimpse how the coimplication of divine creating and being created, "creari in creare,"[40] is mirrored in the coimplication between seeing and being seen. This point is taken up and developed in decisive ways by Eriugena's later medieval, or already early modern, heir, Nicholas of Cusa, who writes in his 1453 treatise *On the Vision of God (De visione Dei)* that "You [God] are visible by all creatures and you see all. In that you see all you are seen by all. For otherwise creatures cannot exist since they exist by your vision."[41] Just as for Eriugena the self-creative God is the placeless place of all places, the seeing Word who runs through all things and is contained in no one of them, so for Cusa, who develops a similar version of the immanence-transcendence dialectic, the creative power of divine vision entails its placeless ubiquity—the inconceivable thought of which stands at the heart of a mystical theology that Cusa develops by means of countless names and images and objects, among which notably the "all-seeing" image or portrait with whose analysis Cusa opens *On the Vision of God.*

In his preface to the work, written to the monks at Tegernsee as an object lesson, or "similitude," for intuiting the logic and practice of mystical theology, Cusa recommends staging an encounter with an all-seeing image or portrait, which he is also sending to the monks, he writes, and which, as he points out, seems to gaze at the individual from no matter what position the individual occupies in relation to the image—and which, more-

---

und éin bekennen und éin minnen" (Pred. 12, DW 1.201.5–8, ed. Quint). For extensive references on this rich history in Christianity, as well as on key Greek precursors, see Beierwaltes, "Cusanus and Eriugena," 130 n. 52; *Identität und Differenz* (Frankfurt am Main: Vittorio Klostermann, 1980), 146 nn. 2 and 3; and *Visio Facialis—Sehen ins Angesicht: Zur Coincidenz des endlichen und unendlichen Blicks bei Cusanus* (München: Bayerischen Akademie der Wissenschaften, 1988), 13–14 n. 21. See also Bernard McGinn's quotation and discussion of Sermon 12, within his thorough and instructive chapter "Nicholas of Cusa on Mystical Theology," in *The Harvest of Mysticism in Medieval Germany,* vol. 4 of *The Presence of God: A History of Western Christian Mysticism* (New York: Crossroad, 2005), 461.

40. Beierwaltes, "Cusanus and Eriugena," 126–27.

41. Nicholas of Cusa, *On the Vision of God* 10.40, in *Nicolas of Cusa: Selected Spiritual Writings,* ed. H. Lawrence Bond (New York: Paulist Press, 1997), 253. In his illuminating commentary on this Cusan contention that "the being of created reality is your vision and likewise your being seen" (*esse creaturae est videre tuum pariter et videri*), Werner Beierwaltes emphasizes the proximity, if not the indiscretion, between the human and the divine in this "being seen," which is to be understood "as divine *and* as creaturely act, in so far as the being of man consists in the vision of God (objective genitive); in it he realizes his being-seen-by-God" ("Cusanus and Eriugena," 130).

over, does so simultaneously for any and all individuals who look at the image. The ubiquitous gaze of the image, moving everywhere at once and hence circumscribed in no one single place, gathers all human individuals as one while sustaining the uniqueness of each. Because there is no possible interchange of the various individual perspectives, the mystical unity of all under the gaze does not suppress plurality but affirms or even requires it, according to a potentiality that emerges thanks only to the reciprocal determination of unique individuals. Along these lines, in his brilliant reading of the mystical logic disclosed through this encounter with the all-seeing portrait in Cusa, French theorist Michel de Certeau highlights the social character of this mystical theology, as well as the mystical character of the social more generally.[42] He notes that the ubiquity of the gaze is in fact not something that can be seen directly by any one individual—since no individual can occupy all positions at once—but is rather a reality constituted and sustained by means of the interrelation of individuals who, finding themselves individually surprised to see the gaze moving always with them, believe the testimony of others that they, too, fall under the same gaze. Such testimony and belief, which evoke, or even constitute, the ubiquity of a gaze that forms a circle whose center is everywhere and circumference nowhere, can never finally or exhaustively make that gaze or its ubiquity present as such. Just as mystical theology, through an endless proliferation of names and images and examples for God, can never finally or exhaustively make that God present as such, and just as the reality of the gaze thus includes within itself the constructive activity of a social interaction, so the reality of theology's mystical God includes the open-ended, creative activity of the human who, through such creativity, evokes endlessly—but never exhaustively actualizes—that reality.

If medieval cosmology, under the influence of Aristotle and Ptolemy, tended to hold at bay the more unsettling implications of Eriugena's early insistence that the world, as self-embodiment of a self-creative God, is infinite and incomprehensible, the later Middle Ages, and in this a pivot to modernity, can be understood to involve a return, within the thought of speculative mystics like Cusa and his heir Giordano Bruno, of the Eriugenian insistence on the infinity and incomprehensibility of the cosmos—and, in turn, on the endlessly creative and self-creative capacity of the human who images an incomprehensible and self-creative God. As Beierwaltes emphasizes, the Cusan understanding of God remains intimately bound to

42. See Michel de Certeau, "The Gaze of Nicholas of Cusa," *Diacritics* 17, no. 3 (1987): 20–21.

Eriugena in several ways, including notably "the characteristic of the God-creator that he *creates himself* and that this creation of himself is identical with his awareness or creative vision of himself (*Sich-selbst-*[Er-]*Sehen*)."[43] Cusa understands the created human both as itself creative, which for him means cultural and historical, and in that degree as participating in the absolute creativity of God. Along these lines he can be understood, as Ernst Cassirer argues in his classic 1926 study *The Individual and the Cosmos in Renaissance Philosophy*, to be an important source for the thought of human creativity central to Renaissance humanism.[44] Under the constructivist influences of nominalism, but seeking to maintain a kind of participatory realism, where the interrelation of individuals yields a unity that requires difference, Cusa develops his understanding of human creativity by rethinking the doctrine of the *imago Dei* as inherited from the mystical tradition of Gregory and Eriugena. A creative freedom from pregiven ideas and the logic of mimesis—a freedom opened in large part by nominalism when, through its emphasis on God's *potentia absoluta*, it frees the play of human thought and language[45]—is for Cusa the function of humanity's status as imitation of a divine creativity that itself, in creating, imitates nothing. The constructive freedom made possible by the lack of a priori givens on this reading proves integral to the unfolding of the real itself. This implies the inclusion within the real, or within nature, of a human—which is to say, a cultural and historical—creativity that not only reflects but advances the divine creativity.

In emphasizing this link between the creative freedom of humanity and its status as *imago Dei*, Cusa can affirm not only the variety and complexity of humanity's historical and cultural being but indeed the creative—and religious—character of everyday life. As Pauline Moffit Watts nicely highlights in her study *Nicolaus Cusanus*, which links Cusa's valuation of everyday creativity, or creative everydayness, to the fictive and literary character of his theology:

---

43. Beierwaltes, "Cusanus and Eriugena," 123.

44. Ernst Cassirer, *Individuum und Kosmos in der Philosophie der Renaissance* (Darmstadt: Wissenschaftliche Buchgesellschaft, 1962), translated by Mario Domandi as *The Individual and the Cosmos in Renaissance Philosophy* (New York: Harper and Row, 1963; reprint, Mineola, N.Y.: Dover Publications, 2000).

45. For an important discussion of the role played by nominalist influence in Cusa, and of Cusa's relation to modernity, see Hans Blumenberg, *Legitimacy of the Modern Age*, trans. Robert M. Wallace (Cambridge: MIT Press, 1983), esp. 483ff.; see also Louis Dupré's treatment of Cusa in *Passage to Modernity: An Essay in the Hermeneutics of Nature and Culture* (New Haven: Yale University Press, 1993), esp. 182–89.

Cusanus' emphasis upon the formative and creative qualities of the mind becomes ever richer and more detailed as his thought develops. His conviction that the mind's creativity is exemplified not simply in the intricate and obscure arguments of philosophers and rhetoricians, but also in the everyday conversations and exchanges of human society becomes increasingly central to his discussion of man. . . . The fact that Cusanus has turned to the dialogue form in [his later work] indicates that he is becoming increasingly aware of the literary and fictional nature of his search for ways in which to overcome disjunction [between man and the unknowable God]. In this too he reflects a humanist influence. As his early works have shown him, the types of answers he seeks are not to be found in logical arguments and proofs. They are instead grounded in the flow of ordinary conversation, in the flurry of commercial transactions that take place in the markets, and in the adaptability and inventiveness of *homo faber*, the artisan.[46]

In and through his theological valuation of human creativity, and in deviation from the common association of everydayness and social existence with vain distraction and curiosity, Cusa is able to affirm the common or the everyday in all of its variability and fluidity—finding even in the flowing mass and in the indistinct murmur of the human multitude an evocation of the mystical presence. Indeed, it is on a bridge in Rome during the Jubilee, amid a crowd of "numberless populations" moving like a "Rhine of human beings," that the philosopher in Cusa's *Idiota de Mente* (*The Layman on Mind*) is astonished to sense what he cannot conceive—a unity within immeasurable multiplicity, "a single faith of all in such a great diversity of bodies."[47] And it is in crossing the ocean, "returning by sea from Greece," that Cusa himself is first struck with his most famous mystical insight: the embrace of "incomprehensibles incomprehensibly, in learned ignorance."[48]

"Learned ignorance" (*docta ignorantia*), the doctrine for which Cusa is best known, constitutes for him the most appropriate relation of the human mind to a God who remains unknowable and ineffable thanks to a divine

46. Pauline Moffitt Watts, *Nicolaus Cusanus: A Fifteenth-Century Vision of Man* (Leiden: E. J. Brill, 1982), 230.

47. De Certeau, "The Gaze of Nicholas of Cusa," 34.

48. Nicholas of Cusa, letter to Lord Cardinal Julian, in the appendix to *On Learned Ignorance*, in Bond, *Nicholas of Cusa*, 205–6. For an informative discussion of the historical and rhetorical senses of this scenario, see Marjorie O'Rourke Boyle, "Cusanus at Sea: The Topicality of Illuminative Discourse," *Journal of Religion* 71, no. 2 (April 1991).

transcendence that is dialectically bound to absolute immanence. Much like Pseudo-Dionysius, John Scotus Eriugena, or Meister Eckhart, all important influences, Cusa figures God as distinct thanks to his indistinction, or as "other" thanks to his being absolutely "not-other," according to what Cusa famously terms the "coincidence of opposites" (*coincidentia oppositorum*) wherein God as absolute maximum proves indistinguishable from God as absolute minimum. As Cusa writes in *De docta ignorantia* (*On Learned Ignorance*, 1440):

> Oppositions apply . . . only to those things that admit a greater and a lesser, and they apply in different ways, but never to the absolutely maximum, for it is above all opposition. Therefore, because the absolutely maximum is absolutely and actually all that can be, and it is without opposition to such an extent that the minimum coincides with the maximum, it is above all affirmation and all negation. It both is and is not all that is conceived to be, and it both is and is not all that is conceived not to be. But it is a "this" in such a way that it is all things, and it is all things in such a way that it is none of them, and it is a "this" maximally in such a way that it is also a "this" minimally.[49]

If Cusa can well be read, as Ernst Cassirer argues, to be distinctively modern in his understanding of the human mind and knowing as creative, he might also be read, I want to argue, and in that very emphasis on human creativity, to resist the logic of machination that we saw Heidegger associate with modern metaphysics and its technological culture. The key to such a reading resides in Cusa's approach to the human as "living image" or "living mirror" of the incomprehensible God who is divine Art—and in his naming of that God in terms of "possibility itself" (God as *posse ipsum*). This naming of God according to possibility itself, which Cusa develops in his final work, *De apice theoriae* (*On the Summit of Contemplation*, 1464), suggests a priority of possibility over actuality and the insurmountable difference between possibility itself and any one of its actual (or actualizable) manifestations. As I will signal in what follows, one might understand this naming of God in terms of absolute possibility to suggest a thinking that deviates significantly from the traditional metaphysical privilege of actuality

---

49. Nicholas of Cusa, *On Learned Ignorance* 2.4.13, in Bond, *Nicholas of Cusa*, 92. Latin version in Nikolaus von Kues, *Philosophisch-Theologische Werke, Lateinisch-Deutsch* (Hamburg: Felix Meiner Verlag, 2002), vol. 1. Hereafter cited parenthetically as *DI*, with book, chapter, and paragraph number from the critical edition, followed by the English edition page number.

and presence—so as even to constitute a version of what Heidegger intends by the "ontological difference" that metaphysics would forget through its reduction of Being itself to *a* being. Furthermore, insofar as the thought of God in terms of possibility can be tied to Cusa's view of the creative humanity made in that God's image, the Cusan anthropology may be seen to resemble models of the human emerging in current theory on technological culture and—like those models—to resist the modern epoch's metaphysics and technological machinations as treated by Heidegger.

⟨∞⟩

Cusa's take on the creative freedom of humanity needs to be understood not only in relation to the incomprehensible God in whose image humanity is made but also in relation to the world where humanity, like God, realizes itself as creative. In his important study *From the Closed World to the Infinite Universe* (1957), Alexandre Koyré emphasizes that Cusa's application to the cosmos of divine infinity marks an important departure from medieval conceptions of the cosmos as limited, qualitatively differentiated, hierarchically ordered, and securely centered. Along these lines, Cusa offers a pivotal expression of the metaphor of an "infinite sphere" whose center is everywhere and circumference nowhere, a metaphor that traverses Western thought from the twelfth-century pseudo-Hermetic text *Book of the Twenty-Four Philosophers* and the thought of Alain de Lille through Pascal to such late moderns as Borges and Joyce.[50] Insofar as Cusa applies to the cosmos itself the divine attribute of infinity, echoing in this as in other things the earlier thought of Eriugena, he is able to understand the cosmos, like God, according to this pseudo-Hermetic formulation, so as to yield a nonhierarchical, thoroughly relational, and perspectival universe: "Since it always appears to every observer," Cusa writes in *De docta ignorantia*, "whether on the earth, the sun, or another star, that one is, as if, at an immovable center of things and that all else is being moved, one will always select different poles in relation to oneself, whether one is on the sun,

---

50. For a wide-ranging and informative history of the infinite sphere metaphor, see Dietrich Mahnke, *Unendliche Sphäre und Allmittelpunkt* (Stuttgart-Bad Cannstatt: Friedrich Frommann Verlag, 1966 [= Faksimile-Neudruck der Ausgabe Halle 1937]). A concise and illuminating treatment of the infinite sphere metaphor in Cusa and in the Pascal from whom he differs can be found in Maurice de Gandillac, "Pascal et le silence du monde," in *Blaise Pascal: L'homme et l'oeuvre*, Cahiers de Royaumont, no. 1 (Paris: Minuit, 1956). Rich discussion of the metaphor can be found also, in its very broad history, in Georges Poulet, *Les Métamorphoses du cercle* (Paris: Plon, 1961).

the earth, the moon, Mars, and so forth. Therefore the world machine will have, one might say, its center everywhere and its circumference nowhere, for its circumference and center is God, who is everywhere and nowhere" (*DI* 2.12.162, p. 161). This immensity of the universe is figured by Cusa very notably in terms of oceanic fluidity, which he evokes in setting up this famous passage by asking "how would a passenger know that one's ship was being moved, if one did not know that the water was flowing past and if the shores were not visible from the ship in the middle of the water?" (*DI* 2.12.162, p. 161).[51] The boundless, oceanic universe, incomprehensibly immense and fluid, renders all knowing for those within the universe thoroughly relational, or relative, and hence provisional—but in such a way that every instance of knowing, indeed every individual, is integral to the incomprehensible whole.[52] Within this universe, as Koyré comments, no one place "can claim an absolutely privileged value (for instance, that of being the center of the universe)," and we thus have to admit "the possible existence of different, equivalent world-images, the relative—in the full sense of the word—character of each of them, and the utter impossibility of forming an objectively valid representation of the universe."[53]

According to the dialectic of immanence and transcendence binding God and world, where world would be the unfolding (*explicatio*) of that which is enfolded in the absolute simplicity of God (*complicatio*), the world for Cusa, while not strictly infinite, is nonetheless thought as unbounded, constituting an image of the infinite God that proves, like the infinite God himself, beyond the objective representation or comprehension of any human mind. "Since it is not possible for the world to be enclosed between a corporeal center and circumference, the world, whose center and circumference are God, *is not understood* [*non intelligitur mundus, cuius centrum et circumferentiam sunt deus*]," Cusa writes; "and although the world is not infinite, it cannot be conceived as finite [*non potest concipi finitus*], since it lacks boundaries within which it is enclosed [*cum terminis*

51. Cusa, cited also with helpful commentary in Mahnke, *Unendliche Sphäre*, 97, and in Gandillac, who contrasts the joy of Cusa with the dread of Pascal before such immensity, in "Pascal et le silence du monde," 359.

52. See, e.g., *DI* 2.11, cited in Gandillac, "Pascal et le silence du monde," 356–57: "We now know that the universe is triple and that there exists nothing that is not one through power, through act, and through the movement of connection; that absolutely nothing can subsist without all of the rest, such that everything is necessarily in everything, with all the variety possible of degrees and of such differences that there can exist nowhere in the universe two realities that are truly equal."

53. Alexandre Koyré, *From the Closed World to the Infinite Universe* (New York: Harper and Brothers, 1957), 16.

careat, intra quos claudatur]" *(DI* 2.11.156, p. 158). By contrast to a modern
metaphysics for which, as according to Heidegger, the world is captured or
grasped as image or picture by the representing subject, to the exclusion of
genuine creativity, the world in Cusa proves beyond representation or comprehension according to a kind of negative cosmology that answers to his
negative theology. As Gandillac notes, "it is precisely because this universe
is infinite and without figure that it expresses and figures the infigurable
Deity."[54] The truth of an infinite God, figured impossibly in the truth of an
infinite universe, teaches the lesson of learned ignorance: that "the quiddity of things, which is the truth of beings, is unattainable in its purity, and
although it is pursued by all philosophers, none has found it as it is. The
more profoundly learned we are in this ignorance, the more closely we draw
near truth itself" (*DI* 1.3.10, p. 91).

To this theologically grounded conception of the cosmos as unbounded
or indeterminate and thus as ultimately incomprehensible corresponds an
understanding of human mind as uncomprehending and also incomprehensible to itself—yielding a view of all human thought as "imprecise" and
hence "conjectural."[55] In his treatment of the nature of human thought as
conjecture, Cusa understands it not only as partial, provisional, or revisable
but also, in the same measure, as fundamentally productive or creative.
The space of human thought as conjecture, which is conditioned by an irreducible ignorance, is one in which the human subject enjoys the creative
potential thanks to which the human is like another God—a human or created god, a finite infinity.[56] As Cusa writes in his main work on the conjectural character of thought, *De coniecturis* (*On Surmises,* 1440–44):

54. Gandillac, "Pascal et le silence du monde," 356.
55. For a helpful discussion of the "negative ontology" operative in Cusa's theology and
anthropology, see also Carlo Riccati's comparative study of Cusa and Eriugena, *"Processio" et
"Explicatio": La doctrine de la création chez Jean-Scot et Nicolas de Cues* (Naples: Bibliopolis,
1983), 265: "The intellect does not grasp any quiddity, not even its own. Our intellect does not
grasp its Being, for the Being from which it derives is not intelligible" (Cusa, *Ven. sap.* 29.h14
n.87 [213v], quoted in Riccati: "Neque intellectus propriam quidditatem et essentiam intra se
attingere potest").
56. See, e.g., *DI* 2.2.104: "Consequently, every creature is, in a certain way, a finite infinity or
a created god" [Ut omnis creatura sit quasi infinitas finita aut deus creatus]. Also *De coniecturis*
2.14.143: "For man is god, but not unqualifiedly, since he is man; therefore, he is a human god.
Man is also world but is not contractedly all things, since he is man; therefore, man is a microcosm, or a human world." *De beryllo* 6 (7 in Hopkins's translation), citing Hermes Trismegistus
(*Asclepius* 1.6), figures human likeness to God in terms of creative capacity, itself linked to an
appreciation of the inherent failure of symbols (or "enigmas") in relation to the divine reality:

Note that Hermes Trismegistus states that man is a second god (*hominem esse secun-*

It must be the case that conjectures originate from our minds, even as the real world originates from Infinite Divine Reason. For when, as best it can, the human mind (which is a lofty likeness of God) partakes of the fruitfulness of the creating nature, it produces from itself, qua image of the Omnipotent Form, rational entities, [which are made] in the likeness of real entities.[57] Consequently, the human mind is the form of a conjectured [rational] world, just as the Divine Mind is the Form of the real world. Therefore, just as that Absolute Divine Being is all that which there is [essentially] in each existing thing, so too the oneness of the human mind is the being of its own conjectures. Now, God works all things for His own sake, so that He is both the Intellectual Beginning and [Intellectual] End of all things. Similarly, the unfolding of a rational world—an unfolding which proceeds from our enfolding mind—exists for the sake of the producing mind. For the more subtly the mind contemplates itself in and through the world unfolded from itself, the more abundantly fruitful is it made within itself, since its End is Infinite Reason.[58]

If, as Beierwaltes suggests, "'self-creation' denies the distinction (Differenz) between creative being and its result,"[59] human mind plays an indispensable, productive role in the construction of a human world, and that world reflects mind back to itself—but in such a way that mind ultimately sees not simply and only itself (as if in an idol) but an image, in itself and its

---

dum deum). For just as God is the Creator of real beings and of natural forms, so man is the creator of conceptual beings and of artificial forms that are only likenesses of his intellect, even as God's creatures are likenesses of the Divine Intellect. And so, man has an intellect that is a likeness of the Divine Intellect, with respect to creating. . . . Therefore, man measures his own intellect in terms of the power of its works (per potentium operum suorum); and thereby he measures the Divine Intellect, even as an original is measured by means of its image. Now, this knowledge [of the divine Intellect] is symbolical knowledge (aenigmatica scientia). Yet, man has a very refined power-of-seeing through which he sees that the symbolism is a symbolism of the truth (aenigma esse veritatis aenigma), so that he knows the truth to be a reality that is not befigurable by means of symbolism (quae non est figurabilis in aliquo aenigmate). (De beryllo, in Nikolaus von Kues, Philosophisch-Theologische Werke, vol. 3; for English see Nicholas of Cusa, Metaphysical Speculations, trans. Jasper Hopkins [Minneapolis: Arthur J. Banning Press, 1998], translation modified).

57. See Idiota de mente 3.72:13–73:3 (Hopkins translation).

58. Nicholas of Cusa, De coniecturis 1.1.5, in Philosophisch-Theologische Werke, vol. 2; quotation from Hopkins's translation (here modified, and with emphasis added) in Metaphysical Speculations, 2:165.

59. Beierwaltes, "Cusanus and Eriugena," 124.

activity, of God's originally creative power and of the incomprehensible character of that power (as if before an icon).

"Things conceptual," as Cusa writes in *De ludo globi (On the Globe Game*, or *On Bowling*, 1462–63), referring in the instance to time as the rational soul's instrument for measuring motion, "insofar as they are conceptual, have this fact from the [rational] soul, which is the creator of things conceptual, even as God is the Creator of things really existent [*quae est notionalium creatrix sicut deus essentialium*]" (*De ludo globi* 2.93, p. 1232).[60] As suggested by the title of this work, where Cusa likens the human creation of conceptual things to God's creation of the real, such creation operates like the invention of a game, where the human constructs a "world" of rules that then make possible, thanks to their constraint, an ongoing and open activity in which the creative human realizes itself—something like the playful game of culture, *homo faber* as *homo ludens*.[61] This is the case, furthermore, not only with the intellectual worlds we create and inhabit but also with our technological innovation, wherein Cusa likewise highlights the human likeness to God: "The soul," Cusa writes, "by its own inventiveness creates new instruments in order to discern and to know. For example, Ptolemy invented the astrolabe, and Orpheus invented the lyre, and so on. [These] inventors created these instruments not from something extrinsic but from their own minds. For they unfolded their conceptions in perceptible material" (*De ludo globi* 2.94, p. 1232). Both in the intellectual creation of notions or concepts and in the technological or the artistic realization of such notions, the human for Cusa exercises a creative freedom that likens the human to God and thus suggests a theological dimension within the creative—and playful—operation of human culture. As Watts nicely makes the point in her chapter "Homo Ludens," "the phenomenon that Cusanus is discussing and analyzing is that of human culture. Culture is not imposed on man by God, nor is its nature or growth in any way necessary or pre-determined. Culture is entirely dependent upon the freedom of man's will, on the freedom of an infinite number of wills, for, as Cusanus often has said, no one ever thinks or does the same thing twice. All forms of thinking, of art, and all other cultural manifestations are, in a fundamental way, games."[62] In Cusa's thought, then, *homo ludens*, the playful humanity

---

60. Nicolas of Cusa, *Dialogus de ludo globi*, in *Philosophisch-Theologische Werke*, vol. 3; for English see the Hopkins translation in *Metaphysical Speculations*, vol. 2.

61. See Johan Huizinga on play and culture in *Homo Ludens: A Study of the Play element in culture* (Boston: Beacon Press, 1955), and Pauline Moffitt Watts's use of Huizinga in her chapter "Homo Ludens," in *Nicolaus Cusanus*.

62. Watts, *Nicolaus Cusanus*, 206. As Watts also notes, referring to Cusa's *De possest*, he

that creates and inhabits a culture that exceeds necessity or predetermina-
tion and thus mirrors God, is endowed with a mind that is, as Maurice
de Gandillac put it, more suggestively than he perhaps could have known,
"the living image of the creative Act, 'humanly' coextensive with the unlimited totality of its virtual constructions."[63]

Cusa's theological and cosmic framing of the intellectual and human
creativity that constitute culture can be read to mark a decisive shift away
from the logic of mimesis operative through much of Western metaphysics. Along these lines, the world-forming operation of the technological
plays a notable role in expressing—and enabling—human freedom. Cusa
understands the technical equipment that humanity devises less according
to its function as instrumental means to determined end within a pregiven
world and more according to the role it plays in actually forming a world
that sustains those structures in and through which the human subject can
think and act freely and creatively.[64] Technological innovations, from this
perspective, like the intellectual conjectures of language, writing, number,
and syllogism, are forms of worldhood, created by humanity, which allow
humanity to engage freely in further creative activity. Like God's own creation of a creative humanity, they are forms that we create in order to make
possible the ongoing freedom of creation.

In relation to this enabling of free—undetermined and open-ended—
creation by means of created technological constraints, one should note
also that, by contrast with much subsequent thought and culture, where
the fine arts and poetry are held higher than the technological, Cusa views
technological innovation as more truly creative than the work of arts like
painting or sculpture, insofar as the latter depend on imitation of nature in
a way that the former does not. As a layman spoon carver argues in Cusa's
Idiota de mente, "If the sculptor and the painter take their models from
the things that they strive to imitate, that is not true of me; I who make
spoons out of wood and dishes and pots out of clay. In this activity I do not

---

"likens the inventive art and freedom of will with which the boy controls the movement of the
hoop [in a game] to the absolute creativity and volition of God."

63. Maurice de Gandillac, *La Philosophie de Nicolas de Cues* (Paris: Aubier, 1941), 154.

64. As Hans Blumenberg highlights, glossing the passages we've just quoted from *De ludo
globi*, and taking technical equipment in Cusa as a form of "world explication," "the astrolabe
of Ptolemy and the lyre of Orpheus are exemplary novelties of invention, which are structurally
closed in themselves and yet at the same time are mediating orientations, reified conjectures, as
it were, for knowledge" (*Legitimacy of the Modern Age*, 536). As I'll elaborate in chapter 4, the
"structurally closed" remains from another angle infinitely open insofar as no one, nor any sum,
of creative expressions—made possible by such structure—would ever exhaust the potential that
its constraints enable.

imitate the form of any naturally given object, since the forms of spoons, dishes and pots arise by virtue of human skill alone. Consequently my art is more perfect than one that imitates the forms of objects, and thus is more similar to infinite art." As Hans Blumenberg helpfully glosses, "to this consciousness of original self-realization belongs the triumphant indication of the realm of technical forms, which are no longer something [the Layman] owes—as having been read from nature—to a piously accepted pregivenness but rather are supposed to have come into existence *sola humana arte* [by human art alone]."[65] The layman, in other words, finds true creativity in freedom from the pregiven and through innovation by human art. It is in that freedom from mimesis, at least in part a function of the nominalist influence in Cusa, that the human most closely resembles—as "living mirror" or "living image"—the God who is infinite art.

These passages from *De mente* on technological novelty, as well as those locating a ground of innovation in the sorts of human deficiency or nudity that call for creative supplement,[66] offer suggestive directions in which to read Cusa's understanding of humanity's creative freedom as an image of God's. Departing from a mimetic conception of creation as the production of images in accordance with exemplars, Cusa allows for intellectual and technical innovation, beyond mimesis, insofar as imitation of God is imitation of the incomprehensible One who himself does not imitate. Human

---

65. For quotation and gloss see ibid., 534–35; subsequent citations of *De mente* use the pagination of Blumenberg's text.

66. See Cusa's *Compendium* 6 and Blumenberg's gloss in *Legitimacy of the Modern Age*, 535: "In *On the Globe Game*, the invention of the new becomes the possibility of self-discovery that the soul practices with itself so as to assure itself of its power, self-movement. The difference between man and beast is sharpened to this very specificity, that man hits upon the idea of inventing new games for himself. Further: Man alone is able, in the absence of light, to help himself and to make vision possible, by the light of a lamp; he alone can aid deficient vision with the eyeglasses and correct the errors of sight by means of the art of perspective." See also Cusa's sermon for Epiphany 1456, whose resonance with Cicero Gandillac notes in citing it, while highlighting that man's status as second God is found in the human capacity as fabricator not only of rational entities but also of artificial forms ("Pascal et le silence du monde," 363):

> The entry of all men into this world is one, but they do not all live in the same way. For even though men, similar to other animals, are born entirely naked, the human art of weaving has clothed them so that they might live in a better way. And likewise they make use of cooked food and live in houses and domesticate horses, and their civilization takes many other forms through which technology adds to nature the means to live better, and which we consider to be great benefits. Let us add that many men live in pain and in sadness, that many are captive and that others suffer in their bodies, while their brethren lead in abundance a life that is joyous and magnificent. It is therefore necessary that man attempt, through some grace or through some technology, to arrive at a life that is more calm and better organized than that which is given him by nature

creation without prior model is itself, for Cusa, participation in divine creativity; innovation beyond mimesis is itself imitation of the divine creativity.[67] Cusa's model of human creativity might well be taken to "break through the principle of imitation, the obligation determining all human productivity since the ancient world," as Blumenberg asserts within a central argument of *Legitimacy of the Modern Age*, insofar as the sole imitation demanded of a creative humanity is the imitation of that creative God who is himself incomprehensible and who himself, in creating, imitates nothing.[68] At least from *Idiota de mente* forward, human creativity in Cusa's thought is freed from every imitation but this one. Cusa's spoon carver, who creates in freedom from any pregiven or natural models, suggests the implications of this view for understanding the power of creating in its active, dynamic character: "You know that our mind is a certain power that bears an image of the aforementioned Divine Art. Hence, whatever things are present most truly in the Absolute Art are present truly in our mind as in an image [of the divine art]. Therefore, mind is created by the Creative Art—as if that Art willed to create itself, and because the Infinite Art is unreplicable, there arose its image. ([The situation is] as if a painter wished to reproduce himself by painting, and because he himself is not replicable, there would arise—as he was reproducing himself—his image]" (*De mente* 13.148, p. 582).

To say, as Cusa does here, that man is an image of God implies not the static copy of any already achieved actuality but a dynamic imitation of the potential for creative activity itself. Consistent with the apophatic attitude, whose reverse side is an infinite naming of God, consistent with an

67. Along these lines, if Cusa struggles in significant ways against a nominalist rending of the natural and supernatural orders by understanding creation to involve the immanent unfolding (*explicatio*) of God's being, he will at the same time, under nominalist influence, sever the tie between sign and signified in a way that opens the space and time for a creativity or poiesis that does not follow a simple mimetic logic. As Louis Dupré emphasizes in his masterful study *Passage to Modernity*, 188: "Though grounding all representations, the divine essence remains hidden. Its presence does appear, not in likeness or image but in symbolic ciphers of the human mind's making. With the nominalists, Cusanus denies any sort of analogy between sign and signified, yet, unlike most of them, he holds that the finite symbols manifest the *presence* of an invisible infinite." If in our creative activity we imitate God by rational and technical as well as symbolic production, we recognize in that production the extent to which every symbol falls short of the divine reality, and in that space of failure the creative freedom remains open for new symbols to be produced. In this way, of course, Cusa thinks and writes in line with a long tradition of mystical theology for which the absolute anonymity of the divine opens space and time for its endless naming, where every figure of God needs to be disfigured. In Cusa's appropriation of that tradition, it bears noting, the logic of endless polyonymy as answer to divine anonymity entails also an affirmation of religious diversity.

68. Blumenberg, *Legitimacy of the Modern Age*, 532.

iconoclasm bound inextricably with iconophilia, Cusa holds that the more perfect image of God is in fact the image that remains always perfectible and hence open to movement—that is, a more *living* image, the *viva imago* whose life consists in the capacity to imitate ever more closely, which is to say ever more creatively, the exemplar who is the absolutely creative art that is never reached in itself and never completed as such. Like the infinite movement of henosis within the Dionysian heritage that is Cusa's, or the Pauline-Gregorian epektasis that is likewise operative in his thought, the dynamic of human creativity in Cusa is valued most in its openness, which entails the endless interplay of kataphasis and apophasis, or figuring and disfiguring. "And because no matter how nearly perfect an image is," writes Cusa, "if it cannot become more perfect and more conformed to its exemplar, it is never as perfect as any image whatsoever that has the power to conform itself ever more and more, without limit, to its inaccessible exemplar. For in this respect, the image, as best it can, imitates infinity [*quae potentiam habet se semper plus et plus sine limitatione inaccessibili exemplari conformandi—in hoc enim infinitatem imaginis modo quo potest imitatur*]" (*De mente* 13.149, p. 582).[69] Movement without limit, suggesting already modernity's infinite progress, defines the essentially creative, irreducibly open life of an image whose exemplar and Creator remains infinitely unimaginable. As Dietrich Mahnke notes, it is in this understanding of humanity as living image (*viva imago*) or as "living and free-working mirror" (*specula viva atque libera*) that Cusa "goes the farthest beyond his precursors," for "it is not the most exact possible passive mirroring of an identical original image [*Urbildes*] but idiosyncratic imitation and active new creation [*die eigentümliche Nachbildung und aktive Neuschöpfung*] that is the highest capacity."[70]

Cusa's affirmation of the human's endlessly dynamic and open creative capacity is tied intimately to the Trinitarian and Christological dimensions of a theology that culminates in a notion of God—and of his image in human mind—as absolute possibility and infinite desire. "The triune and

69. Ibid. See also, along these lines, the passages on the image of an unknown king in *De mente* 3.73, p. 543): "Just as God is Absolute Being itself that is the Enfolding of all beings, so our mind is an image of that Infinite Being itself—an image that is the enfolding of all [other] images [of God]. [The situation is] as if the primary image of an unknown king were the exemplar of all other images depictable in accordance with the primary image. For God's knowledge, or 'face,' is descendingly disclosed only in the mental nature [i.e., in mind], whose object is truth; and it descends further only by way of mind, so that mind is both an image of God and exemplar for all the images-of-God that are [ontologically] subsequent to it" (ibid., 543).

70. Mahnke, *Unendliche Sphäre*. 101–2. See further references to the living image in Cusa at 103 n. 1.

one God," Cusa writes in the final lines of his final work, *De apice theo-riae*, "whose name is 'the Omnipotent one' or 'the Power of all power,' is signified by 'possibility itself.' With Him, all things are possible and noth-ing is impossible; and He is the Strength of all strength and the Might of all might. His most perfect manifestation—than which no manifestation can be more perfect—is Christ, who by His word and example leads us unto a clear contemplative-vision [*contemplatio*] of Possibility. And this contemplative-vision is the happiness which alone satisfies the mind's su-preme desire" (*De apice* 28, p. 1434). The happiness that desire finds in possibility, as suggested by the work's opening evocation of Paul, is the hap-piness of desire's openness and movement, the creative movement of the living image whose cosmic significance and dynamic character are figured in the Christ and Trinity—for "if the Apostle Paul, who was caught up unto the third heaven, did not even then comprehend the Incomprehensible, no one will ever be content not continually and insistently to seek to com-prehend better Him who is greater than all comprehension" (*De apice* 2, p. 1423).

If in Cusa's Christ there appears a contemplative vision of possibility, in which alone the mind's supreme desire finds happiness, that image of possibility lends to our historically and culturally creative humanity a cos-mic scale—for it is the Christ who most fully realizes the coincidence of created and creative being, and it is the human whose creative capacity most closely resembles that of the Christ. Such a valuation of creativity can be read, as Cassirer and Gandillac and others stress, to involve an af-firmative and thoroughgoing engagement with worldly existence, and an interweaving of nature and culture, that deviates from medieval tendencies toward escape from the world and suspicion of human invention. "Just as the Christ is the expression of *all* humanity," writes Cassirer,

> just as He signifies nothing but its simple idea and essence, so does man, too, viewed in his essence, include within himself all things. In man as a microcosm all lines of the macrocosm run together.... In medi-eval thought, redemption signified above all liberation from the world, i.e., the uplifting of men above their sensible, earthly existence. But Cu-sanus no longer recognizes such a separation between man and nature. If man as microcosm includes the nature of all things within himself, then *his* redemption, his rising up to the divinity, must include the ascen-sion of all things. Nothing is isolated, cut off, or in any way rejected; ... Not only man rises up to God through Christ; the universe is redeemed within man and through him.... The union has been completed not

only through God and man, but between God and all creation. The gap
between them is closed; between the creative principle and the created,
between God and creature, stands the spirit of humanity, *humanitas*, as
something at once creator and created.[71]

While Cusa's Christological take on possibility and human creativity
gives to it a cosmic scope that weaves together man, world, and God, and
thus makes culture integral to nature, the Trinitarian angle on creative
capacity likewise calls attention to its fundamentally dynamic and open-
ended character. To think humanity as *imago Dei* in this Trinitarian sense
is to think the human and its creative capacity in terms of ceaseless movement, much like the Pauline and Gregorian epektasis, toward the inaccessible, incomprehensible exemplar that is, as possibility itself, divine art. In
Cusa's Trinitarian formulation, the divine art involves omnipotence, wisdom, and their unity through will or spirit—where spirit means, above all,
motion: "And because of a certain likeness the [divine] will is called spirit,
for without spirit there is no motion. [This latter point is true] to such an
extent that we give the name 'spirit' to that which causes motion even in
the wind and all other things. Now by means of motion all artisans effect
that which they will to. Therefore, the power of the Creative Art (this Art
is the absolute and infinite Art, i.e., the Blessed God) works all things by
his Spirit, or Will" (*De mente* 13.147, p. 581). In answer to the Trinitarian
divine Art, the motion of human mind is figured likewise in Trinitarian
terms—which means endless movement into the divine: "Therefore, the
mind is three and one—having power, wisdom, and the union of both in
such a way that it is a perfect image of the Art, i.e., in such a way that it can
conform itself, when stimulated, ever more and more to its Exemplar. . . .
Hence, in the oneness of the mind's essence there is power, wisdom, and
will. And master and mastery coincide in the essence as in a living image of
the Infinite Art—an image which, when stimulated, can make itself always
more conformed to Divine Actuality, while the preciseness of the Infinite
Art remains always inaccessible" (*De mente* 13.149, pp. 582–83). Suggesting already something of Pico's humanistic understanding of the human
as "work of an indiscrete image," Cusa develops his take on the human as
living image of infinite art by highlighting the "inaccessible" or "unreplicable" character of such art (*De mente* 13, p. 148). Just "as if the primary
image of an unknown king were the exemplar of the other images depictable in accordance with the primary image" (*De mente* 3.73, p. 543), so the

71. Cassirer, *The Individual and the Cosmos*, 40.

human mind is creative image of an unimaginable creator—and for that reason infinitely open.

The human inhabits an infinite openness, or ongoing opening, of creative possibility insofar as it is the image of an inaccessible God, the Infinite Art that Cusa finally names, as I've suggested, "possibility itself," *posse ipsum*, a name that marks the "loftiest level of contemplative reflection, . . . the Possibility of all possibility," which is never exhausted by any one or even all of those possibilities—or actualities—that possibility itself grounds. In this sense, possibility itself is an especially good name for the God who invites or makes possible an infinity of names or representations while (and because) remaining beyond all of them. To see possibility "itself" is to see, in fact, its difference from all manifestations or evocations of it; it is to see, as in Marion's saturated phenomenon, more than we can comprehend. This is why, within the understanding of human creativity as an image of divine creativity, the highest contemplation of that image is the contemplation of possibility itself, where we see disclosed the *difference* between possibility itself, which is the "Quiddity and Basis of all things" (*De apice* 8, p. 1426), and the actual existence of any particular possibility for this or that—beginning with the possibility of our own mind. Indeed, it is in the reflexive structure of finite mind (as image) that the infinite openness of possibility (the inaccessible exemplar) appears to mind: "The mind sees itself. And because the mind sees that its own possibility, or power, is not the Possibility of all possibility (since many things are impossible for the mind), it sees that it is not Possibility itself but is an image of Possibility itself. And so, since in the mind's own possibility the mind sees Possibility itself, and since the mind is only its own possibility-of-existing, the mind sees that it itself is a mode-of-manifestation of Possibility itself" (*De apice* 24, p. 1433). Human mind, then, in its reflexive structure, appears as image of God and hence as a possibility irreducible to the horizon of actuality. As Cusa puts it, "Possibility itself precedes all possibility that has a qualification added, it cannot either exist or be named or be perceived or be imagined or be understood. For that which is signified by 'Possibility' precedes all such things, although it is the Basis of them all, even as light is the basis of [all] colours" (*De apice* 19, p. 1431). Possibility, from this perspective, is disclosed but invisible in all beings (and nonbeings) just as light is invisibly disclosed in all visible things (insofar as we see the things and not the light)—or language silently spoken in all things said, or Being absently present in all beings. Insofar as our mind sees the difference between possibility itself and any given possibility for this or that, which is to say an eventual actuality, it sees more than it can comprehend, or the degree to which it cannot comprehend or represent possibility itself. It is in the human mind's reflexive awareness of its incapacity to comprehend possibility itself that possibility itself shows itself in its incomprehensibility. The negative theology of possibility itself is answered, then, by a negative anthropology. As Alfons Brüntrup nicely highlights in his lucid study of possibility in Cusa's later writings, *Können und Sein,*

> The human mind becomes transparent to itself as image of the absolute *posse.* In the realization of mental acts absolute possibility [*Können*] becomes transparent, and indeed it becomes transparent to the mind itself in its own acts. . . . The *mens humana,* which looks back into its own essence, in a look that is the realization [*Vollzug*] of the mind itself, sees in itself possibility-itself [*das Können-Selbst*]. . . . Setting eyes on the *posse ipsum absolutum* is the highest goal and the final realization [*Vollendung*] of the spiritual nature of man. If the *mens* wants to glimpse in itself possibility-itself, so must it swing upward from the *visio comprehensiva* to the *simplex visio.* Therein the *mens humana* fulfills its meaning, to step beyond its own power of comprehension, in order to see the incomprehensibility of the absolute.[72]

The mind's being-able-to-see (*das Sehen-Können des Geistes*) surpasses its being-able-to-conceive (*Begreifen-Können*), and in that excessive gap, which it sees in looking upon itself, the human mind fulfills itself as image of unimaginable possibility. This status of the mind as image to which the mind itself relates is what gives to it an infinite openness. "The mind knows itself in infinite distance [*in unendlichen Abstand*], so that it seeks after its goal in longing. . . . Straining after a final goal, which is sought in seeing and seen in striving, is the 'fundamental constitution of the mind.'"[73]

⊱⊰

As I've been suggesting, by naming the God in whose image our creative humanity is made with the final name of possibility itself, Cusa departs in a significant way from the metaphysical privilege of actuality and presence. In this context, as Hans-Georg Gadamer notes in a brief study of Cusa in

72. Alfons Brüntrup, *Können und Sein: Der Zusammenhang der Spätschriften des Nikolaus von Kues* (Munich and Salzburg: Verlag Anton Pustet, 1973), 128.
73. Ibid., 129.

modern thought, "the expression 'creative' [*schöpferisch*] means not only making or capable of making [*zum Schaffen fähig*] but a constitution of Being that for its part includes no already-being [*kein Schon-sein*], no pregiven stock [*Vorrat*] but a Being-able [*ein Können*]. . . . [Cusa] does not like the traditional expression of the *actus purus*, in which all *dynamis*, all *potentia* comes to an end in pure presence [*Anwesenheit*]—he seeks *posse* in Being itself."[74] Insofar as he seeks to think possibility at the heart of Being—and beyond the logic of actuality and presence, in terms of a creativity both divine and human—Cusa suggests productive lines along which to envisage, both in the history of theology and in modern technological humanity, alternatives to the Heideggerian account of Christian ontotheological tradition and the modern metaphysics of the technological subject. Indeed, insofar as Cusa articulates the pure possibility of the *posse ipsum* in terms of its difference from any determinate possibility for this or that, he may well foreshadow in theological terms, as Peter Casarella very effectively argues, building on Gadamer, something akin to the "ontological difference" that Heidegger articulates in the name of a possibility that proves irreducible to any determinate actuality—and in resistance, I would emphasize, both to ontotheology in Christian tradition and to its incarnation in the metaphysics of modernity's technological humanity.[75] Likewise linking the Cusan God of possibility to the question of possibility and creativity in a Heideggerian frame, Giorgio Agamben productively highlights that the central Heideggerian notion of facticity is bound to a sense of making or fabrication (*facere*), and indeed of self-making, that is both required and possible only because the existence at stake, Dasein, lacks a proper face of its own. In this way Dasein might be read as a later extension of Pico's indiscrete image, the human who proves creative thanks to its lack of assigned place or definition in the order of nature. In a Cusan heir like Pico, or later Giordano

74. Hans-Georg Gadamer, "Nikolaus von Kues im Modernen Denken," in *Nicolo' Cusano agli inizi del mondo moderno* (Florence: G. C. Sansoni Editore, 1970), 47–48.

75. See Peter J. Casarella, "Nicholas of Cusa and the Power of the Possible," *American Catholic Philosophical Quarterly* 64, no. 1 (Winter 1990), esp. 31: "Possibility itself undermines the pure presence of traditional metaphysics. In fact, by radicalizing the difference between possibility itself and its manifestations, Cusanus even suggests an ontological difference in the Heideggerian sense. Even when using the language of image and exemplar, he does not maintain that the only true being is fully present in possibility itself. What distinguishes possibility itself from its manifestation in possibilities is not the same as the distinction between an idea in which the Being of beings is purely present and the beings which exist as pale copies of true Being. Possibility itself is the hidden ground of its own manifestations. A simple vision of the mind does not 'make present' or 'represent' the ground of all beings as yet another among beings. Rather possibility itself is disclosed through its difference from distinct possibilities of existence."

Bruno, one should indeed be struck by the essential tie between an emerging modern sense of the human as endlessly poetic and a mystical take on
the human as indefinite, indeterminate, or infinite.

Inheriting and building on the apophatic anthropology and cosmology
of earlier thinkers such as Gregory of Nyssa and John Scotus Eriugena, Cusa
thus marks a crucial link between medieval mysticism and modern conceptions of human creativity. Cusa's mystical take on the cosmos as infinite sphere bearing the attributes of God and on the human creature as
"living image" of that God, himself taken as infinite art and absolute possibility, informs significantly the early modern thinking of figures like Pico
and Giordano Bruno on the multiform character of man and on the infinity
of worlds—a thinking decisive in later modernity also, I will argue, for no
less a writer than James Joyce. The capacity of the human for ongoing metamorphosis through creative and self-creative activity is tied in Cusa's heirs
Pico and Bruno, as previously in Gregory and Eriugena, to a deficiency or
indetermination that becomes the ground of human inventiveness. Man becomes creative and self-creative to the degree that "no pattern for this creature has been provided in the original 'world program,'"[76] and that world
now proves to be an unbounded whole in whose ongoing metamorphoses
the human plays an integral part—such that the clear modern division between spirit and nature, or between cultural and natural reality, or between
subject and object, does not hold.

The human lack of essence or program, the indeterminate ground of
invention, is especially notable in Bruno, where it implies the infinitely
plastic character of the creative human: the one who in essence lacks definition can become virtually anything. Like the indefinable divinity embodied absolutely in the cosmos, the human for Bruno proves *omniformis* in
and through the flow of a never-ceasing metamorphosis, where creating and
being-created coincide. As Alfonso Ingegno indicates in his introduction
to Bruno's key dialogue, *Cause, Principle, Unity*, "the divinity is a matter
which creates all and becomes all; thus, the perfect human being is one
who, by elevating himself to the infinite in contemplation of the divine,
actualizing in the infinite his cognitive potency, is capable of assimilating
everything because he knows how to transform himself into it." Extending
the thought of Cusa along these lines, Bruno's human proves *omniformis*
according to "the identity of *facere* and *fieri*, of the potency of creating and
being created," and it does so within a cosmos where the incarnation of di-

76. Blumenberg, *Legitimacy of the Modern Age*, 525.

vinity is no longer localized spatially or temporally in the individual Christ but rather proves to be, like the infinite sphere, everywhere and nowhere.[77]

As commentators often point out, Bruno inherits and extends Cusa's thinking of the infinite even as he modifies it through this rethinking of incarnation in terms of universal and ongoing transformation. Bruno thinks the immanence of God in such a thoroughgoing manner that he collapses the traditional distinction between creation of the world and generation of the Son within the Trinity, such that the world in its very matter comes to be seen as the self-embodiment of a God who holds nothing back but gives all of himself in and through that world, which, in all of its parts, both spatially and temporally, is a ceaseless becoming. This means not only that the world is infinite, as Cusa suggests, but indeed, as Bruno insists, that there must be an infinity of worlds—wherein the ubiquitous presence of God implies an abandonment of any division of the world into ontological hierarchies, any division between natural and supernatural. There remains for Bruno, then, no privileged location, whether spatial or temporal, where the incarnate God enters world and history in a discrete manner so as to constitute a cosmic or historical center. Bruno's thinking of immanence goes hand in hand both with a radically acentric universe and with a conception of time as "the real dimension of the self-reproduction of god, which is continuous, but of equal value in every one of its moments."[78] This conception of divinity as embodied within the infinity of worlds and the movement of time implies the deepest affirmation of endless metamorphosis, according to which—poetic principle par excellence—"anything can become anything."[79] Further, it implies the rejection of that metaphysical principle par excellence, the principle of sufficient reason, which demands that the givenness of things be justified in terms of something outside or beyond the things themselves. As Blumenberg comments, nature in Bruno "is filled with movement and the metamorphosis of forms; consequently—and this is its most radical opposition to Leibniz's universe, which it anticipates in so many ways—it is ruled by the *principium rationis insufficientis*, insofar as one poses any other question than that of the right of the whole to exist."[80]

77. Alfonso Ingegno, introduction to Giordano Bruno, *Cause, Principle, and Unity and Essays on Magic*, edited by Richard J. Blackwell and Robert de Lucca (Cambridge: Cambridge University Press, 1998), xxviii.

78. Blumenberg, *Legitimacy of the Modern Age*, 570.

79. Ibid., 569, 595.

80. Ibid., 569.

Within this infinite universe, unleashed from the centered and hierarchical cosmos of medieval thought and culture, the human can be understood "as one of the endless phases through which nature's self-realization passes,"[81] the worker of an endless and open metamorphosis who finds his likeness to the divine in the freedom of creation, which is a freedom from bondage to that which already exists, actually or ideally, in a pregiven stock of the real. It is a freedom to go beyond the apparent givenness of nature and its order in the creation of another nature, as Bruno puts it in the third dialogue of his *Expulsion of the Triumphant Beast*: "And [Jove] added that the gods had given intellect and hands to man and had made him similar to them, giving him power over the other animals. This consists in his being able not only to operate according to his nature and to what is usual, but also to operate outside the laws of that nature, in order that by forming or being able to form other natures, other paths, other categories, with his intelligence, by means of that liberty without which he would not have the above-mentioned similarity, he would succeed in preserving himself as god of the earth."[82]

If man can be likened to the gods, or be himself a "god of the earth" thanks to his inventive capacity, that capacity also suggests that the course of time as course of endless transformation becomes itself the scene of a learned ignorance that defines the species being of humanity as "transition from one condition of transformation to another."[83] If according to Max Weber the movement of infinite progress is fundamental to modern rationality, one might trace the emergence of that movement not only in a disenchanted and technical rationality but also in a mystical thinking on the intersection of creation and ignorance within a technological humanity that finds its creative freedom in its indefinition or infinitude.

The take on modernity exemplified in Weber, then, as in Heidegger, stands open to a revision that recalls the late medieval and early modern mystics even as it might speak to our world today. Perhaps no mistake that it is a poet, the German writer Jochen Winter, who offers a reading of Bruno that highlights, in this first of moderns, burned for his trouble, a thinker who before the fact goes "beyond" the modernity founded in a calculative and instrumental rationality that places the self-assertive human subject

81. Ibid., 590.
82. Giordano Bruno, *The Expulsion of the Triumphant Beast*, trans. Arthur D. Imerti (Lincoln: University of Nebraska Press, 1964), 205.
83. Blumenberg, *Legitimacy of the Modern Age*, 592.

before a distinct, objective world, or world picture, which itself is then subjected to the representational and technological mastery of that subject. "If
his philosophy possesses an eminent significance," writes Winter in *The
Creation of Infinity*, "that is because it harbors, for the West, an idea of
creation for the period that follows the modern."[84] That idea of creation, a
function of infinity, resists the subject whom Heidegger and Weber place at
the center of modern technoscientific thought and culture, the self-certain
subject of Cartesian tradition, in whose place emerges a thoroughly relational and never wholly discrete self, the self "as point of intersection
within the universal exchange, characterized . . . by a blurredness: because
one cannot see right through all of the references, because the visible leads
constantly to the invisible."[85]

As creatively active within the infinitely dynamic tissue that constitutes and exceeds the self, this relational self lives and moves always by
means of a vision or knowledge that implies blindness and unknowing. It's
knowing and doing will never exhaust the tissue of the real, but as productively participant in that tissue, such knowing and doing imply an infinite
responsibility. As Winter beautifully puts it, "It is precisely by means of
the relative that the individual finds his path toward the absolute, when
he recognizes himself as part of the gigantic organic tissue that, within an
uninterrupted contraction and expansion, transmits messages charged with
meaning." Thus immersed creatively and unknowingly in the infinitely dynamic, cosmic tissue, the self in Bruno is confronted with an obligation to
think in terms of a whole that exceeds the self even as the self participates
in that whole: "Thought is thus obligated to declare the cosmocentric vision as point of departure for its acts. Thus alone does man choose those
gestures that affirm his responsibility in relation to space both close and
far."[86] The infinite, creative, cosmic metamorphosis in which the human
participates with infinite capacity, or totipotence, implies of the human
both irreducible unknowing and immeasurable responsibility. This intersection of unknowing and responsibility is notable also at the heart of
more current theorizations of a technoscientific world that proves to be the
absolutely relative space and time of our indefinite human becoming, our
"hominescence."

84. Jochen Winter, *La création de l'infini: Giordano Bruno et la pensée cosmique* (Paris:
Calmann-Lévy, 2004), 194.
85. Ibid., 193.
86. Ibid., 193–94.

CHAPTER FOUR

Of the Indefinite Human: Religion and the Nature of Technological Culture

The Heideggerian contention that technological culture dehumanizes because it rests overly secure in its conception or definition of the human, according to a logic where too much security effectively uproots and dislocates, is rehearsed and extended at the center of Jean-Luc Marion's 2004 inaugural address as John Nuveen Professor of the Philosophy of Religion and Theology at the University of Chicago Divinity School, a chair held previously by Paul Tillich and Paul Ricoeur.[1] Marion aims in the lecture to establish and elucidate the paradox he believes to be confronted by any philosophy of religion: it has for an object, as Tillich had asserted, something that cannot in fact become an object for philosophy.[2] By insisting on a paradoxical definition of the human as indefinable, as exceeding the stable boundaries of any clear and distinct concept, Marion argues for a thought of the human that unsettles and eludes the reductive objectification of the human exercised by modern technological culture and by the metaphysics of the subject grounding such culture.[3] The failure of modern

1. Jean-Luc Marion, "*Mihi magna quaestio factus sum*: The Privilege of Unknowing," *Journal of Religion* 85, no. 1 (January 2005); hereafter cited parenthetically as PU.

2. "The object of philosophy of religion," as Tillich wrote, "is religion. But this very simple explanation already signifies a problem, *the fundamental problem of philosophy of religions*: with religion, philosophy faces an object that refuses to become an object for philosophy" (quoted in PU, 4).

3. In arguing for the unknowability of the human, and thus against any "clear and distinct" concept that could define the human, Marion is working in relation to the Cartesian horizon that still informs our understandings of "knowledge" and that excludes from knowing any doubt:

> What do we really understand by the verb "to know"? Whether we admit it or not, we mean by "to know" the taking (or producing) of what Descartes called a clear and distinct idea; and we mean this not because we necessarily accept the Cartesian theory

metaphysics, of the natural as well as human sciences it founds, and of the rationalized, technological culture these in concert yield, is, Marion argues, a humanism that in fact dehumanizes precisely by claiming to offer a clear and distinct idea of the human. Any such definition, he insists, seeming to make the human available as an object conceivable to the representing human mind, or subject, thereby opens the deadly possibility of making distinctions between those objectified beings that belong to the human and those that do not: "To claim to know and to define man with a concept leads inevitably to a decision about his objectification," Marion writes, "or rather to a decision about his humanity according to the objectification that we will have produced. Defining man with a concept does not always or immediately lead to killing him, but it does fill the first condition required to eliminate all that does not fit this definition. The danger—having done with some among men because we can define 'man'—is not exaggerated or non-sensical. We experience it directly, as a clear possibility, in all the applications of its objectification" (PU, 11).

Thus extending Heidegger's analysis and critique of modern metaphysics as a thinking that conceives all "being" in terms of objectivity and that understands "truth" to consist in the subjective certainty about such being achieved by the human subject, who thus becomes "ground and measure of all that is," Marion locates the danger of defining the human in the arrogance of decision it implies. If man becomes the measure of all that is, including humanity itself, if the human is a function of our definition or conception, if it is grasped within our measure, then it depends upon our decision—and such decision, Marion insists, will inevitably exclude from the human that which may then, much like Giorgio Agamben's "bare

---

of science but because we share with it its finality: knowing seems to us to be without value if it is not, through this idea, about obtaining "mentis purae et attentae quam facilem distinctumque conceptum, ut de eo, quod intelligimus, nulla prorsus dubitatio relinquator" ("a concept so clear and distinct, produced by a pure and attentive mind, such that no doubt remains about what we are understanding"). What can thus be known (by virtue of idea and representation), in such a manner that no doubt about it subsists, is defined as an object; or, what amounts to the same thing, one may only admit into science that which offers an object that is certain: "Circa illa tantum objecta oportet versari, ad quorum certam et indubitatem cognitionem nostra ingenia videntur sufficere" ("We should attend only to those objects of which our mind seems capable of having certain and indubitable cognition"). (PU, 8)

Marion cites Descartes, *Regulae ad directionem ingenii* 8 (AT 10): 368, lines 15–17, and 2 (AT 10): 362, lines 2–4; for the English translation, modified here for the first quote, see *Descartes: Selected Philosophical Writings*, trans. John Cottingham, Robert Stoothoff, and Douglas Murdoch (Cambridge: Cambridge University Press, 1988), 2:3 and 1.

life,"[4] be given a death that is neither murder nor sacrifice. "To claim to define what a man is leads to or at least opens the possibility of leading to the elimination of that which does not correspond to this definition. Every political proscription, every racial extermination, every ethnic cleansing, every determination of that which does not merit life—all these rest upon a claim to define (scientifically or ideologically) the humanity of man; without this claimed guarantee, no one could put such political programs into motion" (PU, 13).[5]

This death-dealing logic common to racism and other ideologies, on Marion's view, operates also at the heart of our modern technology, an exemplary instance of which can be seen in the medical field, whose ostensible aim is the care and preservation of human life. The "medical definition of my body as an object," Marion warns, "will also allow for the distinction of health from sickness in terms of norms. Thus is opened the fearful region in which man can make decisions about the normality, and thus the life and death, of other human beings—because these other human beings have become simple human objects." Taking the medical field as exemplary of a logic to be noted also in fields such as economic theory (which ignores the gratuity presupposed but not contained by every economy) or politics (which reduces the social being to a political object contained in the comprehensive and quantified identity of the citizen), Marion argues that the greatest danger to "humanity" is its definition—because of the violent, exclusionary decision such definition implies. He insists, furthermore, that the technoscientific machine in modernity is founded on, even as it reinforces, just this kind of definition and thus the project of domination or mastery, decision and death, with which such definition cooperates (PU, 12).

The danger of this "determining" that "amounts to a denying" of humanity, the violence inherent to such determination, is, Marion insists, what any overly secure humanism involves, and it is just such security that constitutes the weakness—or really, the dangerous power—of every humanism:

4. See Giorgio Agamben, *Homo Sacer: Sovereign Power and Bare Life*, trans. Daniel Heller-Roazen (Stanford: Stanford University Press, 1998).
5. The explanation of violence operative here— according to which I must first make other the one to whom, only then, I allow myself to do violence—overlooks the extent to which it can be familiarity more than otherness that yields the greatest violence. In this latter direction, see, e.g., Jacques Derrida's *Voyous* (Paris: ÉditionsGalilée, 2003), 76: "One of the many reasons for which I mistrust the brother and, above all, what can seem to be comforting in the expression 'fraternal dispute,' is that there is no war worse than that of fraternal enemies. There is never any war, or danger for the democracy to come, except where there are brothers."

Not only does it claim to comprehend as a matter of fact what man can and ought to be; but above all it assumes that such knowledge reinforces the humanity in man, when such knowledge instead destroys it or, in any case, threatens it. The weakness of humanism's claim consists in dogmatically imagining not only that man can hold himself up as his own measure (so that man is enough for man), but above all that he can do this because he comprehends what man is, when on the contrary nothing threatens man more than any such alleged comprehension of his humanity. For every de-*finition* imposes on the human being a finite essence, following from which it always becomes possible to delimit what deserves to remain human from what no longer does. (PU, 14)

Much as Emmanuel Levinas argues that my obligation to the other derives not from the category or conception of any general "humanity" to which the other belongs as individual instance but rather from the face of the other in its excessive singularity, so Marion insists here that the distinctive claim of a human person to be loved and not killed—and we can love, he insists, only that which we do not comprehend—is based not in the definition or conception of an individual's humanity but in that humanity's excess over any definition or concept. Assuming the status of what Marion calls the "saturated phenomenon" (PU, 23), the human always gives to thought more than thought can ever intend, conceive, or comprehend—and for this reason, to receive the human other calls first not for conception or definition but for love.[6]

Two points of tension within Marion's subtle analysis bear noting here. Both concern what seem to be gestures of exclusion on which Marion himself relies to save the human from any exclusionary—or murderous—definition, and both relate in significant ways to my own question concerning the indefinite human and the nature of technology in their religious significance.

6. For Marion's fullest treatment of the saturated phenomenon, see his *Etant donné: Essai d'une phénoménologie de la donation* (Paris: Presses Universitaires de France, 1997), translated by Jeffrey L. Kosky as *Being Given: Toward a Phenomenology of Givenness* (Stanford: Stanford U. Press, 2002). On his treatment of love, in addition to his early theological writings, see especially *Le phénomène érotique* (Paris: Éditions Grasset, 2003), now available in Stephen E. Lewis's translation, *The Erotic Phenomenon* (Chicago: University of Chicago Press, 2007). For my take on the interplay between love in Marion's theology and givenness in his phenomenology, see "Converting the Given into the Seen: Introductory Remarks on Theological and Phenomenological Vision," in Marion, *The Idol and Distance*, trans. Thomas A. Carlson (New York: Fordham University Press, 2001).

First, Marion's definition of the human as indefinable presupposes the
anthropocentric and theologically backed discourse of a Christianity that
secures the privilege and dignity (if not the definition or identity) of the
human through an exclusion of other beings, such as the animal, which
in Marion's analysis (as elsewhere in Christian thought and culture)
amounts to a life that is, thanks to a right established by God, subject to
the naming, domination, and indeed killing exercised by the human who
is created in God's image (a reading of human dominion, as we saw, that
can show up in a figure like Gregory, who in other respects seems to call
fundamentally into question any project of human mastery). In light of
Hegel's position on the Genesis account of Adam's right to name the animals, Marion explains that

> Adam gives a name, and thus a definition to the animals, which thus
> become subject to him, because in general all knowledge by concept re-
> duces what is known to the rank of object. Adam thus names in the
> manner by which the *I* knows—by concepts of objects. However, Adam
> has the power thus to name only that which can legitimately become
> for him an object: the animals (and the rest of the world), and perhaps
> the angels, but not God, and not himself. If, moreover, he claimed to
> name them, either this name would have no validity, or, if it had valid-
> ity, what he named would not be man as such (as the unrivaled thinker)
> but merely a thought-object like all others. (PU, 10)

From the logic of this biblical story, where the distinction of the animal
from man and from God works to uphold the definition of man and God
as indefinable, Marion draws the lesson that "it follows from the characteristics of knowledge by concepts that man cannot name man, which is
to say define man, except by reducing him to the rank of a simple concept,
thereby knowing not a man but an object, possibly animated, but always
alienated" (PU, 10).[7] This argument against the alienation of man by his defining concept is the same that Marion makes, at the center of his phenomenological project, in defining and elaborating the saturated phenomenon:
it must be allowed to show itself on its own terms rather than being made
to appear on our terms—according to our conceptions and definitions—and

7. One might ask here whether, and in what ways, the human and God become, according
to this notion of "legitimacy," the sole claimants to the status of saturated phenomenon—which
seems to stand in some tension with Marion's treatments of the saturated phenomenon elsewhere.

thus as alienated from itself.[8] Such avoidance of definition and concept, which would allow the human to give itself rather than to depend for its appearance on an alienating and exclusionary definition or concept given ahead of time, seems to depend nonetheless on a fundamental gesture of exclusion, directed first at the animal, and then, as suggested parenthetically in the same passage, at all other nonhuman and nondivine beings—which are termed the "world."

Indeed, the theological grounding of Marion's anthropology here involves a fundamental distinction between the "human," on one side, and, on the other, "world," and it attributes to the former but not to the latter the traits of the saturated phenomenon:

> if God remains incomprehensible, man, who resembles nothing other than Him, will also bear the mark and the privilege of His incomprehensibility. Put another way: the human being belongs to no species whatsoever, refers to no genus, is not comprehended by any definition of (in)humanity. Delivered from every paradigm, he appears immediately within the light of the One who surpasses all light. Man's face bears the mark of this borrowed incomprehensibility in so far, precisely, as he too reveals himself as invisible, like God.[9] Man is thus radically separated from every other being in this world by an insurmountable and definitive difference that is no longer onto-

8. On Marion's critique of metaphysics for its alienation of the phenomenon, and on the relation of such critique to the question of revelation, see my essay "Blindness and the Decision to See: On Revelation and Reception in Jean-Luc Marion," in Hart, *Counter-Experiences*. It is worth noting here that in his effort to think the phenomenon as self-giving, Marion draws on a Heideggerian definition ("the showing-itself-in-itself," "that which shows itself in itself," *Being and Time*, 54 [31]) that itself recalls the Aristotelian definition of *physis*, as distinct from *techne*, as that which has its principle in itself and thus depends on no other being in its coming to be. For an illuminating study of this contrast and its bearing on the question of nature and technology in metaphysical tradition, see Serge Margel, *Logique de la nature* (Paris: Éditions Galilée, 2000), e.g., 16–17: "Nature unveils that which is produced from and through itself [*ce qui se dévoile de et par soi-même*], every being that carries in itself the principle of its birth and of its death, whereas technology [*la technique*] unveils that which is produced not from itself, but in drawing its principle from another being, from the artist or the technician." See also Stiegler on Heidegger's relation to the Aristotelian distinction, in *La technique et le temps*, 1:23–24.

9. Marion here cites a passage from Levinas that seems to me significant, for reasons that will become clear momentarily: "The face is signification, and signification without context. . . . In this sense one can say that the face is not 'seen.' It is what cannot become a content, which your thought would embrace; it is uncontainable, it leads you beyond" (Emmanuel Levinas, *Ethics and Infinity: Conversations with Philippe Nemo* (Pittsburgh: Duquesne University Press, 1985), 85–86.

logical but holy. No longer does the human being distinguish him-
or herself from the rest of the world as the "Platzhalter des Nichts"
("lieutenant of the nothing") or the "Hirt des Seins" ("shepherd of
Being"), but as the icon of the incomprehensible.[10] Man's invisibility separates him from the world and consecrates him as holy for
the Holy. (PU, 6)

If in his thought of the human as indefinable, or indeed invisible, Marion
here aligns himself with a Levinasian ethic of the holy that aspires to exceed
any Heideggerian ontology, on the question of technology Marion in fact
remains more in line with the Heidegger for whom the essence of technology reduces man, through calculative and instrumental thought, to object
or even to standing reserve.[11] He thus sets himself at odds with the Levinas
for whom technology may in fact cast us outside every horizon and thereby
open the possibility of a "signification without context," which means the
nudity of a face whose significance is absolute and as such ethical. "Technology," Levinas writes, "wrenches us out of the Heideggerian world and
the superstitions surrounding *Place*. From this point on, an opportunity appears to us: to perceive men outside the situation in which they are placed,
to let the human face shine in its nudity."[12] Unlike the Levinas who can see
in technology a liberation of the human from the violence of placement and
definition, an opening to the placeless and indefinable absolute, Marion's
anthropology can only fault technology and its founding metaphysic for setting a definition of the human that effaces the human as indefinable, and in
that reading of technology Marion sets humanity in a radical difference or
separation from "world."

10. The terms "Platzhalter des Nichts" (lieutenant of the nothing) and the "Hirt des Seins"
(shepherd of Being), are Heidegger's, the former from *Was ist Metaphysik?* in *Wegmarken*, vol.
9 of *Gesamtausgabe*. 118; the latter from *Brief über den Humanismus*, in *Wegmarken*, 342. English translations in Heidegger's *Basic Writings*, ed. Krell, 106, 234, 245.

11. On the extension of objectification into the objectlessness of "standing reserve" (*Be-
stand*) see, of course, Heidegger's much discussed essay "Die Frage nach der Technik," in *Vorträge und Aufsätze* (Stuttgart: Neske, 1954), translated as "The Question concerning Technology," in *The Question concerning Technology and Other Essays*, trans. William Lovitt (New
York: Harper Torchbooks, 1977).

12. Emmanuel Levinas, "Heidegger, Gagarin, and Us," in *Difficult Freedom: Essays on Judaism*, trans. Seán Hand (Baltimore: Johns Hopkins University Press, 1997), 232–33.

But is the world in fact any more reducible to an object than is the human? Is it any more comprehensible—or less holy?[13] And if not, if the world is no more reducible to objective definition than the human, might we not understand the incomprehensibility of the human, its lack of definition, as a function of its constitutive engagement with the world—not its separation from the world? And might we not in turn understand such engagement, in and through which we do not in fact comprehend ourselves, to be from the beginning sustained and cultivated by technological means?[14] I pose these questions both in light of other recent theorizations of technological culture, which I believe call for a revision of the Heideggerian analysis on which Marion continues to rely, and in light of the theological traditions on which Marion's anthropology itself directly depends, and of which I gave my own reading in chapter 3. In both contexts, I want to argue, an indefinition or incomprehensibility of the human might be understood as the very condition of technological existence, and vice versa.

In resistance to a technological objectification of humanity, grounded in a humanism that proves to be dehumanizing, Marion deploys a theological perspective on the incomprehensibility of the human as created in the image of an incomprehensible God. A mystical or negative anthropology follows here from a mystical or negative theology. To see humanity as created in the image of God is, from this perspective, not to secure humanity's definition or to conceive its essence (as in ontotheology and its modern translations) but, indeed, to see that the essence of humanity, like the essence of God, is infinite or indefinite and therefore beyond any definition or conception, in excess of any representation or name. Along these

13. Here Marion seems to follow Levinas in the anthropocentric definition of holiness; elsewhere he suggests that the saturated phenomenon is to be generalized as the norm of phenomenality, and not restricted to the human or divine.

14. This is also one of Stiegler's central arguments, made via Heidegger in resistance to Heidegger. See, e.g, *La technique et le temps*, 1:250:

> Not only does Heidegger think the instrument but he thinks *starting from* it. Nonetheless, he does not think it *fully*: he does not see in it the originary and originarily lacking horizon of any disclosure, including the non-foreseeing; he does not see in it that which properly puts into play the temporality of Being, which is constituted techno-logically from access to the past, and hence to the future, and which constitutes therein the historial as such. He always thinks the tool as (only) useful and the instrument as tool, remaining incapable at the same time of thinking, for example, the artistic instrument as world *instructor* [*instructeur* de monde]. Here, the necessary analyses of employability correspond to a utilitarian preoccupation less than ever; and here, more than ever, in the instrumental putting to work, the world-making of the world—and a *rupture*— takes place.

lines, Marion's argument draws on the traditions of mystical speculation in Christian and Neoplatonic thought from the patristic theology of Gregory of Nyssa to the early modern humanism of Giovanni Pico della Mirandola, even into the late modern writing of Friedrich Nietzsche, who appears here as heir to Pico. The first major traditional source on whom Marion draws is Gregory of Nyssa, who, as I've shown, offers in his fourth-century treatise *De hominis opificio* (*On the Creation of Man*, περὶ κατασκευῆς ἀνθρώπού, 379) the classic formulation of a mystical or negative anthropology grounded in a mystical and negative theology (and Gregory, recall, was the first we know in the Christian tradition to have written a systematically negative theology).[15] However, while citing and elaborating Gregory's assertion that the human resembles its divine archetype insofar as it remains, like the archetype, incomprehensible, Marion does not explore the linkage we saw Gregory suggest between the human subject's incomprehensibility and its capacity for creative innovation by technological means. As I sought to show in chapter 3, the human in Gregory who, as image of the incomprehensible God remains incomprehensible, is at the same time a technological being whose creative freedom and dominion over the world likewise derive from the icon-archetype relation, even as that freedom and dominion are realized through a technological innovation that is conditioned by lack. "What seems to be a deficiency of our nature," Gregory posits, noting that we must create technologies to do the work for which animals are naturally endowed, "is a means for our obtaining dominion [πρὸς τὸ κρατεῖν] over the subject creatures."[16]

As I have already argued, a similar linkage between the human lack of definition and its creative, indeed technological, freedom recurs within the Christian, Neoplatonic tradition in pivotal figures from John Scotus Eriugena in the early Middle Ages through Nicholas of Cusa and Giordano Bruno on the eve of modernity. These later thinkers—as interpreters such as Blumenberg and Dupré argue, and as I sought to develop in my own way— in reviving the infinite cosmos and the cocreative humanity of Eriugena, prove especially important to understanding the passage from a limited, hierarchical, and centered cosmos typical of the Middle Ages, in which the nature of man is conceived teleologically, to an infinite and relative universe, itself never fully comprehended by the human, in which humanity

---

15. As Bernard McGinn notes in *The Foundations of Mysticism*, vol. 1 of *The Presence of God: A History of Western Christian Mysticism* (New York, Crossroad, 1991), 141.

16. Gregory of Nyssa, "On the Making of Man," 7.2, in Migne, *Patrologiae Cursus Completus, Series Graeca*, 141B; English translation in Schaff and Wace, *Nicene and Post-Nicene Fathers*, ser. 2, vol. 5.

exercises a creative freedom that is all the more divine insofar as it follows no pregiven paradigms. It imitates nothing other than the freedom and potential of a Creator God who, in his own creating, imitates nothing.

While passing over in silence the technological dimension of creative humanity in the theology of Gregory and his heirs, Marion does signal the issue obliquely in his suggestion that one might hear a modern echo of the mystical anthropology he wants to advance even in Friedrich Nietzsche, who by attesting to man as "the not-yet determined animal" (*das noch nicht festgestellte Thier*) confirms that "the impossibility of assigning him any definition at all fixes the only correct definition of man."[17] In this respect, Marion suggests, Nietzsche would point back also to the Renaissance thought of Pico, whose *Oration on the Dignity of Man* asserts that "man is an animal of diverse, multiform, variable and destructible nature."[18]

If Marion's silence on the technological and creative capacity of humanity in relation to Gregory is striking, it is perhaps even more so in relation to Nietzsche, for whom truth becomes creation, or creation truth, and in relation to his precursor Pico, who in his oration on man argues, as I noted, that the variability of humanity is the function of a human creativity that is grounded in the human's lack of definition or limit, its lack of natural place or law—a lack willed, moreover, by God. Much as Gregory had argued that the poverty or deficiency into which we are born becomes the spur to technological innovation and dominion over the world, and much as his early modern heir Nicholas of Cusa understands the human as "another god" or a "second god" precisely because the human, like God, creates in imitation of nothing, or in freedom from pregiven paradigms (and this especially in the sphere of technological innovation), so Pico, along lines not highlighted in Marion, has God tell Adam, whom God takes as the "work of an indiscrete image" (*indiscretae opus imaginis*), that "we have made thee neither of heaven nor of earth, neither mortal nor immortal, so that with freedom of choice and with honor, as thou the maker and molder of thyself, thou mayest fashion thyself in whatever shape thou shalt prefer."[19] From late antiquity through the late Middle Ages and Renaissance, even into late modernity, the traditions of mystical thought on which Marion

17. The Nietzsche quotation is from the *Nachgelassene Fragmente* (1884), 25 (428), in *Werke* 7.2, ed. Giorgio Colli and Mazzino Montinari (Berlin and New York, 1974), 121; cited in PU, 20.

18. Pico della Mirandola, *De dignitate hominis*, ed. G. Tonion and O. Boulnois (Paris, 2004), 12; discussed in PU, 20. In this direction, especially as it involves the affirmation of infinite metamorphosis within the immanence of a thoroughly relational world, Nietzsche might be seen as heir also to Bruno as we encountered him in chapter 3.

19. Pico della Mirandola, *Oration on the Dignity of Man*, in Cassirer, Kristeller, and Randall, *Renaissance Philosophy of Man*, 225.

draws in his effort to think the human as indefinable will with striking recurrence link that indefinition to creative and technological capacity. Marion's reluctance with respect to the technological question could perhaps be understood to stem from his concern to think the human more in terms of passivity and receptivity than, as is the tendency of modern metaphysics, in terms of activity or productivity. He wants all phenomena— including that of the human—to rely not on the constitution or decision of the human subject but on the unconditional and excessive givenness of the phenomena themselves. His reluctance to think the incomprehensibility of the human as the condition of creative and technological capacity (or vice versa) is consistent with his larger project of critiquing the representational subject of modern metaphysics as analyzed and critiqued in Heidegger— the subject who becomes the ground and measure of all that is. From this perspective, any trace of human self-production threatens to reintroduce a metaphysics of the subject and thus to compromise the unknowing that alone could rightly capture, precisely by not capturing, the indefinition of the inconceivable human. As Marion writes, insisting on the "privilege of positive self-unknowing," "my unknowing of myself—otherwise called the impossibility of my gaining access to myself through any idea, concept, or image that I may produce, except through the image that another gives to me—in no way signifies a flaw or defect in my knowledge, as metaphysics has so often claimed" (PU, 19). Here as throughout his work, Marion aims to undo the self-grounding and representational subject of modern metaphysics, wanting indeed to deprive the subject of any constituting decision.[20] "The nature (and definition) of man is characterized by instability [this we learn from Pico and his heir Nietzsche]—man as the being who remains, for himself, to be decided and about whom one never ceases to be astonished. Man, undecidable to man, thus loses himself if he claims to decide about himself. He remains himself only as long as he remains without qualities, other than those of a 'monstre incompréhensible' ('a monster that passes all understanding').[21] Let us not be mistaken: Pascal here designates a privilege, that of showing forth (monstrare) in oneself the incomprehensible" (PU, 20).

The themes of human limit or finitude, passivity and receptivity, have played a decisive role in twentieth-century Continental thought, but we may be reaching the point, in light especially of recent science and tech-

20. Though as I argue elsewhere, it may well be that the givenness of phenomena in Marion does after all depend for its appearance on my decision or will to see that givenness. See my "Blindness and the Decision to See."

21. Marion is here citing Pascal, Pensées (Lafuma, sec. 130; Krailsheimer, p. 32).

nology, where the obsession with passivity and limit, so intimately tied to reflection on the "impossible," begins to look like a flight from the unnervingly open and seemingly inexhaustible potential that may prove operative in our technoscientific networks themselves. What here calls for consideration, I think, is the intimate interplay between, on the one hand, the human lack of definition, as articulated so richly by Marion and the mystical tradition on which he draws, and, on the other hand, the creative and technological capacity of that same human, a capacity explored by mystical tradition but largely passed over by Marion's reading of that tradition. If the technological can appear to the (in this respect fairly Heideggerian) perspective of Marion and others as grounded in an overly narrow and stable delimitation of the human, one might also argue, from a slightly different angle, that the human, in its very technological existence, builds upon, even as it effects or instantiates—its own lack of definition, the irreducible indetermination that itself opens and conditions our creative capacity.

In the field of religious studies and in the human sciences more broadly, it is a commonplace, of course, to understand "religion" (and just about everything else) as human construction or creation, realized through the social dialectics of "world building." In this humanistic understanding of religion, a thinker like Marion would worry that the human is reduced or effaced through an overly secure definition of the human and thus that the excess of the human—and even more the excess of religion as revelation—would be lost. Now, while one indeed has to acknowledge the common tendency of social scientific thought to involve an overly secure (and thus often impoverished) conception both of the human and of religion—Heidegger does, after all, identify something all too real in his critique of "newspaper science"—I want to note also that the anthropology grounding this understanding of religion as world construction by means of human creativity can itself recall—if in ways unexpected both to the social scientists and to their critics—the anthropology of mystical tradition that I've been sketching out.

For example, when Peter Berger argues in his classic study *The Sacred Canopy* (1967) that man becomes social creature and world builder because he is born "unfinished" and thus lives "constantly in the process of 'catching up with himself'" through the production of a world that itself, in turn, produces man, when he argues that man by nature must form a "second nature," or culture, he is building not only on the dialectics of Hegel and

Marx but also on a kind of negative anthropology found in the work of figures such as Arnold Gehlen and Georges Lapassade.[22] Both Gehlen and Lapassade take their lead from the Dutch anatomist Louis Bolk, who in his 1926 lecture "The Problem of Human Genesis," as I noted in chapter 1, developed the biological and evolutionary theory of human "neoteny," according to which the human, born prematurely (ontogenetically and phylogenetically), remains fundamentally and forever incomplete, maintaining a fetal character even into its (never fully realized) maturity—thus constituting an always open work.[23] In his 1963 book *L'entrée dans la vie: Essai sur l'inachèvment de l'homme*, Lapassade draws on the likes of Marx, Freud and Heidegger to develop Bolk's theory of neoteny in a way that highlights in especially striking fashion the lack of definition to be reckoned with in the central object of human scientific thought. The human sciences in fact imply or require, Lapassade concludes, what I am calling a negative anthropology, precisely insofar as the human, because born premature and thus remaining ever underway and incomplete, lacks any definite or definable "nature." That lack of nature, in turn, is related intimately to the creative and thus to the social and historical, as well as the endlessly pedagogical, capacity of the human—both allowing such capacity and demanding it. "The concept of incompletion," Lapassade writes, "taken at the anthropological level, has the effect of placing into question any *a priori* as to the 'nature' of man and of insisting on the necessity of a history in order for man to be what he is." As historical, then, which is to say, as creative in an open-ended fashion, the human figured in such social scientific thinking exceeds and resists the definition of any concept. "The concept of incompletion is therefore at one and the same time the concept of lack and the lack of a concept. It is the concept of lack: it signifies that man is de-completed [*décomplété*], that he does not find in himself, in his instincts, in an innate know-how,

22. Peter Berger, *The Sacred Canopy* (New York: Garden Books, 1967), 4, 6. See Arnold Gehlen, *Der Mensch* (1940; Frankfurt: Athenaion, 1974); translated by Clare McMillan and Karl Pillemer as *Man: His Nature and Place in the World* (New York: Columbia University Press, 1988), esp. chapter 11, "Bolk's Theory and Other Related Theories." See also Georges Lapassade, *L'entrée dans la vie: Essai sur l'inachèvment de l'homme* (1963; Paris: Éditions Economica, 1997).

23. Louis Bolk, *Das Problem der Menschwerdung* (Jena, 1926), lecture given on April 15, 1926, at the Twenty-Fifth Congress of the Anatomical Society of Fribourg, available in a French translation by Georges Lapassade, "Le problème de la genèse humaine," *Revue Française de Psychanalyse*, March–April 1961. See also Lapassade, "Présentation de Louis Bolk," and Bolk, "La genèse de l'homme," *Arguments* 4, no. 18, 2nd trimester (1960). For an assessment of Bolk's current standing, see Stephen Jay Gould, who accepts Bolk's theory of neoteny but rejects the means by which Bolk argues toward it: "The Child as Man's Real Father," in Gould, *Ever Since Darwin: Reflections in Natural History* (New York: W. W. Norton, 1973).

the meaning [or direction] of his life and the truth of his behaviors, and that the human being can be only an interhuman being. But it is also the lack of a concept: the sciences here show themselves to be insufficient at the same time as they are necessary to 'comprehending' man."[24]

Operative, then, within one of the more influential and commonly presupposed social-scientific theorizations of religion as world building, this figure of the premature human who becomes creative (social, cultural, historical, pedagogical) in the space and time of its natural lack, or lack of nature, can be seen to operate also within more recent philosophical and theoretical attempts to develop, in light of an irreducibly technological existence, a thought of human and world today—a thought, in its turn, that might be seen to assume a fundamental significance for the question of religion, and to reintroduce the question of the mystical both into human-scientific understandings of man as *homo faber* and into the philosophical analysis of emerging technoscientific worlds.

⋄

Jean-Luc Nancy, along Heideggerian lines that diverge in illuminating ways from those followed by Marion, argues in his volume *La création du monde, ou La mondialisation* (2002) that human "nature," from the beginning "technological," must be understood to involve a creative capacity that always already "denatures." That creative capacity—according to which, much as with the temporality of Heidegger's Dasein or Stiegler's Epimetheus, the human never quite catches up with itself—is grounded for Nancy, as for the theorists of human neoteny I've signaled, in the prematurity or aboriginal deficiency of the human. The initial and always ongoing "noncoincidence" of the human with "itself," the dynamic interplay between insurmountable delay and never completed advance, involves an "extreme instability and mutability" that imply the "denaturing" nature of the human—"pretending to believe," as Nancy notes, "that there would have been first an integral and stable 'nature.'" From his perspective, which of course doubts that any integral or stable "nature" can ever define the human, one can say "that 'humanity' is the indexical name of the indeterminate and infinite term of hominoid denaturing" (Nancy, 126–27). The human for Nancy from its (never wholly present) "beginning" inhabits an indeterminacy that yields a technological creativity whose potential remains irreducibly open. "Without principle or end," the "nature" of the

24. Lapassade, *L'entrée dans la vie*, 202, 203.

human, then, consists in its lack of stable or integral nature, and that very lack is understood both to ground and to find sustenance in a technological existence that entails not the mastery of objective knowing or calculative thought but the amazement of an unknowing that demands the endless, ongoing creation of "world."

Just as the human who is "without principle or end," indeterminate and denaturing, escapes the logic of modern metaphysics' representational subject, so the "world" it inhabits is "without preliminary and without model" (Nancy, 63), defined by an immanent and open "sense" always yet to be created, a meaning or direction that refers to no "other world," nor to that first principle or cause named God in whom, beyond *this* world, one might seek this world's reason (according to the alienating logic of metaphysics that Marion elucidates). The God of ontotheology, who conceives or represents and thus creates or produces the world as its efficient cause or necessary reason, thus, as I noted with Heidegger, impedes a genuine thought of creation, which takes place only in the absence of pregiven ends or principles. If a modern metaphysics thinks production through efficient cause according to given ends, the "without model" of a being "without given" opens "the enigma of creation" (Nancy, 89).[25] This enigma, which gives a world and sense "without a why," recalls for Nancy the mystical tradition of Angelus Silesius—which means also that binding the likes of Cusa and Eckhart back to Eriugena and Dionysius—even as it can be tied to a new reading both of modern philosophy and of the essence of technology.

The mystical "without a why" suggests a new sense of the essence of technology, which becomes the name for a "know-how of that which is not already made" (Nancy, 128).[26] The "sense" of the world according to technology, on this reading, implies "the non-necessity and the non-naturality of the world (that is, of the totality of possible significability), which implies also its non-historicity in the metaphysical and theo-teleological sense of

---

25. See also, e.g., Nancy's discussion of the distinctively Christian—and deconstructive—character of such openness in his essay "La déconstruction du christianisme," *Les Études Philosophiques*, no. 4 (1998): 508–9: "My inquiry is guided by this motif of the essence of Christianity as opening: opening of the self and self as opening—under all the forms of opening, in all of its resonances: opening as distension, as gap, but also the 'Open' of Heidegger (which, since the opening of Heidegger, governs a climate of contemporary thought). What is going on with the opening of Christianity or with Christianity as opening? What is going on, and this at bottom is the true question, with *an absolute transcendental of opening*, which does not cease to make all horizons recede or dissolve?"

26. In this sense, Nancy's position resembles that of Stiegler, with the important difference that Nancy highlights and develops in a way that Stiegler does not the theological significance of technological creation. In Stiegler, e.g., see *La technique et le temps*, 1:241.

the word 'history'" (Nancy, 129). If this sense is the function of what Nancy calls an *absens* or an *absenthéisme*, if it excludes the theoteleological conception of history (which is not historical in any decisive sense),[27] it also pertains to the thinking of a creation *ex nihilo* (and perhaps a truly *decisive* sense of "history") at odds not only with appeals to the natural "itself," untouched by technology or culture, but also with the mythico-religious logic of such appeals. "Technology" is a name, Nancy argues, for the "planetary domination of the absence of beginning and end, or of the withdrawal of any initial or final *given*—of any *physis* or of any *muthos*" (Nancy, 114).

From the perspective opened by Nancy, the amazement that Aristotle, following Plato, designates as the origin of philosophy, the amazement for which, as Heidegger argues, machination and newspaper science have no time, can be thought nonetheless as essentially technological, exceeding the bounds of nature and its myths. It signals "nothing other than the specific technology of a non-knowing [*la technique propre d'un non-savoir*]: not the ignorance awaiting a teacher, nor the inexperience on its way to being initiated—which are both modalities of the mythico-religious world— but the knowing that, from the beginning, is articulated around a gap [*une béance*]" (Nancy, 132).[28] In tension, then, with the "mythico-religious," which should be understood here in terms of a closure or constraint within the givens of nature, the meaning of the technological is "denatured" and thus "de-mythified" (Nancy, 130). It operates in conjunction with a non-knowing and a lack of given principles and ends that open and condition a creation that remains infinite. Throughout our technologies—from the

27. Jacques Derrida has done as much as any other recent thinker to signal the paradoxes entailed in a thought of history as involving genuine futurity—which seems to require the kind of openness to decisive events that both enable any history and threaten to tear it apart. See, e.g., along these lines, Derrida's definition of the "messianic" in his seminal essay "Faith and Knowledge," 17: "This would be the opening to the future or to the coming of the other as the advent of justice, but without horizon of expectation and without prophetic prefiguration. The coming of the other can only emerge as a singular event when no anticipation sees it coming, when the other and death—and radical evil—can come as a surprise at any moment. Possibilities that open and can always interrupt history, or at least the *ordinary course* of history. But this ordinary course is that of which philosophers, historians, and often also the classical theoreticians of revolution speak. Interrupting or tearing history itself apart, doing it by deciding, in a decision that can consist in letting the other come." Here, as elsewhere, Derrida extends in his own way a line of thinking woven deeply throughout Heidegger's corpus, beginning notably with *Contributions to Philosophy*, which carries on an extended meditation concerning the relations between decision and history.

28. In "Faith and Knowledge" (e.g., 56), Derrida highlights nicely the intensification—and the mystical character—of such a gap in the technological world where, departing from the disenchanted modernity of Weber, we exercise increasingly powers of know-how for which we lack, insurmountably, the founding knowledge.

supplementations of the body (tools, arms, clothes) through the technologies of production and exchange (agriculture and breeding, money and
writing) to the manipulation and mutation of nature "itself" (biological engineering, etc)—the ungrounded principle and never achieved end would
be for Nancy "the pro-duction of the pro-ducer or the ex-position of the
ex-posed, the 'nature' of man as a denaturing in him of 'nature' as a whole,
what is today called the 'symbolic,' or in other words the opening of an
empty space where there plays (again) the infinite 'creation' of the world"
(Nancy, 133; see also 132). *This* technological humanity and its creation
stand at odds with the reduction of world to worldview, that tendency of
modern metaphysics that Nancy rightly sees also in the mythic appeal to
the *cosmotheoros*:

> A world is traversed from one end to the other. It never passes beyond
> those ends to occupy an overarching position where it observes itself.
> The time has passed where one could represent to oneself the figure of
> a *cosmotheoros*, of a world observer. And if that time has passed, that is
> because the world has withdrawn from the status of any possible repre-
> sentation. A representation of the world, a vision of the world, signifies
> the assignment of a principle and end of the world. This is as much to
> say that a vision of the world is in effect the end of the world seen, in-
> haled, absorbed, and dissolved in that vision. (Nancy, 37–38)[29]

The mythic appeal might be seen, in this light, as reaction against the
modern disappearance of God—which itself can open a thought of creation
beyond the mythic bounds of any total worldview, insofar as "a world removed from representation is above all a world without a God capable of
being the subject of its representation (and hence of its fabrication, of its
maintenance, and of its destination)" (Nancy, 38). Such a modern disappearance of God, I would emphasize, or a world removed from representation, is
deeply consistent with the God and world I have traced in the medieval and
early modern mystics, who likewise see in the "origin" and "end," which is
to say in the infinite God who sees and courses through all, precisely what
cannot be reduced or contained by representation.

This tension between the openness of an infinite creation by means of

---

29. Nancy goes on here to suggest a political significance in Heidegger's attack on the metaphysics grounding the "age of the world picture": "The Nazi *Weltanschauung* wanted to re-
spond to the absence of a *cosmotheoros*. And that is also why Heidegger, in 1938, turning against
that Nazism, exposed the end of the age of *Weltbilder*—of images or pictures of the world"
(Nancy, 38).

technology and the closure of a "mythical" religion bound to the given sheds light both on the traditions of mystical theology I've sketched out, which on the verge of modernity open a thought of creation beyond mimesis of the already given, and on tensions in current technological culture between the unsettling possibilities of radical innovation and reactive appeal to some sense of the given—whether the given of "nature" or of the "human" or of the "tradition" that would keep these safe and sound.[30] "The removal of any given," as Nancy writes, "forms the heart of a thought of creation. This is also what distinguishes it from myth, for which, in general, there is something given, something that precedes, which constitutes precedence itself, and on that basis origination" (Nancy, 91). From this perspective, the unsettling openness of creation—ungrounded and open-ended, open to the infinite multiplication of ends—might be taken to yield flight into the (ostensible) comfort or stability of mythical givens, a flight that senses well something of the *absenthéisme* that Nancy names and elucidates.

∽

Along similar lines, within a quartet of works on our emerging techno-logical world and humanity, which he takes to be undergoing a very real renaissance,[31] Michel Serres detects just the kind of flight perceived by Nancy in the so-called return of the religious, where ostensible threats posed by technoscience to "man" in his very "life" and "nature" provoke reactions aiming to resecure these same categories as "sacred": "The diffuse anxieties today surrounding chemistry or biotechnologies, for example, bring back the old abandoned figures of 'Nature,' of 'Life,' and of 'Man,' [which prove] all the less defined and all the more sacred as these

30. In a similar direction, see, along with Derrida's development of it in terms of immunity and autoimmunity in "Faith and Knowledge," Bergson's distinction between the stasis of the closed society and the openness of a dynamic mysticism in *The Two Sources of Morality and Religion*, trans. R. Ashley Audra and Cloudesley Brereton (Notre Dame: University of Notre Dame Press, 1977).

31. See, e.g., *Hominescence* (Paris: Le Pommier, 2001), the first of the four works: "We are living a Renaissance next to which the one the humanists called by this name is reduced to a mild wrinkle within the flow of time" (332) The three subsequent works are *L'incandescent* (Paris: Le Pommier, 2003); *Rameaux* (Paris: Le Pommier, 2004), which on p. 168 makes similar reference to our renaissant world and humanity; and *Récits d'humanisme* (Paris: Le Pommier, 2006). Serres proposes calling the series as a whole *Le grand récit*. A short essay by Serres bringing together many of the themes on the human woven through this series, "Le temps humain: De l'évolution créatrice au créateur d'évolution," can be found in Pascal Picq, Michel Serres, and Jean-Didier Vincent, *Qu'est-ce que l'humain?* (Paris: Le Pommier, 2003). The individual works of the *Grand récit* will be cited here parenthetically as, respectively, *HOM, INC, RAM,* and *REC*.

fears grow. Let's not touch 'Man,' they say, nor let us violate 'Life' or 'Nature,' whose myths reappear, as so many ghosts [*revenants*]" (*INC*, 29). This return of myth and the appeal to a sacred givenness of humanity, in its life and nature, may well be seen to involve a flight from the human indetermination that I am positing as both ground and consequence of the human capacity for technological creation that is also inevitably self-creation. That same technological capacity, on Serres's analysis, requires us to see the emergence of a world, and of a humanity in and through that world, that can no longer be (if it ever was) understood adequately according to the old divisions of subject and object, activity and passivity, or, correlatively, according to the character and conditions of solely human intelligence and agency—all of whose localities and delimitations may once have served a project of mastery and possession that now grows untenable.

If a certain Heideggerian perspective holds that a technoscientific human subject reduces all being, including its own, to the status of defined object, and if through such objectification the human subject makes itself the measure or even master of all that is, at the cost of a profound dehumanization, Serres might allow us—along lines seen also in Hayles on the posthuman or, closer to the field of religion, Mark Taylor on the network as complex adaptive system—to read technological culture otherwise. Theorizing the "network" already in 1964, in the introduction to the first book of his multivolume work *Hermes*,[32] and insisting throughout his subsequent work that relation and communication are more fundamental than substance or being, Serres productively highlights the operation of an irreducible unknowing within our technological experience, which entails not only creation but also self-creation on the part of a humanity that cannot finally define or comprehend itself. Indeed, the human proves self-creative for Serres in just the measure that it lacks stable definition or strict program. "Man changes," Serres writes, "insofar as one cannot fix for him any definition, which he always lacks or exceeds" (*INC*, 315). This instability, within technological culture, of the human and related categories (such as nature and life) may signal a challenge that is less that of human finitude (surely one of *the* questions in modern and contemporary thought) and more that of human infinitude, which is to say the human indetermination or incompletion that can itself be understood as the ground and condition

---

32. Michel Serres, *Hermès*, vol. 1, *La communication* (Paris: Éditions de Minuit, 1968), 11–20. The subsequent volumes (vols. 2–5) of this work are *L'interférence* (1972); *La traduction* (1974); *La distribution* (1977); and *Le passage du Nord-Ouest* (1980). A very short, one-volume selection of portions from the series appears in English as *Hermes: Literature, Science, Philosophy* (Baltimore: Johns Hopkins University Press, 1982).

of an inexhaustible openness or possibility. Inhabiting such possibility, we find our being less in the category of the human "as such" (as already defined in its nature or its dignity, which means its place or rank) and more in the ongoing process that Serres calls "hominescence," a neologism that highlights the "escence" of the human, its irreducibly inceptive, inchoate, and ever-changing character—and hence the resistance of the human to placement or belonging. Indeed, taken in its hominescence, the life of the human entails its continual departure from any fixed place, whose discrete boundaries and fixed markers spell death. "Our species *leaves*—that is its destiny without definition, its end without finality, its project without aim, its voyage, no, its erring, the *escence* of its hominescence. We leave, and give leave to our productions; we produce, and we produce ourselves, through this incessant movement of leaving" (*RAM*, 173). In a striking revision of the Pauline logic of adoption, which opens a new universalism by cutting ties of blood and other forms of identitarian belonging, Serres argues that any belonging that defines property and place, and any property or place that depends on belonging, are unsettled incessantly by the hominescent human, whose definition is always under construction. "In the interminable process of hominisation," he writes, "we cease to define man, we adopt him. Indeed, we fabricate him" (*RAM*, 100).[33]

Much like the distributed intelligence and agency of the posthuman in Katherine Hayles, or like the nodular subject of the complex adaptive network in Mark Taylor, hominescence in Serres emerges from a fundamentally relational, interactive, and evolving technological and scientific process that, while bringing forth a new humanity, "does not yet know what humanity [*homme*] it is going to produce" and, likewise, cannot possibly know exactly what humanity "does" that producing (*HOM*, 14).[34] As Serres

---

33. Serres should be read in relation to the resurgence of interest in Paul in recent Continental thought. See especially Alain Badiou, *Saint Paul: The Foundation of Universalism* (Stanford: Stanford University Press, 2003), and Giorgio Agamben, *The Time that Remains: A Commentary on the Letter to the Romans* (Stanford: Stanford University Press, 2005). On the notion of spiritual adoption, see also *HOM*, 174–78, where Serres reads in biotechnological development the promise of a liberation from blood and hence a new universality. "Who does not see," Serres asks, in a suggestive contrast to Marion's take on the technological, "that every racism is eradicated through this radical deconstruction of the structures of relation [*de parentés*] founded uniquely on ties of blood?" (178).

34. From this perspective, our relation to the task of human self-creation is much like the writer's relation to his work in Maurice Blanchot's understanding of literature in "Literature and the Right to Death": "Either: as an interior project [the work] is everything it ever will be, and from that moment the writer knows everything about it that he can learn, and so will leave it to lie there in its twilight, without translating it into words, without writing it—but then he won't ever write: and he won't be a writer. Or: realizing that the work cannot be planned, but

elaborates in and through the works that comprise *Le grand récit—Hom-*
inescence, L'incandescent, Rameaux, and *Récits d'humanisme*—we now
inhabit humanly constructed and global systems whose cognitive and agentive capacities not only exceed us but also transform us—and transform
us in such a way that our self-creation transpires always in conjunction
with an insurmountable ignorance or unknowing concerning both producer
and produced. Reshaping our relations to space and time (through digital
technologies, satellite networks, mobile communications, cyberspace), to
intelligence and agency (through cybernetics, artificial intelligence, robotics, prosthetics), to life and death themselves (through genetics and bioen-
gineering, thermonuclear weapons), emerging technoscience should lead us
to see that we are no longer (if we ever were) passive recipients of a nature
that is simply given "out there" but rather nature's "active architects and
workers" (*HOM,* 49). Our distinctive "nature" is "de-naturing" because
birth-giving (*natura*: the things to be born). We give birth to our world and
ourselves by actively interfacing with the given so as to shape and transform
it—only then to be, in turn, reshaped once more by that which we have created: "We are causing to be born, in the etymological sense of the term, an
entirely new nature, in part produced by us and reacting upon us" (*HOM,*
182). Within a process that disturbs modal logic through abrupt transformations of the contingent into the necessary and vice versa, we are becoming
in concrete ways "our own cause, the continuous creator of our world and
of ourselves" (*HOM,* 165), and we do so in such a way that "through new
and unexpected loops, we ourselves end up depending on the things that
depend globally on us"—including, most notably, life's time itself.[35]

The condition of unknowing wherein we are recreated in unexpected
ways by our own creations is one we inhabit suspended—or vibrating—
between contingency and necessity, each of which can slip suddenly and
unexpectedly into the other, as happens with the work of art or the event of
love, which, like any real birth, did not have to be, but which, once having
come to be, contingently, unforeseeably, affects us with the overwhelming
force of necessity. The law can yield event, and the event can become law,
Serres points out, and "from this immense caduceus, where contingency

---

only carried out, that it has value, truth, and reality only through the words which unfold it in
time and inscribe it in space, he will begin to write, but starting from nothing and with nothing
in mind—like a nothingness working in nothingness, to borrow an expression of Hegel's" (in *The
Station Hill Blanchot Reader: Fiction and Literary Essays,* ed. George Quasha, [Barrytown, N.Y.:
Station Hill Press, 1999], 362). See also Stiegler's discussion of related themes and passages from
this important essay in *La technique et le temps,* 1:268.

35. Michel Serres and Bruno Latour, *Conversations on Science, Culture, and Time* (Ann
Arbor: University of Michigan Press, 1995), 172.

and necessity are interwoven, man and his humanism are finally born today" (REC, 187). Inhabiting the vibration between necessity and contingency, between law and event, between the continued redundancies of
format and the cutting singularities of new message, the hominescent can
never be certain whether the one or the other is at stake. "The intoxicating
beauty of the vital adventure, human and global," Serres suggests, "comes
from the fact that we never know whether that which we think, that which
we do, hope, or feel, here, now, or even for a long time . . . stems from
contingency or necessity"(RAM, 187)—and in such unknowing one might
locate a dynamic of faith.

Far from the certainty of salvation on which Luther and Calvin insisted,
with consequences that reverberate all too powerfully today, the faith suggested in Serres entails an unavoidable coimplication of unknowing and belief, as well as of weakness and power. Taking inspiration again from Paul,
Serres notes that credo and πιστεύω, which we translate in terms of belief,
mean at bottom "traversing throughout one's life, hesitating and vibrating, the segment that separates and unites" two positions, one involving
"the objective truth or, from the subjective side, the certitude or conviction
that such truth entails," and the other involving "on the contrary, objective
falsehood or the subjective rejection of such an error." The belief or faith
to be discerned in such hesitation or vibration, suggested by Paul's contention that "we walk in faith, not in the light of reason" (2 Cor. 5:7), concerns
"a contingency where are mixed certitude and doubt, conviction and its
negation, light and darkness, knowledge and ignorance" (RAM, 88). The
first of the three theological virtues, along with hope and love, the belief
in which unknowing or doubt is unavoidably implicated, yields a modern
self and consciousness that "overturns mastery" and unsettles Descartes, a
self whose belief, immersed in doubt, moves in and through a hope without
assurance, and a love—or a generosity—open to all, especially the gentile,
the stranger. "Faith, hope, and charity describe the non-ontology of this
new subject: its non-installation, its non-assurance, its non-being, its nothingness . . . the unbelonging of the soul" (RAM, 89, 91). At the heart of a
technoscientific existence that has been taken by many to stand at odds
with any genuine theology or religious faith, one can in these terms locate
a dynamic of faith, which, above all in the link that it posits between unknowing and creation, recalls in terms of our own emerging world that of
the mystics I've engaged.

The global character of hominescent unknowing, the function of a loop-
ing between that which we create and that which, in turn, recreates us in
such a way as to call into question the assessment of modernity as project

of mastery, is especially notable in what Serres identifies and analyzes as "world objects" (*objets-monde*), which is to say humanly fabricated devices or systems whose scale—in terms of energy, speed, space, or time—reaches a worldly dimension. These technoscientific creations of ours finally exceed us in such a way that, instead of relating to them from a stance of distance and independence (as with the "representational" relation between subject and object, or human and world picture, in Heidegger's account of modern Western metaphysics), we actually live and move within them and find ourselves shaped by them and their own ongoing development. World objects, Serres explains in *Hominescence*, "place us in the presence of a world that we can no longer treat as an object: objective, to be sure, and thus we avoid any animism, but not passive, since it acts, in return, on the global constraints of our survival. We need to think such a return" (*HOM*, 180). At this level, the "object" of human thought and action, much like Hayles's distributed system or Taylor's network, differs from any object that might be set apart and placed securely in front of a self-sustaining or self-possessed subject, defined discretely, circumscribed and hence *located* in such a way as to fall under the conceptual or practical hold, mastery, or possession of that subject.[36] By contrast to Heidegger's world picture, the world object, in Serres, puts us in the presence of an objective world that, in its activity and movement, we can no longer treat as an object, a world no longer passive but actively—interactively—engaged with us and thus not amenable to the modern project of mastery.

The emergence of such world objects, which goes hand in hand with today's technological processes of globalization, yields a new universe that indeed challenges the modern philosophy of domination and possession insofar as that philosophy is founded on a clear and stable division of the subject from the object—a division thanks to which alone the subject might hope finally to comprehend and thereby control an objectified reality (or a reality reducible to the logic of economic calculation and exchange).[37] And just as the character of "object" here changes considerably, so too does that of "subject": the human subject emerging in our technoscientific world is no longer the self-certain or self-possessed individual subject of Descartes

36. It is worth recalling here that the association of location with definition or circumscription is decisive to the mystical insistence that God cannot be located. On this, see my essay "Locating the Mystical Subject," in *Mystics: Presence and Aporia*, ed. Michael Kessler and Christian Sheppard (Chicago: University of Chicago Press, 2003).

37. The world object, as Serres points out, removes the object from service as token or means of exchange: "By reason of their global dimension, the new objects are henceforth, most often, beyond exchange. One can take hold of fixed and locatable springs, but one cannot steal the hazard of the rains" (*REC*, 124).

or Locke, but rather a thoroughly relational and interactive "we," an irreducibly collective and emergent subject whose distributed intelligence
and agency make impossible its discrete or punctual location. This, then, is
the angle from which Serres argues that philosophy needs to reexamine its
basic categories and concepts: "The subject, objects, knowledge, action . . . ,
all [were] constructed for millennia under the condition of localities whose
divisions defined, among other things, a subject-object distance along which
knowledge and action played themselves out. The measure of that [subject-
object] distance conditioned [knowledge and action]. Divisions, proximi-
ties, distance, measure . . . , these finitudes that were preconditions to our
theories and practices are being undone today, where we are passing into a
larger theater and where we are losing our finitude" (HOM, 183).

If, as Serres argues, we are losing our finitude today in demonstrable
ways, if we are indeed undoing or reworking the boundaries of subject and
object, the borders of life and death, and the kinds of spatial and temporal
limit that have long defined us, then the human "itself" likewise grows
increasingly difficult or even impossible to locate clearly or define securely.
The technological humanity that interactively builds and inhabits a world
no longer reducible to object is a humanity whose always-open, creative
potential must be understood to depend on its relative lack of definition
or determination: the more programmed the creature, the less open in its
potential; the less programmed, the more open and adaptable. Insofar as it
remains nothing determined in itself, the human can become virtually all,
and in this respect, we can articulate, within today's technological culture,
a figure who may indeed recall the incomprehensible or indeterminate,
and thereby creative, human of mystical tradition from Gregory and Eriugena through Cusa, Pico, and Bruno. Through a pure but no less wonderful
contingency, one figure associated with that tradition—the Dionysius or
Denys who, as patron saint of France, was long confused with both Dionysius the Areopagite (a convert of Saint Paul) and the actual pseudonymous
author of the Dionysian mystical theological corpus (most likely a late
fifth- or early-sixth century Syrian monk)—was by legend beheaded and,
in depictions of the legend, shown holding his own head in his hand. This
image of a subject whose head has literally been placed beyond him, while
still remaining in his hands, expresses for Serres the interplay between our
human indetermination, or emptiness, and the technological invention related thereto. The beheaded Denys represents the subject "nude and empty,
without faculty," whose cognitive and agentive capacities have been objectified and placed before, which means outside, the subject who nonetheless
depends on them—or indeed lives only in and through them. "All having

become Saint Denises, we henceforth everyday take hold, in order to use it, of this full and well made head that lies before us, carriers of an empty and inventive head on our neck" (HOM, 237).

With this kind of mystical resonance, then, our creative potential stems from our *not-knowing* ourselves, from a deprogramming or forgetting, from the indeterminate ground, adaptive and free, of "exodarwinian" transformations wherein, through the extensions of its mind and body, the creature of evolution becomes evolution's cocreator. "The most mimetic of the beasts starts to propagate messages otherwise than through sex and the body. Through gestures, plaints, cries, music, words, writings, telecommunications . . . humans receive information from people other than their parents, and emit it toward people other than their children. We break open and generalize genealogy through these signs, both carnal and disembodied, circulating by exodarwinian paths, adoptive and free" (REC, 137). The free space-time of adoption, which generalizes genealogy, is one of technical or technological innovation and of the learning that enables and is enabled by such innovation. The indeterminate human, ever being born, must ever be learning precisely insofar as it lacks the fixed and stable channels of any strictly given program; it must invent that which is not given innately. "Apprenticeship departs from a pregiven and programmed niche, a genetic automatism, for an adventure without any clear promise: leap into the unknown!" (RAM, 174)—and in the oceanic freedom of such apprenticeship, the one who learns will rely on those various extensions and instruments, those technologies that themselves will evolve like, but independently of, the bodies (and minds) they supplement and on which they were perhaps first modeled. Thus the technological tool or apparatus (*appareil*) becomes, in the nautical sense, a casting off (*appareillage*). In extending ourselves we depart from ourselves, cast off into an oceanic turbulence whose feedback loops, interacting with navigational systems, modify unpredictably both the inventor and his inventions. And like the rigging that allows a ship to navigate, without controlling or mastering, the oceanic— and climatic—turbulences that are both means of conveyance and constant threat, the technological apparatus becomes the space-time of a cybernetics that entails something quite other than what Heidegger signaled under that name.[38] Abandoning any notion of creation as preformation or providence, or as production by means of stable principle of sufficient reason,

38. See, e.g., Heidegger's letter to Eugen Fink in the appendix to *Fundamental Concepts of Metaphysics*, 368, and the discussion of cybernetics in the Heraclitus seminar Heidegger held with Fink in the late 1960's: *Heraclitus Seminar*, trans. Charles H. Seibert (Evanston: Northwestern University Press, 1993).

we inhabit a new era where "contingent evolution produces a producer of contingent evolution." To inhabit such an era responsibly we need to think an ethics "in the cybernetic mode," which means "governing productions on whose comportment we never decide once and for all and before all"; it means keeping open the kind of responsiveness and attentiveness and adaptiveness that save life on the seas and elsewhere, the "prudence of the pilot" who understands that the real, like the seas, mixes "storm [*houle*] and route . . . responds to the solicitations of the pilot who makes his way, contingent and necessary, by a possible route that bypasses the impossibilities" (*RAM*, 201, 202).

At this point, where the quasi-mystical character of an inventive and evolving and always indefinite humanity intersects with the ethical navigation of a fluid world in and through whose ongoing creation humanity creates itself, I must highlight two lines in Serres's thinking that I believe bear significantly on a reading of religion and technology today. The first concerns the intimate and increasingly complex interplay we need to acknowledge between the sociocultural and the natural-cosmological within our world-building and self-creative activity, and the second, related, concerns our dwelling with time. Both directions, I believe, call for a revision of the Heideggerian orthodoxy that can see technology only or primarily as dehumanizing, as uprooting and "deworlding," because reductive of all possibility to the logic of actuality and its mastery. As Serres argues in *Le contrat naturel* (1990), "The global power of our new tools today gives to us as partner the Earth, which we constantly inform through our movements and energies, and which in turn informs us, through its energies and movements, its global changes. We do not need language, again, in order for this contract to function, as a play of forces. Our technologies [*techniques*] make up a system of ropes/cords [*cordes*] or of lines/traits [*traits*], a system of exchanges of power and information, which goes from the local to the global, and the Earth responds to us, from the global to the local."[39] The ongoing operation of this "natural contract" binds inextricably the natural with the sociocultural and thus suspends forever the simple givenness of any nature "itself" or life "itself," thereby weaving intimately the epistemological and ontological with the ethical and political. The time, or tempo, of nature and of life

39. Michel Serres, *Le contrat naturel* (Paris: Éditions François Bourin, 1990), 170. Hereafter cited parenthetically as *CN*.

"themselves" thus becomes increasingly a time of human making—as, for example, in the time of genetic evolution, or the time of the climate that cools or heats the earth and thereby shapes the flow of its waters.

Through genetic engineering, the almost unimaginably slow and blind time of natural evolution becomes, concretely, the historical and intentional time of human labor and creativity. The time of "life" begins to fall under our influence (which does not mean control), and thus we assume over life a new responsibility (which is not to say mastery). Likewise, through the technological ways of life that yield global warming, a new and truly global human condition emerges, itself the product of a collective humanity that transforms, through its affect on climate or weather the time that passes or flows, the temporality, the tempo, of earth and its waters, which not only sustain life but may well offer an indispensable ground of humanity (as Robert Harrison argues in a beautiful and challenging book, *Dominion of the Dead*, whose arguments I take up in chapter 6). The scope of this new human influence on earth and its time is captured well by the Dutch chemist Paul Crutzen, who suggests that we should rename the geologic age in which we live. We inhabit no longer the Holocene (dated from the last period of glaciation), Crutzen asserts, but instead the Anthropocene, a new age "defined by one creature—man—who had become so dominant that he was capable of altering the planet on a geologic scale." Crutzen thus highlights the temporal import of a similar assertion made by Soviet geochemist Vladimir I. Vernadsky, who some seventy years ago observed that "through technology and sheer numbers . . . people were becoming a geological force."[40]

Philosophical and theoretical analyses of technology, of course, have long noted its distinctive tendency to transform the human experience of time and place, and that tendency has been linked in the major twentieth-century thinkers to a tension or even opposition between technology and "traditional" religious life. If modern technology in its mechanical reproductive forms can seem (as Walter Benjamin emphasized in his classic work) to speed up things that move slowly (time-lapse photography), or to slow down things that move quickly (slow-motion film), that restructuring of time and

40. Crutzen, who won the 1995 Nobel Prize for Chemistry for his work concerning the hole in the ozone layer, is cited by Elizabeth Kolbert in "The Climate of Man," *New Yorker*, April 2005, 54. Kolbert's fine three-part series from the *New Yorker* has now appeared in an expanded book version, *Field Notes from a Catastrophe: Man, Nature, and Climate Change* (New York: Bloomsbury, 2006). Vernadsky is cited in Andrew C. Revkin, "Forget Nature: Even Eden is Engineered," *New York Times*, Tuesday, August 20, 2002, sec. D (Science Times), 1.

place is integral to a decay of the "aura" that thrived in the traditional context of an art that was first religious.[41] If modernity's technological organization of human experience can seem to make near what physically remains distant (the image transmitted by newspaper, television, or Internet),
or seem to make distant what in fact stands physically close (through the
distraction and uprooting, for example, that so worries Heidegger and his
heirs), then it yields a "homelessness" related essentially to human self-
assertion and a correlative flight of the gods. In the directions just noted—
genetics and evolution, climate and geologic time—these tendencies of the
technological to reshape time and to reshape place intersect in the most
concrete and global senses, touching us all directly if indeed variously. At
such an intersection, however, the technoscientific does not simply distract, uproot, or displace; it does not in fact set the human subject at a distance from a world or an earth thus objectified, manipulated, and exploited
by calculative and instrumental means within a human project of mastery.
Rather, the technoscientific binds us in ever more intimate and complex relations with earth and world (whose distinction may itself grow unstable)—
and in a manner perhaps finally, or originally, "religious."

If natural scientific thought can tend to neglect the human or the social,
so the humanistic and social scientific fields have tended to neglect the
natural world and its science. The binding networks of emerging technoscience, however, demand that these often separated fields now be thought
in their intimate interplay: "Through the exclusively social contracts, we
have left the tie that attaches us to the world, that which binds the time
that passes and flows [le temps qui passe et coule] to the weather [le temps
qu'il fait], that which sets in relation the social sciences and those of the
universe, history and geography, right and nature, politics and physics, the
tie that addresses our language to mute, passive, and obscure things which,
by reason of our excesses, recapture voice, presence, activity, light. We can
no longer neglect it" (CN, 81).[42] By highlighting the inextricable tie between
two senses of "time" (temps) at stake in the networks of our technoscientific
self-creation, and in noting the "contractual" character of such networks,[43]

41. See Benjamin, "The Work of Art in the Age of Mechanical Reproduction."
42. Serres has developed this idea elsewhere as well: "No crowd or state in nature; no flora
or fauna in law. On one side things, on the other side men. Today we continue this perilous
acosmist divorce: history forgets geography, neither the social sciences nor politics care about the
planet. Now, not only do we inhabit the world, but we are today weaving with it ties that are so
global and tight that it is entering into our contracts" (RAM, 228).
43. Serres is convinced, admittedly without having any proof, that the rope or cord that ties
is the "first invention of human technology" and "contemporary with the first contract." His

where we are bound not only to one another in our emerging humanity but also to the Earth as global human ground, we might understand such time and its transformations—which always weave chance and necessity, the natural and the cultural—to involve not only something of the technological but indeed something of the religious, which itself proves interwoven with the technological. Within this sense of the religious, human duration, both subjective and collective, is not separable from the time of the world.

Serres develops this understanding of time in a striking way when he argues that the members of a "traditional" religious humanity, through its prayers and rites—such as the chants that open, punctuate, and close the day of the Benedictines—do not simply follow a given time but indeed structure and sustain time. "Their shoulders and their voices," Serres writes of the monastics whose prayers and rites we modern amnesiacs may forget, "from biblical verses to orisons, bear each minute into the next throughout a fragile duration which, without them, would break" (CN, 80). I would add that the time or duration that the monks sustain through their song and prayer is also, in return, the time that sustains them. Likewise, in and through our technoscientific ties, we come to depend now on global temporalities and tempos that depend on us—and that involve both the continuities and cuts that time, in the living contradiction that yields rhythm, entails. Indeed, as Serres puts it in *Récits d'humanisme*, "one of the Greek roots of this word, *teinô*, τείνω, which means to be stretched or extended continuously, as in the long flowing of a paste or liquid, contradicts the other possible root, *temnô*, τέμνω, which means: to cut in thin, almost atomic, pieces, as when one measures duration in centuries, minutes, or microseconds. The same contradiction sculpts the term rhythm, flowing and broken" (REC, 135).[44] In this dynamic, rhythmic tension between the continuities and the cuts

---

beautifully simple example of the interplay between the natural and social contract comes from mountaineering, where, when the climbing grows steep and difficult and potentially deadly, the group ropes up and creates not only a social bind, among the people tied one to another, but also a natural tie, in relation to the rock where the piton is placed as point of attachment for the rope. "The group is tied, referred, not only to itself, but to the objective world. The piton solicits the resistance of the wall to which no one will trust a tie-in except after having tested it. To the social contract is added a natural contract" (CN, 163).

44. See also Serres on the interplay of time and the *récit*, and on that between chronology and meteorology: "Thus, and in its greatest generality, this latter [the *récit*] is constructed as human duration, subjective and collective, and as the time of the world. It is both scientific and literary, cognitive and objective. The two laws that govern it, chaos of random grains and the necessary continuity of a line, meet up with those that found the very nature of time, where, I forcefully underscore again, the time that passes does not differ from the weather outside, where, I'll insist on this for as much time as it takes, physical time is composed in as contradictory a way as human time" (REC, 136).

of time, all time might be understood as a time of faith, as the movement of constant vibration and hesitation between necessity and contingency, between repetition and creation, between knowing and unknowing. And, indeed, in the human work of sustaining time by creating and attending to its punctuations and differentiations, its durations and departures, its flux and reflux, its memories and its forgetting, I locate a basic work of religion, a work that concerns as much the time that passes and flows as it does the climate that interplays with the energies and movements of the earth and its waters. In either sense, one can liken the work of religion to Penelope's incessant weaving: "In the same way [as Penelope], religion presses, spins, knots, assembles, gathers, binds, connects, lifts up, reads or sings the elements of time. The term *religion* expresses exactly this trajectory, this review [*revue*] or this continuation [*prolongement*] whose opposite is called negligence, the negligence that incessantly loses the memory" (*CN*, 80) of those words and behaviors through which the religious give voice to the things of the world and to the time within which they—people and things both—live.

If the reverse side of religion is negligence, where might we see such negligence today? Perhaps foremost, we find it among those who, according to the perilous acosmism about which Serres warns, deny or ignore the increasingly complex and intimate ties binding the social and the natural and hence the local and the global. While those, for example, in the daily news who speak most vocally for the "culture of life" and for the nature and dignity of the human do so more often than not in the name of religion and the "values" of "tradition," known and kept secure by "people of faith," we might well view just such speech, I think, as an acute expression of negligence—in the sense that it involves a distinctive denial or disavowal of those ties that now bind the human to life and to nature, negligent of those processes sustaining and advancing the ongoing contractual exchange in which we become indeed the "continuous creators of our world and of ourselves" (*HOM*, 163). That negligence might also be understood as lack of faith, if by faith we mean the vital vibration between certainty and unknowing, necessity and contingency—in short, the faith that dwells in a time of life.

Such negligence, or unfaith, arrogating to itself the authority and ostensible security of tradition, can also be read, finally, as a flight from the trait of the human that makes something like tradition necessary and possible in the first place, namely, the indetermination and incompletion that call for and condition our technoscientific being, our exodarwinian self-creation. The various myths today that appeal to the human "itself" as "sacred" in its life and nature, myths that claim to know who or what the human is, while pretending to derive such knowledge from tradition, may well ignore not only the complexity and variety of "the tradition" in any given case—a tendency that the ideologues on right and left seem increasingly to share equally with respect to "the Western tradition," for example—but even more the condition of any tradition at all. We can and we must create tradition and all it requires—all the extensions of man: pages, books, images, rituals, archives, networks, and the like—because we remain deficient, indeterminate and incomplete, "in ourselves." Tradition, in turn, its immeasurable memory as well as its immeasurable forgetting, can speak to us and through us in a living way thanks only to such deficiency, and in such a way that wealth and poverty, excess and lack coincide—in a coincidence where life time demands the vibrant uncertainty and unknowing of faith.

CHAPTER FIVE

Here Comes Everybody:
Technopoetics and Mystical Tradition in Joyce

The quasi-mystical character of a technologized media culture and its massive, anonymous chatter is performed, with strikingly Joycean resonance, in a recent collaborative artwork titled *Listening Post*, by Mark Hansen, a statistician-artist, and Ben Rubin, an artist-mathematician-technologist.[1] As stated in the artists' project description, *Listening Post* "is an art installation that culls text fragments in real time from thousands of unrestricted Internet chat rooms, bulletin boards and other public forums. The texts are read (or sung) by a voice synthesizer, and simultaneously displayed across a suspended grid of more than two hundred small electronic screens." By these means, *Listening Post* becomes a work that makes visible and audible the infinite and incomprehensible stream of a global communication whose scale and complexity ultimately elude the bounds of any given speech or visibility. The work thus repeats—unknowingly, one surmises—gestures of thought and language crucial, we've seen, to mystical theology and fundamental also, I'll now argue, to Joyce's *Finnegans Wake*.

Listening Post is machine art whose networked programs articulate the random in all of its banality and all of its surprise. Like the music and poetry of John Cage, himself a devoted and creative student of Joyce, *Listening Post* uses, by means of its data-mining techniques, the formulaic or programmatic to stage or screen the unique and unforeseeable, drawing by means of computer programs ever new and unpredictable sequences from "the stream of world chatter" on the Internet.[2] It gives voice and visibil-

---

1. For information on the work, including artists' statements, images and video clips, see the *Listening Post*, www.earstudio.com/projects/listeningpost.html/.

2. The phrase "stream of world chatter" is from Adam Gopnik, "Chatter: Orange and White," in Talk of the Town, *New Yorker*, March 3, 2003. On Cage's interest in Joyce, see, e.g., Cage's

ity to what might be read or heard as "the world's mind," yielding "all at once" an experience of the "totality of communication" that occurs "at any given moment" in the "myriad chat rooms, message boards, and Internet forums."[3] Coursing across a grid of 231 LED screens—like those of the cash registers where the invisibly massive flow of monetary currency offers glimpses of itself—the samplings of Internet chatter screened by the *Listening Post* are vocalized by means of synthesized voices whose artificial tone can turn musical, even hymnal. These voices of the machine make all the more poignant the deeply human senses of hope and futility they bring to expression—taking on faith that the words spoken are indeed the expression of humans, for as Adam Gopnik points out, "no one, not Hansen or Rubin or even the machine, knows where any of this is coming from."[4] Even if overused, the term uncanny does rightly describe the sense one has in hearing and reading the flow of these uncountable, transient, chorally arranged voices, which seem familiar even as they come from no definable or locatable place or person, and hence seem to come from everywhere, and which speak to me in my distinct present but remain abstracted from any secure context or stable representation. To be immersed in the stream of such voice and image suggests participation—my own and that of a multitude I cannot count but in which I believe—in a totality that no one comprehends but all can sense, a totality that might yield not only the most profound alienation but also, as Peter Eleey puts it, a "transcendent feeling of connection on a grand scale, regardless of what one actually had in common with any of the voices materializing in the installation."[5]

While incapable of ever doing so directly or adequately—according to an impossibility and failure essential to the work's power—the *Listening Post*

---

book *Writing through Finnegans Wake* (Tulsa: University of Tulsa, 1978) and the CD *John Cage: Roaratorio* (Wergo), which contains "Roaratorio: An Irish Circus on Finnegans Wake, for voice, tape, and Irish musicians" and "Writing for the Second Time through Finnegans Wake, for speaker."

3. "The world's mind" is from Gopnik, "Chatter"; I also quote here Kevin Fitchard, "Listening In," telephonyonline.com.

4. Gopnik, "Chatter."

5. Peter Eleey, "Mark Hansen and Ben Rubin: Whitney Museum of Modern Art, New York," *Frieze*, no. 75 (May 2003), www.frieze.com. That sense of transcendence, woven with a certain faith, might prove inextricable too from the kind of paranoia that a writer like Don DeLillo associates with faith within a world of pervasive but incomprehensible systems and powers. Eleey notes just such an ambivalence in this instance of the uncanny, or sublime: "In a perfectly timed Foucaultian twist, *Listening Post* brought to the people a version of the knowledge that government collects on a sublime scale—along with its attendant power, fear and pleasure. Whether the piece ultimately serves more as assuaging entertainment than as provocation is irrelevant to its evaluation, but a fascinating question nonetheless."

"is meant to reveal the sheer magnitude of online discourse, a digital Tower of Babel."[6] As its creator Rubin explains, it means to convey the "yearning" of the "untold number of souls out there just dying to connect." The "scale and immensity of human communication" on the Net,[7] or at least of the yearning for communication, are sensed or felt here without ever being made fully present—sensed or felt in just the measure that one senses how far the actual expression falls short of the immense totality of communication and noncommunication coursing through the ebbs and flows of the network. Fluidity is indeed one of the most striking traits of the work. The "torrent of communication" that the work evokes is likened by Rubin to the wind, and "the sound generating systems are constructed," he notes in his statement on the Web site, "almost as wind chimes, where the wind in this case is not meteorological but human, and the particles that move are not air molecules but words." Most commentators on the work also note the fluidity of its operation, likening it variously to the flow of a river or the meandering of a stream, to the tides of an ocean, to the movement of a dream. *Listening Post* is "about realizing that, if you can hear it all at once, the Internet sounds like the dream of a city."[8]

Hansen and Rubin, who have also in progress a project titled *All the News* for Renzo Piano's new New York Times building, where they will screen in real time the immeasurable currents of the daily news, diverge from the positions exemplified by Kierkegaard and Heidegger on technological culture even as they recall an alternative and more affirmative line of thinking on the press, from the likes of Joyce, or already Stéphane Mallarmé, to Marshall McLuhan. It is no mistake, I think, that the last is not only a founding theorist of contemporary technological and media culture but also a student of the Catholic traditions that decisively inform Joyce. Moreover, Joyce himself was not only a religious writer in the senses McLuhan illuminates, but also one of the first and still most significant writers to articulate the question of the book, as Joyce scholar and media theorist Donald Theall points out, "in a culture which has discovered photography, phonography, radio, film, television, telegraph, cable, and telephone and has developed magazines, advertising, Hollywood, and sales promotion."[9]

6. Matthew Mirapaul, "Arts Online: Making an Opera from Cyberspace's Tower of Babel," *New York Times*, December 10, 2001.

7. Rubin, quoted in ibid.

8. Philip Nobel, "First Take: Philip Nobel on Ben Rubin," *Artforum*, January 2002. I think also of the angels in Wim Wender's *Wings of Desire* (*Der Himmel über Berlin*) as they walk through the library and hear the chorus of countless inner voices.

9. Donald Theall, *James Joyce's Techno-Poetics* (Toronto: University of Toronto Press, 1997), 42.

McLuhan articulates well, and precisely as a reader of Joyce as religious writer, the tension between, on the one hand, "the gloomiest apprehensions in the academic mind"—from Plato through Heidegger tending to react uneasily to media and other technologies, with their attendant risks of inauthenticity—and, on the other hand, "the enthusiastic attention of poets and aesthetes" for "the popular press as an art form."[10]

Hansen and Rubin's *Listening Post* signals the manner in which the Internet and its culture extend and amplify what Lamartine was famously able to see of the press in his "epoch," in 1831, fifteen years before Kierkegaard's *Present Age*:

> Do not perceive in these words [declining to write for the *Revue Européenne*] a superb disdain for what is termed journalism. Far from it; I have too intimate a knowledge of my epoch to repeat this absurd nonsense, this impertinent inanity against the Periodical Press. I know too well the work Providence has committed to it. Before this century shall run out journalism will be the whole press—the whole human thought. Since that prodigious multiplication which art has given to speech—multiplication to be multiplied a thousand-fold yet—mankind will write their books day by day, hour by hour, page by page. Thought will be spread abroad in the world with the rapidity of light; instantly conceived, instantly written, instantly understood at the extremities of the earth—it will spread from pole to pole. Sudden, instant, burning with the fervor of soul which made it burst forth, it will be the reign of the human soul in all its plenitude. It will not have time to ripen—to accumulate in a book; the book will arrive too late. The only book possible from today is a newspaper.[11]

What Lamartine presciently and cuttingly says of the relation between book and newspaper in his time might be said today, in turn, of the relation between newspaper and the electronic media network, for which the Internet is perhaps only the most automatic figure. His position resonates with those of the anxieties I highlighted in Kierkegaard and Heidegger and kin: the threat of totality (the whole of human thought), the subjection to repetition or reproduction and uncontrolled dissemination (the prodigious

10. Marshall McLuhan, "Joyce, Mallarmé, and the Press," in *The Interior Landscape: The Literary Criticism of Marshall McLuhan, 1943–1962*, ed. Eugene McNamara (New York: McGraw-Hill, 1969), 5.

11. Lamartine, quoted in ibid.

multiplication that art has given to speech), the erasure of real time and space (thought spread abroad in the world with the rapidity of light) to the point of instantaneity and ubiquity (instantly conceived, written, understood at the extremities of the earth), and the human will to mastery (the reign of the human soul in all its plenitude) whose full extension could well yield an extreme emptiness.

In Heidegger and Kierkegaard and their heirs we can hear echoes, indeed, of Plato's old lament, to which McLuhan (like Derrida) calls attention, that the media supplement gives "not truth but the semblance of truth" in such a way that "hearers of many things will have learned nothing; they will appear omniscient and will generally know nothing; they will be tiresome company, having the show of wisdom without the reality."[12] By contrast, as McLuhan notes, Mallarmé, affirming productively the modern conditions of thought and expression that Lamartine articulates, manages to formulate "the lessons of the press as a guide for the new impersonal poetry of suggestion and implication"—the kind of poetry whose more contemporary version Hansen and Rubin bring to expression in a medium where letter and image and sound intersect and interplay in such manner as to recall and give voice to the medieval illuminated manuscript, such as the Book of Kells, which serves as model for Joyce's *Wake*. Hansen and Rubin could well be taken to stage in "real time" something akin to the voice and vision of the *Wake,* as voice and vision of a mass subject never able fully to recollect or comprehend itself, but creative and self-creative in just that space-time of incomprehension. If Mallarmé stands out as one of the "resourceful technicians among modern poets and painters," Hansen and Rubin stand out as resourceful poets and painters among modern technicians.[13] Mallarmé saw "that the scale of modern reportage and of mechanical multiplication of messages made personal rhetoric impossible," and hence that the task of the artist was to "manipulate the low current of casual words, rhythms, and resonances to evoke the primal harmonies of existence or to recall the dead."[14] Similarly, in Rubin and Hansen's vision, the incalculable currents of Web traffic and chatter become an evocative work of art that confronts us with our own incomprehensible global being by staging, in audio and video,

12. Plato, *Phaedrus,* in ibid.

13. Victoria Vesna is another figure whose work unsettles clear distinctions between artist-poet and technician-scientist, even as it calls us to reimagine and reconceive the interplay of nature and culture, science and art—an interplay that might be taken as central to the religious. Visit her work site VV, at http://vv.arts.ucla.edu/.

14. McLuhan, "Joyce, Mallarmé, and the Press," 11, 12.

the impossibility of that being's full or final expression or representation, whether visual or audible.

Against the kind of "moral and aesthetic horror" that one senses in a Heidegger or a Kierkegaard "at the ignobility of the popular scene," where leveling and inauthenticity threaten genuine creation, Mallarmé can find in the mass (as does another Heidegger I pointed to), precisely as scene of banality and boredom, the indeterminate ground of possibility for poetry. As McLuhan glosses Mallarmé's "Etalages," "A shop window full of new books prompts his reflection that the function of the ordinary run of books is merely to express the average degree of human boredom and incompetence, to reduce to a written form the horizon of the human scene in all its abounding banality. Instead of deploring this fact as literary men tend to do, the artist should exploit it: 'The vague, the commonplace, the smudged and defaced, not the banishment of these, occupation rather! Apply them as to a patrimony.'" What McLuhan calls these "vast territories of stupefaction" (very close, I think, to the technological bewitchment of which Heidegger speaks) become, thanks to a work of creative screening, the ground of poetic potential. Holding that Joyce was "the only person to grasp the full artistic implications of this radically democratic aesthetic," which probes "the aesthetic consequences and possibilities of the popular arts of industrial man," McLuhan underscores that if the press is for Mallarmé that "ultimate book" in which the "whole world" is meant to result, the work is one whose writer is self-effacing; it is a book that "does not admit of any signature." Rewritten in the flowing light and hum of an emerging electrified media network, which itself uncannily echoes and images the infinite universe of Christian mystical tradition, that book could be titled *Finnegans Wake.*[15]

In and through the language of an "inauthentic" mass subject—its idle talk and chatter, its clichés and commonplaces, its everyday formulae and conventions—Joyce brings to expression a singular creativity. In the banal and repetitive language of the mass he finds a vulgar eloquence, an immeasurable ground of ongoing creation, where through ever new combinations and associations, which exploit the formulaic while departing from it, the singular can emerge. In this direction, Joyce opens for us the possibility of reading anew the interplay of authenticity and inauthenticity in a Heideggerian or post-Heideggerian framework, and thus a new perspective on the creative potential of technological culture. If Heidegger critiques the anonymous public language that assumes immediate intelligibility and accessi-

15. Quotations from ibid., 13, 15.

bility to everyone, eclipsing authentic existence and genuine creation, Joyce appropriates, intensifies, and reshapes that anonymous public language to the verge of inaccessibility, and in such a way as to make everyday chatter the existential ground of creative voice. The distinction of the human, then, is tied intimately to its capacity for indistinction. If, furthermore, influential analyses of the technological tend to highlight its deracinating effects and its unsettling of "tradition," I would also argue that the condition of possibility for any tradition is the same that gives rise to technological existence itself. Traditionalists who see technology primarily as (mournful) threat to tradition and technophiles who see technology as (utopian) liberation from tradition fail equally, and in similar ways, to consider either the technological dimensions of temporality and tradition or the temporal and traditional depths of technological networks—both of which stem from the human as an open, ongoing work of the indiscrete image.

·◌·

The human as indiscrete image, elusive intersection of the mystical and technopoetic, finds one of its most significant and influential enactments in the work of Joyce. *Finnegans Wake* above all, in a writing and a voice that may indeed be seen and heard as revelation after the death of God, not only stages the interplay between tradition's immeasurable wealth and creative humanity's indetermination but also, in doing so, solicits a religious, mystical resonance in the technological mass culture of an emerging postmodernity. Situating Joyce in the Christian epic tradition of Dante, Milton, and Blake, Thomas J. J. Altizer, the foremost death-of-God theologian, sees and hears in Joyce an expression of the "total presence" that would constitute the reverse side of God's kenotic self-realization through self-negation. "The *ipsum esse* or existence itself of Being or God," Altizer writes in "Joyce and the End of History,"

> is now fully passing into actual speech, and nowhere so fully as in
> *Finnegans Wake*, a passage or metamorphosis which resurrects the
> body as word or speech. The "nullification" of God embodied in the
> Resurrection of Book Four of the *Wake* is thereby, and precisely thereby,
> a realization or self-realization of God wherein the whole perfection of
> being realizes itself in the pure actuality of the *ipsum esse* or existence
> itself. But that actuality is here realized not simply through language
> and speech but *in* and *as* word and speech, for now God is fully and fi-
> nally *logos* or "word." That "word" is pure immediacy, an immediacy

which is darkness and light, and pure darkness and pure light, a light
which is the cosmic and apocalyptic sacrifice of God.[16]

While Altizer reads the death of God, as embodied in Joyce, in terms of
pure actuality and immediacy, my own reading of Joyce and of the death of
God tends more toward an insistence on infinite mediation and irreducible
possibility. If Joyce's text is pure actuality, it is a pure actuality of possibility itself—a possibility that eludes final closure and closed finality. Along
these lines, I take the "absolute absence of the Absolute" in Joyce according to Samuel Beckett's understanding of the formulation, whose meaning is "purgatorial," evoking "the cyclic dynamism of the intermediate,"
which entails an "endless verbal germination, maturation, putrefaction."[17]
By contrast to the purgatory of Dante, which, as conical, "implies culmination," the purgatory of Joyce "is spherical and excludes culmination. . . .
In the one, absolute progression and a guaranteed consummation: in the
other, flux—progression or retrogression, and an apparent consummation.
In the one movement is unidirectional, and a step forward represents a net
advance: in the other movement is non-directional—or multidirectional,
and a step forward is, by definition, a step back." As if performing a version
of the faithful time I developed in my reading of Serres, the continuities
and cuts of Joyce's temporal flow exclude the fullness or presence of any
culminating actuality, whether that of heaven or that of hell, both of which
amount to stasis. "In what sense, then, is Mr. Joyce's work purgatorial? In
the absolute absence of the Absolute. Hell is the static lifelessness of unrelieved viciousness. Paradise the static lifelessness of unrelieved immacula-
tion. Purgatory a flood of movement and vitality released by the conjunction of these two elements."[18] The vitality of the *Wake*, then, the life whose
possibility the work keeps open, is the function of a tension, and hence a
difference, whose ongoing play alone sustains life, a differential tension be-

16. Thomas J. J. Altizer, *History as Apocalypse* (Albany: State University of New York Press,
1985), 250.

17. Samuel Beckett, "Dante . . . Bruno. Vico . . . Joyce," in *Our Exagmination Round His
Factification for Incamination of Work in Progress*, ed. Sylvia Beach (Paris: Shakespeare and
Company, 1929; reprint, Norfolk, Conn.: New Directions, 1939), 22 and 16, respectively. As my
remarks here should suggest, my reading of Beckett on Joyce diverges from Altizer's contention
that the absolute absence of the Absolute means "a total emptiness" that "becomes actually
and factually present" (*History as Apocalypse*, 226), for the purgatorial suggests a differential
dynamic that would in fact be closed or ended by an emptiness (or presence, which here amounts
to the same) that could be judged total. For a similar differential reading, developed in a Derridean register, see Mark C. Taylor's response to Altizer (which does not engage the *Wake* at length)
"p. s. fin again," in *Tears* (Albany: State University of New York Press, 1990).

18. Beckett, "Dante . . . Bruno. Vico . . . Joyce," 21, 22.

tween the necessary and the contingent, the type and its infinite variations, the formula and the singularity.

Such life in Joyce has both mystical and technopoetic dimensions, which are interwoven. Working in the tradition of McLuhan and tracing the vulgar eloquence of an everyday life shaped intimately by mass media and related technoscience, Donald Theall elucidates in Joyce a technopoetics that I understand also as a mystical poetics, which Joyce works out under the inspiration—and through a recapitulation at once satiric and deathly serious—of the mystical thinking whose tradition flows not only from Dionysius and Eriugena through John of the Cross, Nicholas of Cusa, and Giordano Bruno but also into Joyce's other, historically more proximate influence along these lines, Giambattista Vico. From Vico especially, Joyce receives not only a cyclic conception of historical movement but also an understanding of that movement as fundamentally poetic or creative— and as founded in ignorance and operative in the vulgar (what Beckett calls Joyce's desophistication of language, a latter-day version of Dante's vulgar eloquence).[19] The *Wake* itself can be read as an open-ended performance of Vico's insight into the principles of history's "poetic wisdom," which figure the human in terms of self-creation and which trace that creation to an immemorial ignorance recurrently recalled, to an inherited—or, in Joyce's terms, "immermemorial"—human infancy that grounds and keeps open the massive historical memory (field also of immeasurable forgetting) in and through which human genesis takes place. Influenced equally by the resonance of mystical tradition and by the rumorous hum of modernity's mass culture and its emerging media and technoscience, Joyce's *Wake* embodies the complex structure and temporality of a self-creative and modern humanity whose abyssal ground of creative potential—a historical burial ground of human ignorance and infancy—mirrors the comprehensive but incomprehensible nothing from which, or as which, the God of mystical tradition creates both world and self.

⌒∞⌒

If in the course of Christian tradition Augustine is the name of that one man, an individual someone, who comes to stand as singular model for all, or everyman, and if he thus signals already what becomes a recurrent

19. See, e.g., ibid., 15, 18. In this way as in others, Joyce is indeed heir to Dante, whose *De vulgari eloquentia* argues that "only the living vernacular remains theologically creative" (Dupré, *Passage to Modernity*, 107). The importance of vernacular languages in the formation of mystical theologies has drawn a good deal of attention in recent decades.

instability, within a stream of influence from Augustine to Heidegger, in the distinction between authenticity and inauthenticity, or between the singular and its replications, the ubiquitous but elusive "subject" of the *Wake*, "Here Comes Everybody" or HCE, is a no one who embodies everyone, or an everyone who amounts to no one—and who does so in utterly singular, not to say authentic, fashion. HCE is indeed singular in its seemingly infinite capacity for variation in and through repetition, which yields a multiplicity of variants that defy counting.[20] What appears to be most authentic or proper to HCE is a singular and irreducible inauthenticity or impropriety, which suggests that the best theological analogue here is less the God who, for Augustine and his heirs, isolates and individuates the person around a private interior than the cosmic God of mystical tradition, whose own ubiquity and evasiveness, whose polyonymous anonymity, are mirrored in the polyonymous anonymity of the human who likewise defies location—a mystical tradition, as I've suggested, in which the unknowing of God and of humanity alike is the condition of their self-creation.

At the center of the *Wake*, which like that of the mystical cosmos can seem to be everywhere and nowhere, lies the indeterminate body of a self "buried in sleep" and dreaming, one through whom virtually all of history and culture come to expression and unfold in an ever-shifting but ever-recurring movement that combines and confuses the sacred and profane, high and low, modern and archaic, memory and forgetfulness, waking and sleeping, birth and death. Through an endlessly layered play of the *coincidentia oppositorum*, the multilingual, transhistorical, and transcultural babble of the *Wake* constitutes a kind of vulgar eloquence. The transient idle talk and inauthentic chatter of yesterday's pop culture blurs with the depths of world tradition and the most far-ranging references of its high culture—and in such a way that their indiscrete interplay yields a genuine creative power. The ground of such creation is a "self" or "subject" absent to itself, through whose body and mind the *Wake* world streams, much as world and history in Eriugena's thought can be understood, as Borges notes, as "an extended dream of God's, one which eventually devolves on God."[21]

20. For a list of HCE's variants, from Howth Castle and Environs to Humps cumps Ebbly-bally and so on, see the wonderful Web page H.C.E. in Finnegans Wake, http://mv.lycaeum.org/Finnegan/HCE.html/.

21. Jorge Luis Borges, "Ireland," in *Atlas*, trans. Anthony Kerrigan (New York: E. P. Dutton, 1985), 14.

If Eriugena offers in the early medieval context a strikingly modern vision that understands world and self as the ongoing, infinite creation of a sub-ject (divine and human) incomprehensible to itself, then Joyce's *Wake* in the modern context offers a strikingly mystical, medieval vision, where the ongoing self-expression of an absent subject (not quite human, not quite divine, and never fully comprehensible to itself) can well be taken as the creative ground of an apophatic and mystical cosmos. In and through that cosmos, the subject ceaselessly composes, decomposes, and recomposes it-self in an ongoing metamorphosis whose distinctly modern sense begins to emerge theologically in Eriugena's later heirs Cusa and Bruno, who also shape Joyce's work in decisive ways.[22] And if Joyce does articulate some-thing of our late modern or postmodern technoscientific and media net-works, even as he simultaneously recapitulates key themes of mystical tra-dition from Dionysius and Eriugena through Cusa and Bruno, a reading of his work in light of that tradition can amplify the mystical resonance I have noted in those forms of human self-creation, especially the technological, that frame our current situation. That resonance proves to be inseparable from the satiric voice in which Joyce writes, a voice whose critical force is directed as much toward the hierarchies and proprieties of Christian (and other) tradition as toward, in Theall's words, "the spirit of technology and the fetishization of organization" that define a "secularized" modernity.[23] That critical force turns productive, I think, by awakening us to the cre-ative possibilities of rereading each anew in light of the other, and such awakening might open to us a middle course between overwhelming anxi-ety and unrelieved boredom.

Like the infinitely and incomprehensibly theophanic universe of Eriu-gena and Cusa, the endlessly variable world of *Finnegans Wake* seems to show or to say both everything and nothing. Because the work draws on

22. In a fine essay titled "Images of Iron: Ignatius of Loyola and Joyce," in *Religion and Media*, ed. Hent de Vries and Samuel Weber (Stanford: Stanford University Press, 2001), Burcht Pranger also highlights the connection of Joyce to Eriugena. See especially 185–87, where Pranger emphasizes the singularity of both Eriugena and the Joyce of *Finnegans Wake*: "The ninth-century Irish thinker Johannes Scottus Eriugena produced the boldest overview of a universe that, in a spectacular sequence of divine manifestations (and as many withdrawals), contains both God and the creation, both being and nothingness. In its scope, boldness, uniqueness, and, not least, experimental nature—in Christian thought no attempt to embrace God and man in a single con-cept of nature had ever been made, nor was it to be made again—it reminds one of that other bold and experimental work by Scottus' twentieth-century compatriot James Joyce: *Finnegans Wake*" (185).

23. Theall, *Joyce's Techno-Poetics*, 9

sixty or seventy languages while fully respecting the rules and boundaries of none, the barely—because excessively—readable language of the *Wake* offers an incalculable syntactic complexity and semantic density, exemplified above all in the pun, within whose immeasurable network of possible relations and hence possible meanings all culture and history, all humanity and divinity, seem to appear and disappear at once. Because it can seem to say everything, the *Wake* can seem also to say nothing, and vice versa; it plays along the unstable border between noise and information, slipping constantly from one into the other. From this perspective, the *Wake* can be taken to recall for a distinctly late modern or postmodern world the kind of coimplication between polyonymy and anonymity that I pointed to in the mystical tradition, where the God who is both all in all and nothing in anything is reflected in a human subject—or *imago Dei*—through whom divine creation and self-creation unfold.

If the mystical cosmos of the medievals finds its principle in the reason or logic of the Word, Joyce's modern "chaosmos" finds its "buginning" in the dissemination of the "woid." The ambivalent expression of both word and void, shifting unstably between the proliferation and defeat of meaning, and hence between laughter and dread, the *Wake*'s language world amounts to a "Soferim Bebel" or a writers' (Hebrew *soferim*) Babel/babble in which "every person, place and thing in the chaosmos of Alle anyway connected with gobblydumped turkery was moving and changing every part of the time."[24] Because the *Wake* remains without stable plot or characters, time or place, and because every event, personage, moment, and location that emerges in the work conjures immediately (much like the open network of tradition's scripture) a measureless web of allusions and resonances, every event or personage, every moment or location, is always (like tradition as such) both more and less than itself—always virtually other than itself within an uncontainable flow of substitution, displacement, movement, and change (both linguistic and conceptual).[25] The writer's Babel/babble

24. James Joyce, *Finnegans Wake* (New York: Penguin Books, 1999), 118; hereafter cited parenthetically by page number.

25. As Joyce scholar John Bishop notes, the *Wake* does of course have some structure and order to it, which are helpful to know about in making one's way through the work and through discussions of it. For a wonderfully clear but no less rich overview of the determinate and linear order that can be glimpsed in the work, see Bishop's summary in his introduction to the 1999 Penguin edition of *Finnegans Wake*, xviii–xxv. Bishop points out that the structure of the book is readily repeated in the experience of the reader, "since even the briefest contact with the *Wake* tends to put one into reverie gear and to induce internally the process of bewildering self-loss, semantic recuperation, and eye-opening reawakening that is mapped out over the book as a whole. A book about 'Here Comes Everybody,' once again, *Finnegans Wake* delves into the

of the *Wake* is also a kind of Bible in motion, a whirlwind "tour of bi-bel" (523): its "proteiform graph" constitutes a "polyhedron of scripture" (107) in which one encounters "the continually more and less intermisun-derstanding minds of the anticollaborators, the as time went on as it will variously inflected, differently pronounced, otherwise spelled, changeably meaning vocable scriptsigns" (118). In short, because "every word will be bound over to carry three score and ten toptypsical reading throughout the book of Doublends Jined" (20), the endlessly changeable, shifting meanings of the "scriptsigns" in this "seemetery" (17), or "semitary of Somnionia" (594), give us a "world, mind," that "is, was and will be writing its own wrunes forever, man, on all matters that fall under the ban of our infrara-tional senses" (19–20). It is a book that lends itself to infinite, and necessar-ily creative, reading, and as such it demands, in the midst of what threatens to be overwhelming noise, attentiveness, patience, and humility.[26]

most common and darkest of experiences, and is a book that many more people can and should enjoy" (xxv). For Bishop, the structure of the book as a whole is well understood in terms of the central figure's descent into and reemergence from the depths and darkness of sleep:

> The linear movement or "plot" of *Finnegans Wake*, from this perspective, might be un-derstood simply as one of deepening embedment (Book I) and resurrection (Books II–IV). The book follows the course of a downward-plunging parabola, in this view, descend-ing from the fall into sleep at its beginning into a darkest center and then reascending toward dawn, light, and reawakening as it nears its end (Joyce likened this trajectory to the boring of a tunnel through a mountain). At the beginning of the book, as its central figure undergoes a "knock out" "early in bed" and so loses consciousness, his percep-tions close to the object world and withdraw into the interior of his body, where the world (now "whirled," "whirlworlds" [17.29, 582.20]), introjected as representation, is motivated by desire and re-created in image, memory, and language. At the end of the book, complementarily, following its last word (the definite article "the") the definite-ness of the daytime world and conscious perception returns. In between, within the dreamer's rubbled body of matter—variously characterized throughout the book as a mound, a dump, a hump, a middenheap, a "mudmound" (111.34), "*the Bearded Moun-tain*" (222.12)—this sleeping figure muses, as if within a "museomound" (8.05), on materials that have gathered within him from a past that is at once personal, cultural, and lingusitic. (xviii–xix).

26. In *Joyce's Book of the Dark: Finnegans Wake* (Madison: University of Wisconsin Press, 1986), Bishop nicely highlights the force of humility in the encounter with the *Wake*—and the relation of humility to the ego-logical themes I've been tracing throughout the present book:

> Although the deformations of English integral to the work have caused some readers to regard it as the product of a furious egocentrism, nothing could be further from the truth. No defense of Joyce's aesthetic methods will make a first reading of *Finnegans Wake* less tortuous and frustrating than it may perhaps be: it is humiliating for some to be reminded that one does not know everything in the world, or even in the fractional part of the world that Joyce managed to assimilate. But even a tortuous first reading of the *Wake* should suggest that few books are less egocentric: dead to the world, its "be-lowes hero" has no consciousness of himself as an "ego" or an "identity" at all. (214)

As in Eriugena's simultaneously scriptural and cosmic exegesis, where
every sign points the soul onward toward other signs within a *transitus*
that never reaches or comprehends the God who simultaneously reveals
and conceals himself in all signs, and as in the infinite sphere of Cusa,
where all human knowing is relational and conjectural and immersed in
unknowing, and where every sign falls short of—even as it participates creatively within—the reality whose center is everywhere and circumference
nowhere, so the connectivity of Joyce's *Wake* world generates an endless
movement among possible meanings that cannot be fixed or unified by reduction to one stable, comprehensible ground or principle. At this level,
the medieval quality of Joyce's language is striking: the endless "interpre-
tive labor" required by the *Wake*, as Umberto Eco notes in his wonderful
study *The Aesthetics of Chaosmos*, "reflects a medieval taste, the idea of
aesthetic pleasure, not as the flashing exercise of an intuitive faculty but
as a process of intelligence that deciphers and reasons, enraptured by the
difficulty of communication."[27] At the same time, as I'm suggesting, the
linguistic and cultural complexities of the *Wake*'s writing and exegesis are
also markedly modern—evoking pervasively the operations and effects of
our increasingly automated and global technological systems.

 Already in 1962, Eco understands the *Wake*'s operation according to its
"cybernetic" quality, which, *contra* Heidegger and more recent critics of
our technological prisons, entails its character as a radically "open work"
insofar as its structure—which could be taken as an irreducibly complex
set of enabling constraints[28]— puts into motion "a machinery of suggestion, which, like any complex machine, is capable of operating beyond the

---

In his theologically attuned and religiously astute work *Joyce's Messianism: Dante, Negative
Existence, and the Messianic Self* (Columbia: University of South Carolina Press, 2004), which
traces in the *Wake* "the negative existence of a Messianic self," a self neither caught simply in
the all too mundane nor escaping metaphysically to the otherworldly (4), Gian Balsamo nicely
articulates the importance of attentiveness, or responsiveness, in reading the *Wake*: "One cannot
read *Finnegans Wake* without feeling the obscure and recurrent impression that one is not reading it for the first time. Given its procedures of character amalgamation and temporal destabiliza-
tion, both rooted . . . in the sepulchral burrow of our archaic past, one will never be done with
reading *Finnegans Wake* in a conclusive, exhaustive, hermeneutic manner. One will have always
only been reading it—in a responsive attitude to one's vestigial memories and their sepulchral
intimations" (127).

 27. Umberto Eco, *The Aesthetics of Chaosmos: The Middle Ages of James Joyce*, trans. Ellen
Esrock (Cambridge: Harvard University Press, 1989), 81. For another illuminating work treating
Joyce's relation to medieval thought and culture, and especially mystical aesthetics, see Colleen
Jaurretche's *The Sensual Philosophy: Joyce and the Aesthetics of Mysticism* (Madison: Univer-
sity of Wisconsin Press, 1997).

 28. On the notion of enabling constraint, see Mark C. Taylor's introduction to *Critical Terms
for Religious Studies* (Chicago: University of Chicago Press, 1998).

original intentions of its builder." Insisting on the interplay between the structure and play of the work, between determinacy and possibility, or between format and event, Eco argues that "the force of the text resides in its permanent ambiguity and in the continuous resounding of numerous meanings which seem to permit selection but in fact eliminate nothing."[29] In his extended treatment of the logic and operation of such openness, Eco's book *The Open Work* emphasizes that the *Wake* is a "major example of an 'open' mode," and in exploiting Joyce's version of that mode, he highlights the cosmic intersection between the closure or finitude of the work and its irreducible openness or infinitude: "In *Finnegans Wake* we are faced with an even more startling process of 'openness': the book is molded into a curve that bends back on itself, like the Einsteinian universe. The opening word of the first page is the same as the closing word of the last page of the novel. Thus, the work is *finite* in one sense, but in another sense it is *unlimited*. Each occurrence, each word stands in a series of possible relations with all the others in the text. According to the semantic choice we make in the case of one unit," Eco continues, "so goes the way we interpret all the other units of the text," and if Joyce clearly introduces a certain sense into the work, "this particular 'sense' has the richness of the cosmos itself."[30]

Twenty years later, Jacques Derrida takes a similar approach by likening the *Wake* to a computer (*ordinateur*)[31] with respect to whose "wiring" (*câblage*) he can ask, "How to calculate the speed at which a mark, a marked piece of information is related to some other within the same word or from one end of the book to the other? At what speed, for example, is the Babelian theme or the word Babel, in each of their components (but how to count these?) coordinated with all the phonemes, semes, mythemes, etc., of

---

29. Eco, *Aesthetics of Chaosmos*, 67.

30. Umberto Eco, *The Open Work*, trans. Anna Cancogni (Cambridge: Harvard University Press, 1989), 10. See also 175–76: "*Finnegans Wake* speaks of the structuring of a circular universe in which it is possible to establish multiple relationships among the various elements, and in which every element can assume different meanings and relational capacities depending on how we want to understand the context—and vice versa. What attracts us most in this text is not so much an actual pun as the possibility of a complete language based on puns, a multiformity of language that will almost appear as the image of the multiformity of real events." I will return below to the significance of the pun for understanding not only the synchronic but also the diachronic, temporal and historical complexity of networks, linguistic and otherwise.

31. It is worth noting that the French term for computer, *ordinateur*, was proposed for such use on April 16, 1955, in a letter to Christian de Waldner, president of IBM in France, from the Latinist and Sorbonne professor Jacques Perret, who thought the term especially fitting given its prior meaning as an adjective designating the God who puts order in the world. For the story, see the blog L'ancien et le moderne, http://ancienetmoderne.blogspot.com/2007/05/lordinateur-ou-dieu-metttant-de-lordre.html/.

Finnegans Wake?" And in response he concludes that "to count these connections [*branchements*], to calculate the speed of the communications,
would be at the least impossible, in fact, inasmuch as we would not have
constructed the machine capable of integrating all the variables, all the
quantitative and qualitative factors. This is not going to happen tomorrow,
and that machine in any case would be but the double or the simulation
of the 'Joyce' event, the name of Joyce, the signed work, the Joyce *logiciel*
today, the *joyjiciel*."[32] Both Eco and Derrida recognize—and highlight
through the technological analogy—that the excess and incalculability of
the *Wake*'s language issue from the irreducible complexity and connectivity of that language and its world. Every word in the *Wake* is a "crossroads
of meaning" within the flow of an ever-evolving and unpredictable "communication network" whose multiple linguistic and cultural registers can
never be translated into the unity of any one language (a unity that no language in fact ever has). This, indeed, is at the heart of Derrida's decisive and
influential engagement with the work: the paradigm of *Finnegans Wake*,
which repeats before the fact the logic of today's computers and networks
(and whose strategy stands in contrast to Husserl's search for a transparent,
univocal language) "repeats and mobilizes and babelizes the (asymptotic)
totality of equivocation, it makes this its theme and operation, it attempts
to make emerge the greatest synchrony possible, at full speed, the greatest
power of the significations hidden away in each syllabic fragment, splitting
each atom of writing in order with it to overload the unconscious with the
entire memory of man: mythologies, religion, philosophies, sciences, psy-
choanalysis, literatures. This generalized equivocation of writing does not
translate one language into another on the basis of cores of common meaning, it speaks several languages at once, draws on them parasitically."[33]
Hence, on the one hand, scriptural and indebted to the depths of tradition
and, on the other hand, already cybernetic and opening the unforeseeable
technological future, the *Wake* forces us to reflect on the resonance between two logics often dissociated in twentieth-century thought: the exegetical logic of a mystical cosmic vision and the differential technologic

---

32. Jacques Derrida, "Deux mots pour Joyce," in *L'Herne: James Joyce* (Paris: Éditions de
l'Herne, 1985), 205–6.

33. Derrida, "Deux mots pour Joyce," 207. For a concise, lucid discussion of the interplay
of Husserl, proponent of univocity, and Joyce, genius of plurivocity, in Derrida's thought, which
shows that pure univocity would entail empty repetition, just as a thoroughgoing plurivocity
would amount to noise, see the chapter titled "Re-Joyce, Say Yes," especially 182–84, in John D.
Caputo, *Deconstruction in a Nutshell: A Conversation with Jacques Derrida* (New York: Fordham University Press, 1997).

that seems to appear in Joyce and that frames our virtual worlds today. To the degree that the *Wake* gives a world that "is, was and will be writing its wrunes forever," it runs between, or around, the ruins of our modern and technological chaosmos and the deepest mysteries flowing though traditional and archaic religion, myth, letters, and poetry.[34]

Inheriting and elaborating insights like those of Eco and Derrida, and extending the work of McLuhan, who not only saw in Joyce the "prehistory of cyberspace and virtual reality" but read him at the same time in light of Catholic tradition,[35] Donald Theall argues in *James Joyce's Techno-Poetics* that the technological implications of Joyce's thought and writing are intimately related to his religious sensibility—one that would, something like Walter Benjamin's "profane illuminations," secularize the sacred or solicit the sacred character of mass culture's everyday life, effecting a profane transubstantiation by "converting the bread of everyday life into something that has permanent artistic value of its own."[36] Theall's analyses are especially suggestive in highlighting the interplay within human and divine genesis and metamorphosis of the religious or quasi-theological, on the one hand, and the technopoetic or machinic, on the other. The "'man-god' that is Joyce's primary imagination, *deus sive natura*" cannot, as Theall emphasizes, be separated from the "complex, multiplex, perplexing assemblage" of a "god-machine or machine god—'vrayedevraye Blankdeblank, god of all machineries' (253.33)—characteristic of a post-Nietzschean or 'antechristian' (114.11) world."[37] Joyce figures the mechanics of such a man-god, however, in terms of the vital dynamics of an ongoing composition, decomposition, and recombination that might be read not only, as Theall rightly notes, as a "deliberate satiric revision of the central organic and spiritual theme of Romantic poetics and Hegelian aesthetics" but also as a revision of the traditional motif (to which the Romantics and Hegel are notably indebted) of a mystical (Neoplatonic, Christian) movement of procession and return, efflux and reflux, which recurs also in Vico, and where the flow of

34. See the various senses of "rune" as related to the Old Norse *run* or *roun*, meaning secret, writing, or runic character; the Finnish *runo*, poem; and the Old English *ryne*, meaning course, movement, or flow.

35. I quote Theall's "Beyond the Orality/Literacy Dichotomy: James Joyce and the Prehistory of Cyberspace," *Postmodern Culture* 2, no. 3 (May 1992): 1. In the direction of technological and media culture, see McLuhan's "Joyce, Mallarmé, and the Press," and in the direction of Catholic tradition, see his "James Joyce: Trivial and Quadrivial," both of which appear in *The Interior Landscape*.

36. Joyce, quoted in Theall, *Joyce's Techno-Poetics*, 105.

37. Ibid., 68.

creation finds its ground and end in the emptiness or indetermination of the unimaginable and incomprehensible.[38]

Along multiple, wandering, and intercrossing lines, which evolve in and through endless repetition and infinite ramification, the *Wake* articulates, in a repetition of Vico, "a theory none too rectiline of the evoluation of human society and a testament of the rocks from all the dead unto some the living" (73). It seeks (and seems), in its endless circularity or closedness, to encompass or remain open to all of human and divine history, from the age of fallen Adam to the age of the annihilated atom. Flowing from "the obluvial waters of our noarchic memory" (80), the "immermemorial" (600) *Wake* seeks to evoke or enact both the deepest recesses of our forgetting and the endless potential of recollection. To the degree that it draws its dynamism from the vibrant oscillation between forgetting and recollection, between our sleeping and awakening, between "feeling aslip and wauking up, so an, so farth" (597), the *Wake* constitutes a world that remains comprehensive and repetitive but also open and evolving. It is the "same anew" in whose riverlike recurrence and branchings, in whose pervasive influence, in whose "chittering waters . . . rivering waters of . . . Night!" (215–16) one can see or hear Vico—"Teems of times and happy returns. The seim anew. Ordovico or viricordo" (215)—and in whose logic one can read also a version of the interplay I sketched out above between being-there and being-away, between self-absence and awakening in Heidegger's thought, where philosophy itself entails the ongoing need to think the same anew.

In exercising and exploiting this interplay between comprehensive memory and creative openness, between tradition and innovation, Joyce indeed draws deeply on the poetic principle that courses through Giambattista Vico's thought and writing of history as a *ricorso* that is best figured by the spiral (a figure that is central to the thought and writing also of Pseudo-Dionysius). As Giuseppe Mazzotta explains in his illuminating study of Vico, *The New Map of the World*, "by its interweaving of circle and line, which produces the spiral, the *ricorso*, thus, is the simultaneous figuration of closure and openness of a circle that repeats itself with a difference, is always out of place and is eccentric to the other circles in the series." Elucidating this interplay between repetition and openness in Vico, Mazzotta could just as well be commenting on the "vicociclometer" that is *Finnegans Wake*:

---

38. Ibid., 69–70. The alternative Theall suggests between creation *de deo* and creation *ex nihilo* (68) may be, in light of my analyses here, an unstable one.

Together with the *ricorso*, the *cursus* suggests Vico's spiral style of writing and spiral style of thinking, the poetic art of connecting events or words remote from one another. Both are marked by a steady recurrence of topics, by a desultory mode of argument aimed at shattering the idea of discursive linearity or merely circular order. The eccentricities, obscurities, and convolutions of Vico's language, for which he has been chastised by his readers even while he was alive, are real: it is a language that leaps over conventional connections, that slides, like a cursor, backward and forward, pursues seemingly random but rigorously elliptical orbits in a series, and creates a special place for a discourse whereby a new, all-encompassing configuration of the past, present, and future can appear before our eyes.[39]

If Vico's comprehensive *ricorso* can thus be taken "as the thought of the possible new beginnings of history,"[40] if it places the poetic at the heart of historical being, it serves also as one of the recurrent figures for Joyce's own navigation of the creative interplay between memory and forgetting, which makes a point much like Mazzotta's while pushing the spiral manner of writing and thinking to an extreme:

> Forget, remember! . . . Our wholemole millwheeling vicociclometer, . . . autokinatonetically preprovided with a clappercoupling smeltingworks exprogressive process . . . receives through the portal vein the dialytically separated elements of precedent decomposition for the verypetpurpose of subsequent recombination so that the heroticisms, catastrophes and eccentricities transmitted by the ancient legacy of the past, type by tope, letter from litter, word at ward, with sendence of sundance . . . all, anastomosically assimilated and preteridentified paraidiotically, in fact, the sameold gamebold adomic structure of our Finnius the old One, as highly charged with electrons as hophazards can effective it. (615)

The flux of decomposition and recombination signaled here within a passage that moves from Adam to the atom by means of type/tope and letter/litter and word/ward and sendence/sundance applies to the *Wake* as a

---

39. Giuseppe Mazzotta, *The New Map of the World: The Poetic Philosophy of Giambattista Vico* (Princeton: Princeton University Press, 1999), 228.
40. Ibid.

whole, a work or world whose whole is operative in every part, and one that not only names but performs the "exprogressive process" of an ever-recurring, ever-differing, cosmic and world-historical decomposition and recombination on the part of its central but indeterminate character's self-expression and recollection.

The influence of Vico is especially significant here, as the etymological ground of his work, which finds in the depth-network of words the key to sociohistorical institutions, is appropriated by Joyce, in whom every word is enabled by the conditions of the pun and thus implies the immeasurable cultural-historical network in which we are, individually and collectively, always already netted. Joyce intends the *Wake*, as Eco notes, "to imply the totality of space and time, of all spaces and all times that are possible. The principle tool for this all-pervading ambiguity is the pun, the *calembour*, by which two, three, or even ten different etymological roots are combined in such a way that a single word can set up a knot of different submeanings, each of which in turn coincides and interrelates with other local allusions, which are themselves 'open' to new configurations and probabilities of interpretation."[41] The possibility of instantaneous leaps and connections across unthinkable distances of time and space, history and culture, is operative, in fact, in every word, for every word harbors the conditions of the pun—and those conditions yield the endless readability and revisability of the *Wake*, which in this respect perhaps only calls attention to what is operative at least implicitly in any linguistic work, or indeed in any network. And just as in Vico, where human poetics would find their irretrievable origin in human ignorance and infancy, so in Joyce the ground of endless creativity and revision is an elusive nullity.

As the *Wake's* central "Night Lessons" will suggest within a discussion of the polyonymously anonymous "median, hce che ech" (284), the simultaneously self-identical and self-differing nightworld of the *Wake* is infinitely multiple and revisable because it stems, absurdly, from the nullity or voicelessness of a "surd." For "whereat samething is rivisible by nightim, may be involted into the zeroic couplet, palls pell inhis heventh glike noughty times 8, find, if you are not literally cooefficient, how minney combinaisies and permutandies can be played on the international surd" (284). The "samething" (or something) of the *Wake's* nighttime would be repeatedly visible (or risible) and endlessly revisable because it marks the infinite and infinitesimal multiplication of a silent nullity, which allows for countless many (and minute) combinations and permutations, wherein "the mystery

41. Eco, *The Open Work*, 10.

repeats itself" (294). Here and elsewhere, the *Wake* enacts that to which it calls attention—its own infinite revisability—and highlights the sense in which the work and its world constitute a "contonuation through regeneration of the urutteration of the word in progress" (284). From the continuous regeneration of the primal iteration of this word in progress would issue a "work in progress" (the *Wake*'s earlier working title), a "whorled without aimed" (272) that is a "whirled without end to end" (582).

Opening such an excessive field of potential combination and permutation, (de)composition and recombination, the *Wake* might be read, as I've suggested, both in quasi-anthropological and in quasi-theological directions, both as the "meandertale" (18) of "morphyl man" (80), who as the "truly catholic assemblage" of "Here Comes Everybody" (32) is also the anonymous "quisquis" of "mister-mysterion" (301) *and* as the story of "Ouhr Former who erred in having" (530), or "oura vatars that arred in Himmal" (599), the "Great Sommbboddy" (415) and "Pantokreator" (411) "in whose words were the beginnings" (597) and in whose sacrament we would consume "Real Absence" (536). The two stories imply and repeatedly blur into one another. As of the "four claymen" in their "starchamber query" on "Yawn," so we might say of the interplay between human and divine in the *Wake*'s meandertale (and hence in our own): "he was ever their quarrel, the way they would see themselves, everybug his bodiment atop of anywom her notion, and the meet of their noght was worth two of his morning" (475). If in this "meet" of their "noght" (naught/knot/night) we might see that "we haply return . . . to befinding ourselves when old is said and done and maker mates with made" (261), then the *Wake* might tell the tale of the infinitely open repetition of the decomposition and recombination of the human and divine in relation to one another. It would do so, however, in such a way that the human is never fully or clearly identifiable as human nor the divine fully or clearly recognizable as divine: each would just barely appear only in order then, of course, to slip away—so that each would reflect the polyvalent nullity or abyss of the other, as in the mirror relation Borges imagines between Shakespeare and God, or as in that between some anonymous "I" and the axolotl he meets in Paris. Just as "Fidaris will find where the Doubt arises like Nieman from Nirgends found the Nihil" (202), so the divine and human here, in the meet of their naught/knot/night, where "maker mates with made," would find in each other the abyssal mirror of their own endlessly imaged obscurities. The *Wake*'s take on this meet can well be read as a late modern version of Eriugena's insight that the incomprehensible and anonymous God shows himself infinitely or abyssally in, through, and to the self-creation of a human subject who proves likewise incomprehensible and anonymous. "The one the pictor of the other and the omber the *Skotia* of the one" (164), Joyce might put it, "each was wrought with his other . . . no thing making newthing wealthshowever" (252–53).

Now, if in the medieval-mystical context of Eriugena and his heirs the self-creation of an incomprehensible God occurs in and through the self-creation of his incomprehensible human image, these two movements, which would stage the "wealthshow" of a theophanic and theocryptic cosmos where "no thing" really does make "newthing," are, as I've suggested, essentially bound within the cyclic or spiral dynamic of a procession and return that itself recurs in Joyce through multiple references, from the hierarchies of Dionysius and cosmic movement of Eriugena through Cusa's infinite sphere and the spirals of Vico's *ricorso*, into the Romantic and Idealist imaginings and conceptions of organic life. If the recurring structure of *Finnegans Wake* is most famously inspired by the poetic-historic cycles of Vico's *New Science*, which treats the "uncertain, formless and obscure material" of human and divine institutions in their historic interplay, it is structured also according to various movements of descending and ascending (298), catastrophe and anabasis (304), systole and diastole—or "systomy dystomy" (597)—that can be taken to flow from "the babbling pumpt of platinism" (164) on which Vico also draws. All of this now recurs, however, within a chaosmos that undermines the clear divisions and hierarchies that a Platonic and Christian culture cultivated between the base levels of material existence and the more elevated and refined levels of the spiritual. Much like Vico, Joyce locates our poetic ground in the body, which is presupposed but never fully expressed, or which is indeed forgotten, in the creative act (much as the bodily ground of technology is forgotten thanks to what that ground enables).

As Bishop notes, the primary unconscious meaning that Joyce, with Vico, discerns beneath all language is the "meaning" of the human body. "Just as *Finnegans Wake* takes place inside the body of a sleeping giant, so too the whole of evolved human language and the reality it shapes arises from the bodies of man's unconscious human ancestors."[42] The linguistic mind, immersed in the incomprehensible networks whose entire evolution speaks in and through any given expression of mind, is immersed likewise in the bodies that have grounded and sustained such evolution; hence the sleeping body at the center of the *Wake* (a center that is nowhere) figures the immeasurable body of "giantle" humanity. "Buried everywhere beneath the *Wake*'s letters lies the form of a sleeping body, HCE. Since

---

42. Bishop, *Joyce's Book of the Dark*, 197.

all abstract language derives from an 'ur sprogue' (507.22 [Danish *ursprog*, 'original language']) in which this body is merged with everything exterior to it, all human language, in both *The New Science* and the *Wake*, etymologically conceals the unconscious 'presence (of a curpse)' out of which all gentile humanity evolved."[43] The currents and cycles of efflux and reflux in Joyce must be read, then, as much in terms of the body, in all its depth and fluidity, as in terms of spiritual aspiration, as much in terms of the flesh's ingestion and expulsion as in terms of the soul's katabasis and anabasis. In the manner of Rabelais, who himself makes burlesque use of the mystics' infinite sphere, the *Wake* revises a dynamic of procession and return that pervades Christian mystical tradition from the likes of Dionysius and Eriugena, who both appear in the opening pages of the *Wake*, to Cusa and Bruno, who themselves, along with Vico, recur throughout the *Wake* and inspire its repeated enactment of coincident opposition and the infinity of worlds.[44]

In the *Wake's* first pages both the Dionysian and Eriugenian visions appear explicitly, announcing the sense in which the work's endlessly shifting and all-encompassing world, "the miraculous meddle of this expending umniverse" (410), originates (almost) from (next to) nothing. Like the polyonymous HCE (here, "Haroun Childeric Eggeberth"), "Bygmester Finnegan" "would caligulate by multiplicables the alltitude and malltitude until he seesaw by neatlight of the liquor wheretwin 'twas born, his roundhead staple of other days to rise in undress . . . a waalworth of a skyerscape of most eyeful hoyth entowerly, erigenating from next to nothing and celescalating the himals and all, hierarchitectitiptitoploftical, with a burning bush abob off its baubletop and with larrons o'tollers clittering up and tombles a'buckets clottering down" (4–5). A distorted, drunken, or dreamlike image of the Dionysian and Eriugenian cosmos, the world of the *Wake* will "eriginate" "from next to nothing" (suggesting the Eriugenian understanding of creation *ex nihilo*), and its movement, "clittering up" and "clottering

---

43. Ibid., 198.

44. The structure of procession and return can be seen likewise, note, in less apophatic thinkers such as Augustine, whose "every man" in the *Confessions* follows the path of descent and ascent, and Aquinas, whose *Summa Theologica*, while famously informed by Aristotle, is also structured according to the Neoplatonic movement of procession and return. On Rabelais, see Maurice de Gandillac in "Pascal et le silence du monde," 355, referring to Rabelais's *Pantagruel* (chap. 13, bk. 3): "Our soul, when the body sleeps, lets itself go and sees again its country which is the sky, and from there receives participation and sign of its prime and divine origin and in its contemplation of that infinite and intellectual sphere, whose center is in every part of the universe and whose circumference nowhere at all—this is God according to the doctrine of Hermes Trismegistus—notes not only things past."

down," will recapitulate and at the same time unsettle the well-ordered hierarchies of the medieval, Dionysian cosmos ("celescalating the himals and all, hierarchitectitiptiploftical") by dispersing their members throughout a complex and fleshy network that lacks the linear or sequential coherence, and the aspirations of spiritual purity, of traditional hierarchy. In this network the mystical cosmos and its dynamic of procession and return blur into the modern city of skyscrapers, the mass culture of consumerism (Woolworth's/waalworth), and the popular children's tales of Humpty Dumpty or Jack and Jill —riffing at the same time on the childhood incident that opens Vico's autobiography, where he falls from a ladder, cracks his skull, loses consciousness, develops a tumor, and leaves his surgeon to give the prognosis of death or idiocy.[45] Like the mystical cosmos or scripture in its infinite multivalence and polysemy, so the *Wake*, as a whole and in all of its parts, can never be reduced to any single message or code. "Panangelical" (407), the *Wake* is suffused by angelic messengers whose displaced, distorted light and language render them "holy messonger angels" (405). As the function of an ever-evolving network, every message can and must be read here in multiple directions at once—and hence every message always harbors the potential of the *mensonge*. The messonger angels and their dispersed hierarchies appear, then, throughout the work—from its initial "erigination," where the angels celescalate the himals and all, through book 4, where the celestial and ecclesiastical hierarchies punctuate St. Kevin's rafting trip, and perhaps most notably in the central "Night Lessons," where the name and movement of HCE himself are signaled by "The Ascending. The Descending." (298) of the angels (from Jacob's dream in Gen. 28:12) or of Vico (the poor kid) along the "Ecclesiastical and Celestial Hierarchies" (298). And like the electronic angels of Serres's global city, who communicate, through complex interactions and across unthinkably immense distances, instantaneously or at the speed of light, so every node in the *Wake*'s network can effect multiple leaps or connections across spatial-temporal or cultural-historical distances by eliciting and exploiting the sedimentation—or burial—that enables and speaks (if silently) through every word. If the "natural" or unintentional course of such sedimentation transpires over unthinkably long and dispersed stretches of time, much like the natural evolution of living organisms, it thereby enables a writer like Joyce to exploit such sedimentation intentionally and thus to "effect in a

---

45. See *The Autobiography of Giambattista Vico*, trans. Max Harold Fisch and Thomas Goddard Bergin (Ithica: Cornell University Press, 1944), 111.

few minutes what it has sometimes taken centuries to bring about."[46] In this way the poetic operation effects a compression of time that is as unsettling, and as full of potential, as the compression of time operative in genetic engineering, which the poetic here so closely resembles. As the nodal function of networks that are themselves multivalent, any given linguistic term—such as the original, the natural, the genuine, the genital, the gentile, the genealogical, the ingenious, or ingenuous, the engineered, or any other of the immeasurably pregnant ramifications of the *gen*—expresses or brings to presence, if for the most part invisibly and inaudibly, temporal and cultural and ethnic and religious and geographic and climatic and other depths that enable what will, itself, never comprehend or fully actualize those depths.[47]

Vico's influence in the Wake is especially powerful in such exploitation of the etym, insofar as Vico's etymological method in the *New Science* "treats modern languages as if they were the language of *Finnegans Wake*—as blurred, polyglottal compacts of dozens of strange and foreign languages."[48] Such compacts, significantly, are not only constitutive of language but also, in some deep sense, constitutive—and characteristic—of the human, for they transport, or preserve, as both buried and alive, the histories and the evolution of peoples in their transgenerational self-making.

---

46. Joyce, quoted by Jacques Mercanton, quoted by John Bishop, in *Joyce's Book of the Dark*, 197.

47. See Bishop's wonderful etymological chart tracing the ramifications of *gen*-, ibid., 200–201.

48. Ibid., 207. It is worth noting too that, while Joyce writes by combining and overlaying a multiplicity of languages, even within single words, the polyglottal character of his text would prove operative already in any "one" given language, such as, e.g., the English language that some in the United States today hope to keep safe from foreign threats. As Bishop continues:

> The earliest known inhabitants of England were eventually displaced by people who spoke a Celtic tongue descended from the proto-Indo-European hypothetically spoken somewhere, most likely, in Eastern Europe—a Celtic related to the Welsh, Scottish, Breton, and Irish still in existence today. But the Roman invasions overlaid this British Celtic with some Latin and a new civic consciousness, and marauding Angles and Saxons, pressured from behind by invading tribes from the East, moved in to override almost entirely the original British Celtic with an extensive Old Teutonic base. Invading Danes and Norsemen added a different complexion yet to the Anglish and Saxon already spreading outwards toward the frontiers of the island. Missionaries of the medieval Church made universal Latin the language of the literate and educated, and the Norman invasion brought, with its laws, the whole consciousness of the Mediterranean and Romance languages into England and then into Ireland—where the hybrid Anglo-Irish known by day to the hero of *Finnegans Wake* acquired a polyglottal texture already densely riddled with historical tensions.

"Like *The New Science, Finnegans Wake* also tries to fathom 'the obscure soul of the world,' (*U*, 27), the force of a fumblingly made history in which generation after generation of billions of ephemeral individuals born in unconsciousness engendered, by their groping efforts, the conscious present in which one lives. A book about rapidly vanishing dreams and 'darkness shining in brightness which brightness could not comprehend' (*U*, 27) *Finnegans Wake* explores, after the example of Vico, *all* the dark, unconsciousnesses that underlie its hero's thinking and enable it to be what it is."[49] Our language and consciousness, "living and evolving forces made by men, but beyond any individual's control,"[50] are immersed in, or sustained by, an unconscious not internal to the human mind (taken in the narrow but perhaps most common sense) but indeed operative in the extended, distributed networks, operative synchronically and diachronically, in which all "individual" minds—and bodies—are netted, constituted, and constantly reshaped. Along these lines, the humanism of Vico, especially as redeployed and refashioned by Joyce, may not be so far from more recent posthuman perspectives where the networks we generate and inhabit but do not comprehend or master are the unknowing conditions of our human self-creation.

Such self-making in both Vico and Joyce can be seen to flow from a primal indetermination and unknowing of the human, the ground and condition of poetic wisdom, in whose first axiom Vico posits that "when man understands, he extends his mind to comprehend things; but when he does not understand, he makes them out of himself and, by transforming himself, becomes them." If, according to Vico, "rational metaphysics teaches that man becomes all things through understanding, *homo intelligendo fit omnia*," it is "with perhaps greater truth" that Vico's "imaginative metaphysics shows that man becomes all things by not understanding them, *homo non intelligendo fit omnia*."[51] Just as in Vico the indetermination of the mind becomes ground of creation, so in Joyce the creative word flows from and returns to a figure who is at once excessively significant and irreducibly indeterminate. Erigenating from (next to) nothing, and moving ultimately back into the abyssal (and endlessly regenerative) waters of "salvocean" (623), the logos or word of the *Wake* belongs to an anonymous "somwome" neither fully divine nor fully human whose relation to "that base anything" comes in the end to "nullum." The movement of proces-

49. Ibid. Bishop's citations here of *Ulysses* are from the 1961 Random House edition.

50. Bishop, *Joyce's Book of the Dark*, 208.

51. Giambatista Vico, *New Science*, trans. David Marsh (New York: Penguin Books, 1999), 405, according to the marginal pagination.

sion from and return to this nullum ("my safe return to ignorance" [446])
can be read equally well from the angle of the human ("the man, Humme
the Cheapner, Esc" or "the youman form" [29, 36]) and from the angle of
the deity ("dayety" [143])—and in both directions a tie might be established
between the creative power of language and the nothingness that grounds
it. Such a tie recurs everywhere in the "nat language" of the *Wake*'s "Nich-
tian glossery" (83), and it is indispensable to the understanding of creation
that takes shape there.

If, as Bishop convincingly argues, the world of the *Wake* is created (and
ever recreated) in the "image, memory and language" (xix) of an "absent
subject" who is "unconscious of and to himself" (xix) and whose "elusive
presence is felt everywhere throughout the book but who is nowhere within
it definitively characterized or even given a stable name" (xvii), and if, as
the *Wake* itself suggests, its "disunited kingdom" has been reared "on the
vacuum" of "your own most intensely doubtful soul" (188), then we might
indeed see here a repetition or shadow or image of the mystical sense of
creation *ex nihilo*. Here both God, as the placeless place of places, an indefinable nothing, and the human subject, as incomprehensible image of that
placeless nothing, alike signal the ground out of which creation issues, and
to which it returns, through the multiplicity and simplicity of the Word.

Word, indeed, proves excessively creative throughout the *Wake*, as
throughout mystical tradition from Eriugena through Cusa, and into Vico's
philology, by virtue of its proximity to the void. The *Wake*'s overall "systomy dystomy, which everabody you ever anywhere at all doze" (597) can
be taken to signal the multiple goings and comings of Here Comes Everybody out of and into the obscurity and unknowing of that void, which itself
assumes multiple forms, from drunkenness and sleep, through death and
the oceanic, to rebirth. "In the buginning is the woid, in the muddle is the
sounddance, and thereinofter you're in the unbewised again" (378). Emerging out of the void/word as "everabody . . . anywhere" in the "muddle"
of the "sounddance," HCE incessantly slips back into that void as a "nomad . . . nomon" (374) who, "touring the no placelike no timelike absolent"
(609), appears nowhere. "Who was he to whom? . . . Whose are his place-
wheres? . . . [T]he unfacts, did we possess them, are too imprecisely few to
warrant our certitude" (56–57). The indeterminate "subject" in or through
whose mind and body the *Wake* world appears finds reflected there an image of its own chaotic nullity, for "an you could peep inside the cerebralised
saucepan of this eer illwinded goodfornobody, you would see in his house
of thoughtsam . . . what a jetsam litterage of convolvuli of times lost or
strayed, of lands derelict and of tongues laggin too" (292). Just as the divine

or human subject in mystical tradition constitutes the placeless place of places in whose absent presence everything and nothing would appear, and just as in Vico the etymological perspective brings to light the indeterminate mass and the historical depth from which any individual would come, so the "goodfornobody" at the heart of the *Wake* marks a void out of which and into which the multivalent thoughtsam and jetsam of the *Wake* world flow.

Joyce himself makes this connection between creative expression and mystical void in a 1912 text that relates the art of William Blake to the theology of Pseudo-Dionysius. Attempting "to paint his works on the void of the divine bosom," Joyce's Blake gives expression to the infinitely unnameable within a creative process that recalls the apophatic ascent into God as imagined by the traditions of Dionysian mysticism:

> Dionysius the pseudo-Areopagite, in his book *De Divinis Nominibus*, arrives at the throne of God by denying and overcoming every moral and metaphysical attribute, and falling into ecstasy and prostrating himself before the divine obscurity, before that unutterable immensity which precedes and encompasses the supreme knowledge in the eternal order. The mental process by which Blake arrives at the threshold of the infinite is a similar process. Flying from the infinitely small to the infinitely large, from a drop of blood to the universe of the stars, his soul is consumed by the rapidity of flight, and finds itself renewed and winged and immortal on the edge of the dark ocean of God.[52]

Artistic creation, on this reading, is endlessly open and on the move, "renewed and winged and immortal," to the degree that it—like the whole of the *Wake,* or like a "rough breathing on the void of to be" (100), or like "a flash from a future of maybe" (597)—rests "on the edge of the dark ocean of God." As in Dionysius and Eriugena, where bottomless denial and unknowing go hand in hand with endless affirmation and imagination, and as in Cusa and Bruno, where the absence of archetype opens infinite creation and where the infinite implies a coincidence of the minimum and the maximum, so with Blake and Joyce ceaseless creation renews itself on the edge of a void whose unutterable immensity, whose darkness and depth, escape both the infinitely small and the infinitely large—which thereby come to intersect or coincide, both equally approximating and falling short of the

---

52. James Joyce, untitled manuscript on William Blake, in *Critical Writings,* ed. Ellsworth Mason and Richard Ellmann (Ithaca: Cornell University Press, 1989), 222.

void-immensity. Just as the infinitely small and the infinitely great can intersect or coincide within the Romantic vision, and just as the human can
contain the universe in mystical tradition, so in every word of the *Wake*,
part and whole intersect or coincide, for "it will remember itself from every sides . . . in each our word" (614). Likewise, the immensity of human
consciousness and language, thought in its temporal depth with Vico, suggests the intersection of the minute or the trivial with the massive or world
historical; in every word as in every individual, unthinkable collectivity,
and hence a deeply anonymous memory, comes to creative expression. This
condition of profound unknowing, this unconscious, is not so much within
us as around us, both behind and ahead of us, or beneath us, in such a way
that it sustains us.

As I've been suggesting, the intersection of the minute and the massive, fundamental to the *Wake*'s "imaginable itinerary through the particular universal" (260), can be traced both to a Romantic vision like Blake's
and to other influential heirs of Dionysian and Eriugenian tradition like
Nicholas of Cusa and Giordano Bruno, for whom "in each thing is realized
everything and everything is in each thing. Each thing finally appears as a
perspective on the universe and a microcosmic model of it." Cusa's infinite and perspectival universe, answered by conjectural thinking immersed
always in unknowing, and having as ground the inaccessible coincidence
of opposites, gives Joyce inspiration for the "polydimensional reality" of
the *Wake*, which like Cusa's universe entails "the infinite possible perspectives of a universal form that can be seen under different visual angles, in
endless and complementary profiles."[53] Just as the *Wake* world seems to
express all things and nothing in the chaotic language of a late modern vision, so the Cusan maximum expresses in early modern, humanistic terms
the coincidence or indiscretion of everything and nothing. Joyce reads this
Cusan doctrine in light of Bruno's insistence that "it is necessary that of
the inaccessible face of God there be an infinite simulacrum (*simulacro*)
in which, as infinite members, are found innumerable worlds."[54] As Eco
elaborates, the *Wake* is able itself to suggest that "the dialectic of the finite
and infinite is accomplished only in the ceaseless process of cosmic metamorphosis. Each being has in itself the seed of future forms that guarantee
its infinity. Joyce had read Bruno's *De l'infinito universo e mondi*, and one
of the most implicit and explicit axioms of the *Wake* is that of the infinity

53. Eco, *Aesthetics of Chaosmos*, 73.
54. Giordano Bruno, *De l'infini, de l'univers et des mondes*, vol. 4 of *Oeuvres Complètes*, ed.
Giovanni Aquilecchia (Paris: Belles Lettres, 1995), 77.

of worlds, unified by the metamorphic nature of each word, the willingness of each etymon to immediately become something else and to explode in new semantic directions."[55] If, as Eco highlights, Joyce uses Bruno to "cast the stable and circumscribed universe of scholasticism into doubt,"[56] in doing so he recapitulates a stream of thought, suppressed by the traditional mainstream, where the cosmos is understood as limited, but nonetheless flowing through medieval thought from Eriugena to Cusa, where the intimacy of God and world, as we saw, yields the impossibility of circumscribing the latter as much as the former. It is against this deep background that one must read the *Wake*'s mystical poetics, which follow the "tendency of Frivulteeny Sexuagesima to expense herself as sphere as possible, paradismic perimutter, in all directions on the bend of the unbridalled, the infinississimals of her facets becoming manier and manier as the calicolum of her umdescribables . . . shrinks" (298).

As heir of Cusa and Bruno, Joyce extends and amplifies the consequences of the break with scholasticism effected by Cusa's humanistic affirmation of creative freedom. Inspired thus by Cusa and Bruno, the infinity of possible worlds opened or embodied by the *Wake*, wherein finite and infinite, part and whole, ceaselessly cross and recross, is a function of the linguistic explosion (itself socio-cultural-historical in a global sense) upon which the work is based. As with the fission of the atom, where the infinitely minute can prove unthinkably powerful and globally binding, so the smallest linguistic units in the *Wake*, reflecting the whole of the work's reality within themselves, split, explode, and scatter in a process of creation from annihilation, or of annihilation that enables creation: "The abnihilisation of the etym . . . expolodotonates through Parsuralia with an ivanmorinthorrumble fragoromboassity amidwhiches general uttermosts confussion are preceivable moletons skaping with muliculos" (353). Norman O. Brown is right to note in this regard that the tie between creation and annihilation—of the atom or of the etym—is fundamental to the *Wake*:

That's what *Finnegans Wake* is about:
smashing the atom.
Etyms are atoms.
Annihilation of language:
   he would wipe alley english spooker, multa-
phoniaksically spuking, off the face of the erse.

---

55. Eco, *Aesthetics of Chaosmos*, 73.
56. Ibid., 74.

Annihilisation of language so that it can be abnihi-
lated again; created out of nothing.
Out of thunder.[57]

Thus, echoing the language of late medieval and early modern mysticism and humanism (Cusa, Bruno, Vico) in combination with that of modern calculus (evoked by Frivulteeny Sexuagesima above) and technoscience
(the annihilation of the atom here), the *Wake* heaves "alljawbreakical expressions out of old Sare Isaac's universal of specious aristmystic unsaid"
(293)—and according to that "aristmystic" the nothing out of which creation issues entails an endless naming or linguistic dissemination to the degree that the nothing can be approached asymptotically but never reached—
as with the multiple mathematical figures that Cusa deploys to evoke the
incomprehensible infinity of God.

This word/void through which creation issues, both in Joyce and in the
mystical traditions, can be read or heard as, among other things, the self-
expression of the God who in Exodus 3:14 announces himself as "I am that
[or as] I am," which, as Meister Eckhart well puts it, is the most appropriate
name for God because it says everything and nothing at once. The "I am"
in Joyce can also be heard in its specifically Vichian tone, where creative capacity is bound to ignorance and infancy and their embodiment. As Bishop
highlights, "the 'giantle' world of Vico's *New Science* . . . originates exactly
as the world originates in the Book of Genesis, and exactly as it always and
only originates in the minds of human infants. 'Lost in ignorance,' 'buried in
the body and immersed in the senses,' these impercipient, space-pervading
giants, informed by *Jov(e)* or *J(eh)ov(ah)*, rise from an unconsciousness that
only knows 'I AM' into 'gentile' human 'nature' by gathering from dark
formlessness the etymologically related property of physical 'nature.'"[58]
The "I am that I am" takes numerous forms in the *Wake*—for example, "I
yam as I yam," "I am yam," "I am, I am big alltoogooder," "what I (the person whomin I now am)," "thou-who-thou-art," "we there are where are"—
and if read in its apophatic sense it would constitute one of the most powerful figures for the coimplication or coincidence of (not quite) divine and
(not quite) human anonymity within the cosmic process of a self-creation
whose ground is dark and inarticulate, like an infantile body immersed in
sensuous sleep. "A being again in becomings again" (491), the "I am that
I am" of the *Wake* constitutes a "howtosayto itiswhatis hemustwhomust

57. Norman O. Brown, *Closing Time* (New York: Random House, 1973), 88.
58. Bishop, *Joyce's Book of the Dark*, 190.

worden schall" (223) whose "darktongues, kunning" (223) give expression both to a multivalent and not quite human figure and to a multivalent and not quite divine figure who, imaging or imagining each other, indiscretely, and by means of "ineffable tries at speech unasyllabled" (183), create, undo, and recreate themselves endlessly within "the untireties of livesliving being the one substrance of a streamsbecoming" (597).

Seeming to include while dissolving the history of all theological and anthropological imagination, this being in becoming, this "constant of fluxion" (297) that defines the *Wake*'s countless goings and comings, grounds (and unsettles) the chaosmos of All within which the human and divine I or "Egoname" (485) seem to be embodied, put to death, and resurrected eternally.[59] The polyonymous anonymity of this I, which travels "the void world over," signals, then, in both modern and mystical language, the immanence of a self-less "Allself" who echoes the mystical "I am":

> for Earl Hoovedsoon's choosing and Huber and Harman orhowwhen theeuponthus (chchch!) eysolt of binnoculises memostinmust egotum sabcunsciously senses upers the deprofundity of multimathematical immaterialities wherebejubers in the pancosmic urge the allimmanence of that which Itself is Itself Alone (hear, O hear, Caller Erin!) exteriorises on this ourherenow plane in disunited solod, likeward and gushious bodies with (science, say!) . . . intuitions of reunited selfdom (murky whey, abstrew adim!) in the higherdimissional selfless Allself. (394–95).

If "that which Itself is Itself Alone" expresses itself today, "on this ourherenow plane," it does so in the polyonymous anonymity of just such a selfless Allself, which is named (and unnamed) throughout the *Wake* not only by the countless names of world-historical gods, angelic hierarchies, or sefirothic emanations, but also, equally, by the innumerable "illassumed names . . . of a tellafun book" (86)—the all too human, endlessly multiplied, and undifferentiated names of a modern mass culture. The anonymity that comes to expression in the *Wake*, indeed, draws not only on the deepest memory of archaic and traditional religion, myth, and ritual, but also on the culture of electronic networks wherein televocal and televisual media

---

59. For a theological reading of Joyce emphasizing the bodily sacrifice repeated in the liturgical and sacramental, see especially Altizer's *History as Apocalypse* and Balsamo's *Joyce's Messianism*.

give voice and visibility to the nameless and faceless Allself of everabody anywhere, who as such is a nomad nomon nowhere.

"As modern as tomorrow afternoon and in appearance up to the minute" (309), the *Wake* is a world in which "wires hummed" (98) and "aerials buzzed" (99), and the oscillations of a modern "dielectrick" throughout that world render word televocal by means of a "tolvtubular high fidelity daildialler . . . equipped with supershielded umbrella antennas for distance, getting and connected by the magnetic links of a Bellini-Tosti coupling system, with a vialtone speaker, capable of capturing skybuddies, harbour craft emittences, key clickings, vaticum cleaners, due to woman formed mobile or man made static and bawling the whowle hamshack and wobble down in an eliminium sounds pound so as to serve him up a melegoturny marygoaraumd, electrically filtered for allirish earths and ohmes" (309–10). As televocal, modern word or speech here is "electrically filtered" for all humanity, whose earth and home are electrified by means of network linkages and coupling systems through which emissions and transmissions cover unseen distances like angelic "messongers." Indeed, this is the world in which "we are now diffusing . . . the dewfolded song of the naughtingels" (359), and in such a world, where technology can turn nightingales into naught angels, where the interplay of technology and nature proves religious, the comings and goings of electrified "messongers," like the epic comings and goings of the *Wake* as a whole (from Adam to the atom, through the obluvial waters of noarchic memory), are contained in a "harmonic condenser enginium" equipped with a "gain control of circumcentric megacycles, ranging from the anttidulibnium onto the serostaatarean" (310). With a Vichian sense of memory, Joyce lights up the diachronic and hence cultural-historical depth and complexity of those techoscientific networks that can seem so often, for critics and enthusiasts alike, to involve a flattening or erasure of time and memory (or what amounts to the same: an eternal present, a perfect memory), or a simple discharge of the past opening to the apocalyptic present or utopic future. Thus charged with modernity's dielectrick pulse, which nonetheless continues to recall the archaic depths of human memory, the *Wake*'s all-encompassing machinery of suggestion becomes, "in cycloannalism, from space to space, time after time, in various phases of scripture as in various poses of sepulture" (254) a "radiooscillating epiepistle to which . . . we must ceaselessly return" (108).

Now, if it is true that the electrified scripture of the *Wake* becomes a radiooscillating epiepistle giving voice to a networked telephony, it is also true that "television kills telephony in brother's broil" (52), and hence that the word and voice of the *Wake* become also—like the mystical God who "runs" through all things—image and sight. While the *Wake* is famously and rightly known as a "lingerous longerous book of the dark" (251), a "funnaminal world" that "darkles" wherein "we are circumveiloped by obscuritads" (244), it is also illuminated throughout by the resplendence of photographic, filmic, and televisual image—the electronic light-writing of our late modern mass culture: "In the heliotropical noughttime" of the *Wake*, indeed, "the bairdboard bombardment screen . . . tends to teleframe and step up to the charge of a light barricade. Down the photoslope in syncopanc pulses. . . . Spraygun rakes and splits them from a double focus: grenadite, damnymite, alextronite, nichilite: and the scanning firespot of the sgunners traverses the rutilanced illustrated sunksundered lines" (349). Just as the "nighttime instrument" or "faroscope" (150) of television shoots a stream of electrons upon a screen where images constantly appear, shift about, transform, and disappear, ad infinitum, so the *Wake* shoots upon the reader's mind a stream of words and letters that become, like the words and letters in the illuminated Book of Kells, light and image—appearing, shifting about, transforming, and disappearing within the endless spirals and interlacings of color and shape, sound and smell, place and time, plant and animal, humanity and divinity. As Beckett puts it, "here words are not the polite contortions of twentieth-century printer's ink. They are alive. They elbow their way on to the page, and glow and blaze and fade and disappear."[60] And just as the reader might indeed see traces of theological light and vision throughout the *Wake*, so does the *Wake* see in its own television that "A gaspel truce leaks out over the caseine coatings. Amid a fluorescence of spectacular mephiticism there coaculates through the iconoscope stealdily a still, the figure of a fellow-chap in the wholy ghast" (349). Thus, in the "chiaroscuro" (107) of the *Wake*'s "philophosy" (119), "revealled by Oscur Camerad" (602), we become, along countless twisting paths of an endless "photophoric pilgrimage" (472), "searchers for tabernacles and the celluloid art" (534)—and so the darkness of mystical interiors merges with superficial screens of photoplay where "flash becomes word" (267).

Along these lines, Joyce's *Wake* reads like the enactment of Taylor's "screening" in and through a Vichian exercise in memory (or vice versa). Just as Taylor will argue that "I" am a function of the ever shifting remembering and forgetting of an excess that flows through me, so for the Vico who recurs throughout Joyce, the human, individually and collectively, en-

---

60. Beckett, "Dante . . . Bruno. Vico . . . Joyce," 15–16.

tails a self-creation in which the generations work through me as much as I through them, in the dynamic and unwieldy interplay of memory and forgetting. Transgenerational, the genesis of human "nature" could never be mechanically genetic nor straightforwardly genuine; the ongoing genera- tion of the human in its "nature" involves an ongoing birth whose matrix is the anonymous depth of an excessive and always troubled memory. "Just as human nature, in Vico's gentile history, is made wholly by people," writes Bishop,

> so HCE's whole nature is unconsciously defined and structured by oth- ers both within and far beyond his immediate circle of acquaintance. It was from Vico that Joyce learned . . . that no infant born into the world of gentile nature can even remotely attain a "personality" without the prior existence of scores of people in the world immediately around it, and of billions of others buried in the night of a historical past ordinarily lost to consciousness: all of human thinking comes from someone else. In reconstructing the "indentity" of a man whose conscious identity has dissolved in sleep, *Finnegans Wake* structurally treats its central figure as the raddled blur of millions of persons, most of whom are completely absent from the consciousness that they unconsciously helped shape. "As a singleminded supercrowd" (42.22), our hero is "more mob than man."[61]

Like the abyss of the soul imaging the abyss of God in mystical tradition, the Vichian Joyce figures the self-creative human, the ongoing birth of human nature, as the interplay of ignorant donation and ignorant reception—the very life of what some call the gift. "Genuine" birth thus always implies a transgenerational ground that remains inappropriable, and Joyce allows us to see the sense in which an emerging technological culture highlights this human ground far more than freeing, or tearing, us from it.

In the electrification of voice and the illumination of word, then, the "daynoight" (412) of the *Wake* promises "new worlds for all"—worlds that would be "scotographically arranged" according to the measureless anonymity of a "scripchewer in whofoundland" (412). Perhaps indis- tinguishable from the creative divinity who is all in all and nothing in anything, the humanity that creates and inhabits these worlds might re- semble a "new 'electronic' humanity . . . whose depth is indistinguishable from its surface or mask. . . . Its actual name would be everyone and no one

---

61. Bishop, *Joyce's Book of the Dark*, 213.

at once, an everyone who can only be no one."[62] As appearing in Joyce, this superficial humanity is shadowed and shaped always by an immeasurable historical and cultural depth, which so many fear lost in the posthuman technological scene, a depth signaled in part by the persistence of mystical tradition in that very work which writes the prehistory of our postmodernity. If read as an inchoately postmodern rendering of the interplay between polyonymy and anonymity within the process of (post)human self-creation, the *Wake* offers to this humanity, as did Eriugena's cosmic God to every soul, or as did Cusa's infinite sphere, its abyssal image—where we would stare into "that multimirror megaron of returningties, whirled without end to end" (582). In doing so the *Wake* signals, among other things, the excess of every tradition beyond the grounds where its self-proclaimed defenders, as well as its dismissive critics, want and need to place it. In order to inhabit that world—which means in order endlessly to create and recreate both that world and, through it, ourselves, we need, while ever bound to traditions that exceed us just as we exceed them, to become "the readers of tomorrow . . . the readers of a possible society in which exercise in the multiplication of signs will not appear as a game for the elite but as the natural, constructive exercise of an agile and renewed perception."[63] And if the *Wake* can teach us to become such readers and thus to renew—to re-awaken—our perception, it does so by forcing us to recognize ourselves "in the ignorance that implies impression that knits knowledge that finds the nameform that whets the wits that convey contacts and sweeten sensation that drives desire that adheres to attachment that dogs death that bitches birth that entails the ensuance of existentiality" (18).

62. Thomas J. J. Altizer, *The Contemporary Jesus* (Albany: State University of New York Press, 1997), 187.

63. Eco, *Aesthetics of Chaosmos*, 85.

CHAPTER SIX

To Inherit: The Birth of Possible Worlds

The anxieties surrounding recent scientific and technological development seem especially acute in relation to the fields of biological science and genetic technology, which have become in the United States and
elsewhere fields whose religious charge is especially notable. Resistance to
the cloning of human stem cells and to genetic engineering more broadly
(human or not), often assumes its loudest voice in the name of religion,
and of tradition, and in that name it speaks to defend and protect what, in
our very "life" or "nature," is believed to define us as properly "human."
Technoscientific intervention into the genesis of biological life reaches (or
threatens to reach) a level where it can appear only as a violation of the
basic nature—or of the property—that would make and keep us "human,"
and the desire to save the human is often bound to the desire to save or
return to some tradition that purports to guard and transmit the human. At
stake, from this perspective, is a delimitation and defense of human nature
as human property, as something that the human must continue to possess and protect in order to remain human. The concern to guarantee such
possession over time, across generations, is a concern to guard nothing less
than the genetic inheritance of humanity. Such inheritance, however, is
not solely biological or "natural," as my explorations here should suggest,
but also inextricably and concretely sociocultural—and the conditions of
human transmission, the conditions of tradition, as I've been emphasizing,
involve both chance and risk, each a condition of the other. If in order to
preserve itself, or to stay alive, human tradition must reproduce or replicate
itself, that reproduction always entails, as according to the logic of iterabil-
ity that Derrida and his heirs have so well elucidated, the risk of a mimetic
repetition that could turn overly strict and all too automatic, such that the
ostensible life and continuity of the human and its tradition would give

in fact a kind of death. The vitality of deconstructive thought, as Jean-Luc Nancy points out, stems from its passage between the insufficient alternatives of lifeless perpetuation of tradition and sheer death-giving destruction:

> "Deconstruction" has as its distinctive trait, if one takes into view its origin in the text of *Sein und Zeit* where the word appears, that it is the latest state of the tradition—its latest state as a retransmission, to us and through us, of the whole tradition with the purpose of bringing it entirely into play or of putting it entirely at stake again [*la remettre en jeu*]. To bring the tradition into play or to put it at stake again according to deconstruction, according to *Destruktion* (the term Heidegger held to guard against *Zerstörung*, that is against "destruction," and which he characterized as *Abbau*, "dismantling") means neither to destroy in order to refound nor to perpetuate—two hypotheses that would imply a system given as such and untouched as such.[1]

From this Heideggerian perspective, Nancy suggests that there is no tradition given as such, no tradition "untouched" or intact in such a way that it can ever be either simply destroyed and dismissed or perpetuated in its static self-sameness. Tradition is living tradition only insofar as it maintains the kind of opening, or indiscretion, in which it finds itself by differing or departing from itself—that is, by differing or departing from the image it forms of itself, or from the model on which it imagines itself.

⁘

The redundancy of code or codification, while indispensable to all forms of transmission, tends also toward emptiness and death; the repeatable code or format indispensable to life needs also the singular and the unforeseeable, the new message. There must be branching of the stem—not only law but event, the necessary and the contingent, which can slip each into the other, in a kind of ceaseless vibration that we might inhabit like a kind of faith. Such a vibrant faith would be the condition of any vital humanity or tradition, which would mean those that are open to birth, and hence rebirth— the joys of any faith, or life, worthy of the name. Birth, however, can be as unsettling, and as hard to locate, as death, its intimate partner; it entails the unavoidable disquiet or anxiety of genuinely living thought, or thoughtful

1. Nancy, "La déconstruction du christianisme," 511–12.

living. "In distancing ourselves from deadly equilibrium," as Serres puts it, "disquiet gives us birth" (*RAM*, p. 152), and he is right to suggest that a God of birth, a God who thinks and creates, would be one who "loves to sow everything with the new and the unexpected," one who stands at odds, then, with any "redundant omniscience" or any "repetitive paradise" (*REC*, 166), which could only amount, really, to blindness and hell. The disquiet of birth and the fluidity of life that Serres affirms at the heart of his thinking operate also, I have argued, in the world of Joyce's *Wake*, in whose author Samuel Beckett rightly finds a "biologist in words" and in which work he sees, well and richly, the "purgatorial," in the sense of "the absolute absence of the Absolute." Contrasting the conical Purgatory of Dante, which achieves culmination, and the circular purgatory of Joyce, which excludes it, Beckett's insistence on the purgatorial, we saw, eluding the static lifelessness both of pure heaven and of pure hell, affirms "a flood of movement and vitality released by the conjunction of these two elements."[2] In the midst of that flood of movement and vitality, in the midst of life, one never can (and never should) count on the simple coincidence of life—or, as Joyce's *Wake* also shows, of tradition—with "itself," for "life" might always also be "Lff," and tradition "taradition" (151), ever recurring and ever adapting, ever awakening us anew, like the river, in the course of a time that both flows or continues (*tempus* as from τείνω) and cuts or interrupts (*tempus* as from τέμνω). "Thus the time that passes, *time, Zeit*, would come close to the *weather, Wetter* [*le temps qu'il fait*], about which one knows that it mixes hot and cold, dry and humid, darkness and light. When we say that time flows [*coule*], we forget that the Latin verb *colare* means to filter a mixture. Thus it percolates more than it flows: it filters. It passes and does not pass" (*RAM*, 149).

From this perspective, genuine life time, the time of genesis for that human being who, by definition, is always leaving, courses in resistance to the secure placement of "life," as "human" or as "traditional," in any pregiven niche whose boundaries would define the human by locating it. It is from within this thinking on life that any overly secure placement or location appears as the mark of death: "What is death? What takes place: here lies [*ci-gît*]. From where to leave? From place [*place*]. A tomb marks place [*le lieu*]. Death marks belonging and its lethal *libido*: to belong, to die. What is a place [*Qu'est-ce qu'une place*]? The place [*lieu*] that a tomb marks" (*RAM*, 206). The logic of placement or location, the logic of definition, and hence belonging, tends toward the kind of property that would

2. Beckett, "Dante . . . Bruno. Vico . . , Joyce," 19, 22.

restrict or suffocate the vibrant displacement and disquiet that are vital to genuine human life and time, in all of their generosity. One should ask, then, or already doubt, whether the human, in its life and time, is rightly understood in terms of such property and its possession. Does the transmission, or tradition, of "humanity" over time in fact depend on a logic of property and possession, whether biological or otherwise? Is the technological dimension of human existence, in particular, of which genetic technology is only one telling instance, to be understood so readily as threat to our human property—and hence to the inheritance of humanity, to its tradition? The hypothesis I've been working out here, through the twofold path of mystical theological tradition and more recent posthuman discourse, is that the human, precisely as creature of inheritance, or of tradition, is inevitably technological—and that the founding condition both of inheritance and of technological existence should be understood not in terms of human property and possession, definition or measure, placement and belonging, but rather, indeed, in terms of an indetermination, a lack of measure or of property, a displacement and dispossession that enable and demand the creative—or the genetic—capacity of the human.

Of course, genetic technology is only one of the more pressing points at which our technological existence might be understood to threaten our humanity by threatening our heritage. Anxiety surrounding biological forms of human heritage can never be neatly separated from anxiety surrounding seemingly distinct, cultural, forms of heritage—such as those ostensibly threatened by media culture and its technologies. Attending to the resonance between cultural and biological operations of reproduction and the dangers they can seem to pose thanks to their own replicating capacities, one can note that the conditions of biological life are repeated in cultural life and entail the same coimplication of chance and risk. The utterly inimitable, without any replication whatsoever, simply cannot live, no less create, but the perfectly replicable, or strictly replicated, flattens or erases any genuine, authentically creative life. Such life needs to find the singular in and through replication, and it requires the capacity to repeat those singular moments that yield creation. A living tradition would need dynamically to bridge those two logics, of the imitable and the inimitable, which we traced in the mystical dialectic of distinction and indistinction, and which prove indeed already operative, as Serres points out, in the "idea" as discovered by Plato. The idea "would present two faces: its meaning, its content, its density, indeed its beauty, its inimitable character, its very universality even, on the one hand; and on the other its driving power of propagation, its imitable character, hence another universality, making the bridge between the inimitable and the imitable" (*RAM*, 172). The appeal to "tradition" (often quasi-automatic, as one can imagine the genetic to be) in order to save the "natural" (for example, the genetic "itself," whose natural replications must in fact be repeatedly broken through the processes of branching or ramification) needs to be thought today in terms of the increasingly intimate interplay and slippage between the natural and the cultural, as between the universal and the singular—and not only because those seeking to save the biological heritage of the human will inevitably appeal to the resources of culture (values, tradition, etc.) but also because the natural and the cultural, thanks to the technological, inform one another in ever more intimate ways. Ostensible threats to the biological heritage of humanity and ostensible threats to the cultural heritage of humanity are increasingly interwoven thanks to technoscientific development itself, and thus it is understandable that resistance to the technological is so often voiced in the name of saving the human and its traditional inheritance.

Among the more nuanced and far-reaching arguments made along these lines recently is that of Robert P. Harrison, professor of French and Italian at Stanford University, in his 2003 book *The Dominion of the Dead*.[3] Aiming to bring a "philological certainty," which is to say an institutional and historical grounding, to the "truth" of Heideggerian philosophy, Harrison's work draws deeply on Vico's *New Science* to elucidate an essential tie between "humanity" and "inheritance," according to what he will call the "law of legacy." To be human, for Harrison, means above all, and fundamentally, to inherit: to be indebted, always already, to those who come before, and to be obligated or bound, through such inheritance, to those who come after. The ground of inheritance, Harrison argues, following Vico, is to be found, quite concretely, in the distinctively human institution of burial for the dead. From this perspective, Harrison argues, "humanity is not a species (*Homo sapiens* is a species); it is a way of being mortal and of relating to the dead. To be human means above all to bury. Vico suggests as much when he reminds us that '*humanitas* in Latin comes first and properly from *humando*, burying' (*New Science* §12)" (*DD*, xi). From this perspective, our being human consists at bottom in our being related to the humus, to the earth, through mortality and through our retention of the dead in that earth.[4] Such retention of the dead through burial is the first

<hr />

3. Robert Pogue Harrison, *The Dominion of the Dead* (Chicago: University of Chicago Press, 2003). Hereafter cited parenthetically as *DD*.

4. On the tie between humanity and humus, see also Heidegger's analysis of the fable of *Cura* (§42 of *Being and Time*): "And because there is now a dispute among you, let it be called '*homo*,' for it is made out of *humus* (earth)." Heidegger's interpretation of the fable could be taken

form of retention in which human memory can find its necessary ground, for "burial does not mean only the laying of bodies in the ground" but also, in a broader sense, thanks to this, "to store, preserve, and put the past on hold" (*DD*, xi). Pivotal to Harrison's argument here is the twofold contention that such burial of the dead allows (even as, according to a significant ambiguity, it may require) a cultivation and preservation of "place," and that such place is threatened or undermined by those forms of technological existence associated with the "posthuman."

Burial of the dead and cultivation of place go hand in hand, and such cultivation is the function of a distinctively human temporality that is created and sustained through the activity of memory—which itself rests in the deeper ground of retention established through burial:

> For what is a place, if not its memory of itself—a site or locale where time turns back upon itself? The grave marks a site in the landscape where time cannot merely pass through, or pass over. Time must now gather around the *sema* and mortalize itself. It is precisely this mortalization of time that gives place its articulated boundaries, distinguishing it from the infinity of homogenous space. As the primordial sign of human mortality, the grave domesticates the inhuman transcendence of space and marks human time off from the timelessness of the gods or the eternal returns of nature. That is why gods are not the original founders of place—mortals are. (*DD*, 23).

The foundation of place, then, contrary to classic accounts in the history of religions (such as that of Mircea Eliade),[5] here consists not in the presence

---

to stand in tension with Harrison's linkage of the human to the *humus* insofar as for Heidegger it is care, and not *humus*, that is distinctive to the Being of the human: "This pre-ontological document becomes especially significant not only in that 'care' is here seen as that to which human Dasein belongs 'for its lifetime,' but also because this priority of 'care' emerges in connection with the familiar way of taking man as compounded of body (earth) and spirit. '*Cura prima finxit*': in care this entity has the 'source' of its Being. '*Cura teneat, quamdiu vixerit*': the entity is not released from this source but is held fast, dominated by it through and through as long as this entity 'is in the world.' 'Being-in-the-world' has the stamp of 'care,' which accords with its Being. It gets the name 'homo' not in consideration of its Being but in relation to that of which it consists (*humus*)" (*Being and Time*, 243 [198]).

5. See, e.g., Eliade's classic account of sacred space and time in *The Sacred and the Profane: The Nature of Religion*, trans. Willard R. Task (New York: Harcourt Brace Jovanovich, 1959): "Revelation of a sacred space makes it possible to obtain a fixed point and hence to acquire orientation in the chaos of homogeneity, to 'found the world' and to live in a real sense" (23). Given the flow of time and the human capacity to forget (or the divine capacity to disappear) over time, of course, religious life must enable repeated return to such founding moments: "It is easy to

of the gods *in illo tempore* but in the mortalization of time, the transformation of homogenous diachronic passage into the differentiated, recollective or reflexive temporality of human memory, which itself requires the "humic foundations of our life worlds," foundations "whose contents have been so buried that they may be reclaimed by the future" (*DD*, x).

It is important to note, I think, that this burial of the dead, first in terms of the body set into the ground and marked by the grave, but then including also, by extension, the countless forms of retention and transmission operative, for example, in languages, practices, and institutions, implies for Harrison a distinction between the natural-biological species-being of *Homo sapiens* and the cultural-historical being of the human: "As *Homo sapiens* we are born of our biological parents. As human beings we are born of the dead—of the regional ground they occupy, of the languages they inhabited, of the worlds they brought into being, of the many institutional, legal, cultural and psychological legacies that, through us, connect them to the unborn" (*DD*, xi). From this perspective, Harrison, like Serres, contends that the defining property of the human, or its "nature," must be understood according to the etymological sense of this latter term, which derives from *nasci*, "to be born": it is our nature to be born, and such birth, beyond the biological, is made possible by the institution of burial, which establishes and keeps the legacies whose retrieval and renewal alone open a future. Though Harrison does not quite put it in these terms, we might read him to say here, in effect, and perhaps despite himself, that the difference between the human (as cultural-historical) and *Homo sapiens* (as natural-biological) is the irreducibly prosthetic or technological character of the human—and we can thus understand the institution of burial as a first form of "genetic technology."

I intend such a reading in resistance to that line within Harrison's analysis that sees the technological primarily as uprooting or delocalizing, and hence as threatening to the ground of humanity in its defining location, its place of burial and retention. Insofar as it distances us from the earth (not only as destination of the corpse but also as provenance of food), Harrison argues, modern technology threatens the distinctively human temporality and hence the discrete boundaries of actual, as distinct from virtual, place. That threat, he asserts, involves a flight from death that undermines, then,

---

understand why the memory of that marvelous time haunted religious man, why he periodically sought to return to it. *In illo tempore* the gods had displayed their greatest powers. *The cosmogony is the supreme divine manifestation*, the paradigmatic act of strength, superabundance, and creativity. Religious man thirsts for the real. By every means at his disposal, he seeks to reside at the very source of primordial reality, when the world was *in statu nascendi*" (80).

the very condition of "humanity" (and in passing we might well acknowledge the rhetoric, often thoroughly gnostic, of timelessness and immortality among contemporary technophiles): "The destruction of place that is occurring almost everywhere at present . . . is linked in part to an anxious and frenzied flight from death. We are running away from ourselves, not so much in the sense that we are abandoning our traditional homelands but in the sense that we are forsaking or destroying the places where our dying can make itself at home" (DD, 32).[6] From this perspective, Harrison insists, we face a choice: either "the human," kept or preserved in the keeping or preservation of earthly place, where our dying can be "at home," or the "posthuman," uprooted from the earth, without place and hence without the possibility of human inheritance. At stake for Harrison in the virtuality of technological existence is the property of the human, both as the nature defining us and as the possession we must keep, and therefore "each one of us must choose an allegiance—either to the posthuman, the virtual, and the synthetic, or to the earth, the real, and the dead in their humic densities" (DD, 35).

Is the choice, however, so clear—even on Harrison's terms? Is the distinction between the real and the virtual, or indeed between the dead and the synthetic, actually tenable? It may be, in fact, according to Harrison's analysis itself, that the basic conditions of retention and memory, through which the human is constituted, call deeply into question the division between real and virtual—just as they would call into question any secure location or placement of "the dead" (whether their burial be "actual" or not) and their dying (and there is in Heidegger, thanks to the impossibility of making it present or actual in any experience, always a virtual character to death, and hence an irreducibility of death to discrete place). To sketch such an argument, I should first elaborate a bit Harrison's theory concerning "world" as the creative expression of human mind, whose primordial need can be understood, he contends, as an originary generosity.

Thanks to burial, Harrison argues, the dead bestow on us the obligation of memory and the reward of futurity, two sides of the same inheri-

---

6. See also, e.g., the work coming out of the Netherlands Organization of Scientific Research (NWO) research program *Cyberspace Salvations: Computer Technology, Simulation, and Modern Gnosis*, started in April 2004 and led by Peter Pels in cooperation with Stef Aupers and Dick Houtman. As both Hayles and Taylor convincingly argue, the various forms of technognosticism, speaking of virtual immortality and the like, tend to involve a dualistic thinking that relies on the reduction of mind to code and then assumes the indifference to code of its instantiation or embodiment. The more compelling positions, such as those of Hayles and Taylor, insist on the constitutive interplay of code and embodiment.

tance: without meeting the former, we do not gain the latter—and also the reverse, one would have to say, since the past is a function of the future just as much as the future is a function of the past. Inheritance binds together the fundamental modes of temporality in their distinctively human form such that the human is essentially indebted or bound both to the past and to the future. The debt—or the guilt—of inheritance, however, in and through which we receive ourselves as human, does not, for Harrison, mark a deficiency but indeed a founding generosity of the human. That generosity, he insists, is indispensable to the creative, distinctively human activity of world building:

> If guilt is radically relational—if in fact it underlies the relations I maintain with both neighbor and predecessor—it is because it throws me into, and keeps me bound by, my need for help. The need both to give and to receive help belongs to Dasein's essence, as it were. To speak with Vico (who was no Hobbesian), the need for help is the basic condition without which families, cities, and commonwealths would not have come into being. That need does *not* devolve from some intrinsic privation or lack in human nature. On the contrary, it devolves from the generosity of humanity itself—a generosity that puts us at the disposal of others and that, through the *ingenium* of the human mind, generates the social world. Humanity means mortality. Mortality in turn means that we repossess ourselves only in giving ourselves. For even receiving help is a mode of self-giving, just as the refusal of help is, or can be, a failure of generosity. Whether we receive help or give it, we share in the world-engendering generosity that flows from the sources of primordial guilt. (*DD*, 157)

Harrison is arguing here against Heidegger's contention that in my guilt, signaled above all in my Being-toward-death, I am utterly isolated, deprived of those supports—worldly relations and beings—on which I normally and more or less successfully rely in my day-to-day existence.[7] He does so within a conception of mortal human relation as fundamentally generous—founded in, and reinforcing, a plenitude rather than a lack. Within this plenitude, to give is already to receive and to receive—above all to receive oneself—means already to give (and along these lines Harri-

---

7. See, e.g., *Being and Time* §58 on conscience, as well as the many passages on the nonrelational character of death, famously criticized by Levinas also, such as *Being and Time*, 354 [307], 294 [250], or 297 [253].

son's thinking proves suggestively resonant with Marion's phenomenological treatment of reception as, at bottom, a giving). If such a perspective on
the reception of self in and through self-giving may already be operative in
Heidegger in a way that Harrison does not develop (the Heidegger whom I
showed, in chapter 2, to posit that human Dasein comes to itself in departing from itself), his analyses do draw very deeply, in their conception of
worldhood, on the Heideggerian perspective. In that direction, the conception of worldhood with which Harrison is operating, much like the Heideggerian analysis to which it is indebted, proves to be, despite what Harrison
himself believes about his opposition to the "posthuman," deeply consistent with the kind of thing a posthuman theorist like Katherine Hayles en-
visions in terms of distributed and emergent systems, or Mark C. Taylor in
terms of the complex adaptive network, or indeed Michel Serres (to whom
Harrison's own previous book *Forests* is dedicated)[8] in terms of the global
technoscientific network in which humanity's own ongoing self-creation
or "hominescence" transpires—a network involving a "natural contract"
that is also "virtual," insofar as it binds us and world within a temporality
where those to come, culturally and naturally, would, as much as do the
dead, voice a claim to our attention: "To the scandal of many," Serres notes,
"I recently proposed that one accord to 'nature' the status of a subject of
right. Let us understand the term in the strict sense: the things and persons
to be born" (*RAM*, 227). Insofar as the natural contract bears strictly on that
which is to be born, it constitutes also a virtual contract, bearing on the
possible worlds, and their eventual inhabitants, for whose birth our technoscientific networks are responsible—and hence regarding which all should
have a right to speak, precisely because of those networks' distributed, collective character.[9] Within such networks, now the inescapable ground or
condition of human inheritance, we are dealing with prosthetic, relational,
interactive, and emergent systems where the discrete location of thought
and agency, or indeed of any self-identical human subject, is called into
question, and where the "nature" of the human itself needs to be understood not in terms of any stable property or category but in terms of ongo-

8. Robert Pogue Harrison, *Forests* (Chicago: U. of Chicago Press, 1992); Serres had previously dedicated his work *Le contrat naturel* to Harrison (Paris: François Bourin, 1990).

9. Serres devotes a section in *Rameaux* to the virtual contract (*RAM*, 225–28). A deep rethinking of the ethical and political dimensions of science, and of its interplay with the humanities, is called for along these lines, insofar as the powers unleashed by scientific knowing stand
to affect all of us in the most concrete ways, even as the specialization of science leaves the
development of such knowing in the hands of the smallest elites. Serres is one of the strongest
guides we have in this direction.

ing birth. Something like this networked understanding of the human as inheritor is central to Harrison's analysis, much as it is to the worldhood analyzed in *Being and Time*.

As Harrison writes, elucidating the conditions of retention thanks to which alone the constitutive memory of humanity may be cultivated (and advancing thus a significant critique of any psychologism in the definition of human mind), "Does retention then belong to what psychology calls the unconscious? Hardly. The mind's synthetic activity extends well beyond our psychic life in its totality, be it on the conscious or unconscious levels, if for no other reason than the human mind is a self-externalizing phenomenon that *creates* its places of retention outside its psychic interiorities. Indeed, its creative activity is largely a world-forming, that is, retention-creating activity. Our institutions, laws, landscapes, cities, statues, scriptures, houses, books, ideologies—these are among the many places in the secular topography where the human mind stores both the past and future of what it retains" (*DD*, 83–84). Much as in posthuman discourse, or in its Joycean prototype, so here in Harrison, the human mind, thanks to its creative and necessarily prosthetic capacities, inherits and retains far more, in fact, than it could ever realize in the discrete presence of any conscious memory. Memory requires retention, but not all that we retain is in actuality remembered; all memory implies a forgetting, all knowing an unknowing. The temporality of memory is one that filters. Retention, then, the basic operation of burial, in fact exceeds us and dislocates us in much the way that the networks of posthuman discourse—or the mystical universe—can exceed and dislocate us.

The "generosity" of the human, which "is above all a transgenerational giving and receiving between the dead and the living" (*DD*, 157), is made possible only by the systems or networks of retention in which human mind always exceeds itself, receiving and retaining more than it could ever actually re-collect or re-present.[10] But if this is so, then Harrison's insistence

10. In this, one could productively read Harrison within a long line of reflection on excess as constitutive of the human—from the theological anthropology of Augustine, for whom my memory contains more than I can comprehend, to the recent phenomenology of Jean-Luc Marion, for whom the self is constituted in and through the excess of "givenness" over the capacity for reception. Mark Taylor makes explicit the resonance between the excess of memory in Augustine and the excess of network culture over those who dwell in it. See *Moment of Complexity*, 200–204, the following passage in particular:

Paradoxically, as his self-consciousness grows, [Augustine] becomes less and less comprehensible to himself. Through images that are as provocative as they are evocative, Augustine restlessly probes what he cannot comprehend. In the endless "caverns and abysses" of his memory, he discovers "secret, numberless, and indefinable recesses."

on the place of memory, which lives only in and through such generosity, seems to grow questionable, as does his desire to set the securely placed, earthly, rooted human in clear distinction to the uprooted, delocalized post-human. As a function of memory that is made possible by retention, itself the function of the human prostheses constitutive of any world, "place-ment" of the dead begins to appear just as "virtual" or "synthetic" as the "posthuman." It is only what Harrison himself calls the synthetic activity of mind that creates a world in which memory can be kept. The extrapsy-chic and exosomatic capacities of the human articulated in Harrison's ac-count of retention, and hence the ground of human legacy or inheritance in his analysis, imply an immeasurable network of institutions, languages, and practices that sustain human memory over time. This means, I think, that burial and retrieval themselves are always already "virtual" in a man-ner Harrison's analysis requires but avoids—and perhaps requires for rea-sons relating to the fact that death "as such" never becomes actual in the full presence of any present.

The difficulty of placing or locating death is related in Heidegger's thought to the open character of worldhood as structure and temporality of existence as possibility. While Harrison hopes to save place in order to make us "at home" in our dying, and while he is no doubt right to note an anxious flight from death that pervades modern and contemporary culture, one can still ask whether the desire to be at home in our dying might not it-self involve some avoidance of the uncanny character of death—my "own" death, on which Heidegger focuses, but also, in the end, the death or demise of others. As a possibility that I can never realize "as such" in any present presence, my death signals the strange possibility of an impossibility, the uttermost "not yet," which never becomes actual, for me, in any experi-ence. That strangeness, as the possibility of an impossibility, and hence as irreducible to actuality or experience, is inextricably tied to the character

---

Awestruck by his own incomprehensibility, he calls out to God: *How great, my God is this force of memory, how exceedingly great! Like a vast and boundless subterranean shrine . . . the mind is not large enough to contain itself. . . .* Long before Freud, Jung, and Lacan, Augustine recognizes the force of unconscious *thinking*. Since "the mind is not large enough to contain itself," thinking can exceed consciousness as well as self-consciousness. This awareness only deepens the mystery of subjectivity. . . . This is not, of course, the end of Augustine's journey. Eventually he passes beyond the "huge court of memory" to the throne of God, where every mystery disappears. When the last screen is lifted, knowledge and self-knowledge form a perfect union. (201–2)

As this last line suggests, the apophatic element in Augustine does reach its limit—in a way that it does not, I believe, in a thinker like Eriugena, for whom even God never comprehends himself, or already in a precursor to Eriugena such as Gregory.

of worldhood as a totality of referential relations that open and sustain possible ways of being—no one of which, nor even the total sum of which,
can ever make fully present or actual the world "as such," which as open
structure and temporality of possibility is nothing susceptible to the logic
of actualization or presentation.

If burial implies a gathering and retention made possible thanks to the
prosthetic and distributed worlds we create and sustain, inherit and pass
down, then burial seems in fact to resist or unsettle secure placement of
the dead—and of our dying—and hence to call into question the location
of heritage itself. It is along these lines, note, that Harrison himself will
distinguish authentically human inheritance from mere genetic lineage,
insisting that the former always exceeds the latter because of its worldly
character: "However vast or narrow their field of operations may turn out
to be, genes remain at best only one among countless dwelling places where
the ancestor carries on an afterlife. If the dead restricted themselves to our
genes history would be a simpler and no doubt saner story, but for better or
worse the dead are not content to reside in our genes alone, for genes are not
worlds, and the dead seek above all to share our worlds" (*DD*, 84). If Harrison signals here the narrowness of the gene in order to distinguish it from
world, which has the broader, networked character that may well unsettle
what Harrison wants to argue about place, one can also wonder whether
the relation of gene and world is not more intimate than this distinction
suggests—and one can ask, in turn, what such intimacy implies about the
interplay between the human and technology, genetic and otherwise.

First, if indeed genes are not worlds, they can perhaps no longer be figured simply as the given real, or as a nature wholly distinct from culture,
insofar as emerging genetic technologies increasingly make of the gene
something more like another element of humanity's retentive and projective world-creating activity. The genetic "itself" becomes something to be
written and rewritten, along with the other elements of worldhood that Harrison signals. Genetic technology, like much else in our emerging technoscientific networks, confounds any clear and stable distinction between a
given or automatic nature and a created, and freely creative, culture. Indeed, it seems no longer simply the case that culture marks our "second"
nature. It is also the case, increasingly, that nature itself is already cultural,
and vice versa, and this not merely in the sense of the naive cultural constructivism that shapes so much recent academic work in the humanities.
Second nature is already first, just as first nature is already second, in such a
way that neither the naive constructivism of many humanists nor the naive
realism of many scientific types is adequate. Insofar as the genetic in its

"natural" sense becomes a function of human creative capacity, the weave between nature and culture becomes inextricable, and the gene is no longer wholly separable (if it ever really was) from the structures and temporality of human worldhood.

Second, while the technological capacity thanks to which the nature of genes becomes increasingly cultural can seem to threaten the property of the human, so as to call for resistance in the name of tradition or of legacy, it may well be that such capacity is in fact a requirement of any tradition at all—and that it is grounded, in fact, in an essential lack of human essence or definition, an indetermination of the human thanks to which alone the human can, or indeed must, become technological.[11] Thanks to such an indetermination, the property of the human may be neither fixed in itself nor transmitted over time with the automatic character that many would imagine the gene to possess—and which many would hope to find also today in the kind of tradition that would save us from technology's dangers.

The appeal to tradition and its codified values can tend in the direction of a reproductive logic that wants to be as automatic (or as "natural") as the "genetic" reproduction of a species may seem to be (according to a kind of genetic literalism or fetishism that Donna Haraway, among others, productively calls into question).[12] What such a tendency of tradition ignores, however, is the indetermination and freedom that alone first demand and then enable something like human tradition, itself perhaps a redundant formulation. Maintaining throughout its (never actually achieved) maturity the indeterminate potential of its (eternal) infancy, the human as indiscrete image, or as neotenic, while inheriting an immeasurable memory of history and tradition (natural and cultural, the two increasingly interwoven), proves endlessly plastic, innovative, and endowed with potential thanks precisely to its lack of fixed nature, essential definition, or lawful program. The human lack of specialization or program, its relative freedom from any proper place, thus becomes the very condition of inventive capacity, the ground of human world building. To be world building is in fact not to have or possess a proper place, but always already to be creating, and hence leaving, place—in such a way that I cannot ever possess what I truly create. The ground of such creation is an indetermination that guards the openness of potential that is "proper" to the human—which can be taken to mean that

11. This lack, furthermore, might prove to be a point where the human, as creature of culture or worldhood, and *Homo sapiens*, as natural species being, condition one another in intimate ways.

12. See Donna Haraway, "Deanimations: Maps and Portraits of Life Itself," in *Picturing Science Producing Art*, ed. Caroline Jones and Peter Galison (New York: Routledge, 1998).

what is most proper to the human is its impropriety, what most distinctive its indistinction. These are pivotal themes, of course, in twentieth-century post-Heideggerian thought and themes developed also, I've tried to suggest, in the course of mystical tradition.

Such openness is tied essentially both to the mortality of the human (Being-toward-death as the horizon of a never actualized possibility) and, correlatively, to its freedom from the automatic repetition of code or law. Giorgio Agamben, implicitly extending lines of analysis from Heidegger's *Fundamental Concepts of Metaphysics*, associates such a code repeatedly with the genetic—and with the animal as defined by blind subjection to genetic repetition within a fixed environment: "Animals are not concerned with possibilities of their soma that are not inscribed in the germen; contrary to what might be thought, they pay no attention whatsoever to that which is mortal (the soma is, in each individual, that which in any case is doomed to die), and they develop only the infinitely repeatable possibilities fixed in the genetic code. They attend only to the Law—only to what is written."[13] By contrast to the animal, which is programmed rather strictly to repeat an already written code, and thus to inhabit an already fixed environment (making the animal, as Heidgger puts it, "world poor"), the neotenic human, because forever incomplete or indeterminate, must invent language and world, must become technological, within the irreducible openness of mortal potential. "The neotenic infant . . . would find himself in the condition of being able to pay attention precisely to what has not been written, to somatic possibilities that are arbitrary and uncodified; in his infantile totipotency, he would be ecstatically overwhelmed, cast out of himself, not like other living beings into a specific adventure or environment, but for the first time into a *world*" (*IP*, 96).

To be cast out into world, and into language, of course, is to be cast out into tradition, or into the conditions of inheritance I am exploring here with Harrison. Much in line with Harrison, indeed, Agamben locates the distinctively human within the exosomatic networks of world and language that make possible something like the retentions and transmissions that we call legacy or tradition. Such retention and transmission are grounded

13. I cite here Agamben's *Idea of Prose*, trans. Michael Sullivan and Sam Whitsitt. (Albany: State University of New York, 1995), 96; hereafter cited parenthetically as *IP*. For a more explicit and extended engagement with Heidegger's *Fundamental Concepts of Metaphysics*, see Agamben's *The Open: Man and Animal*, trans. Kevin Attell (Stanford: Stanford University Press, 2004), both of which are given a lucid and productive reading in relation to Rilke and German-Jewish thought in the opening chapter of Eric Santner's *On Creaturely Life: Rilke, Benjamin, Sebald* (Chicago: University of Chicago Press, 2006).

in an openness, or a potentiality, that distinguishes a genuinely living tradition from "every specific destiny and every genetic calling" (*IP*, 97). In this respect, Agamben's analysis highlights a trait of the human implied but underplayed by Harrison, and as I've suggested, operative at the heart also of posthuman configurations and mystical anthropologies alike: the human indetermination that would be required by any heritage or tradition that does not degenerate into lifeless (or death-dealing) repetition or self-replication. The openness of the human, within whose potential alone tradition might take place, is not something that can be located, and it is not inscribed, like a fixed code, within man. It never becomes present itself. It consists, indeed, in a kind of generative forgetting or thoughtlessness, an absence of man to himself—but a forgetting that makes memory possible, and an absence in which the human would find itself: "This is why before handing down any knowledge or tradition, man has to hand down the very thoughtlessness, the very indeterminate openness in which alone something like a concrete historical tradition has become possible" (*IP*, 97; translation modified). I read Agamben here to signal something akin to what Harrison envisages in terms of burial and retention, which are fundamental to memory and tradition but never exhausted by memory and tradition, which itself, in one common extreme, can bury, or close off, the open potential of burial.

Indeed, if such openness enables—and demands—tradition, tradition at the same time always threatens to close that openness through the all-too-certain, quasi-genetic effort to preserve and to transmit tradition's codified values, categories, or concepts. This is the danger of tradition about which Heidegger warns in *Being and Time* and elsewhere: the danger that things will be handed over to self-evidence and thus find only an inauthentic, not truly decisive, reception; the danger that "rootedness" in "authentic" tradition will become a more radical form of uprooting or inauthenticity, a kind of bewitchment akin to that of technological modernity, or even to the animality that such bewitchment can resemble.[14] As Heidegger notes, when tradition "becomes master, it does so in such a way that what it 'transmits' is made so inaccessible, proximally and for the most part, that it rather becomes concealed. Tradition takes what has come down to us and hands it over to self-evidence; it blocks access to those primordial 'sources' from which the categories and concepts handed down to us have in part been

---

14. The political dangers in this direction can be as acute as those one might identify in the mystification of a technoscientific and rationalized culture that does not know itself to be mystified. On this see, e.g., Stiegler, *La technique et le temps*, 1:25.

quite genuinely drawn."[15] Much like newspaper science's assumption that all is immediately accessible and understandable, the self-evident givenness toward which tradition can tend blocks a vital reception of tradition as something actually living and undergoing its own recurrent birth—which is genuine birth only if it could not have taken place, or if it could have been otherwise. The continuity of genuine tradition requires the possibility of its suspension, just as much as liberation from tradition must at the same time appropriate and sustain it. "Liberation from the tradition," as Heidegger writes in *Fundamental Concepts*, "is an ever new appropriation of its newly recognized strengths" (*FC*, 352), and genuine appropriation needs to be liberating. The vitality of a tradition, as lived historically, requires the possibility of its suspension. The alternative is clearly formulated: either the possibility of suspension or the suspension of possibility. In the latter case, a real and common one, no doubt, tradition ceases to be vital and turns into deadening and deathly rote.

Those speaking most vocally in the name of tradition today—often on the very question of genetic technology, but also on so much else—can well seem to tend in that direction. They appear to want to keep "traditional values" as inviolate and automatic as the genetic lineage they might also want to defend (and I set aside for now the often fantastic or illusory character of the tradition evoked). What they ignore, if we can follow analyses like those of Agamben or Harrison, both deeply indebted here to Heidegger, is that a genuine living tradition must keep continuity while remaining open to the unprogrammed, that it must see not life but death in any overly automatic transmission of its "values." The tendency toward an overcertain transmission or an automatic repetition or mimetic replication, often thought (or hoped) to preserve the values or property of a tradition, can well be read as a sign of cultural degradation. As Agamben notes, "genuine spirituality and culture do not forget this original, infantile vocation of human language, while the attempt to imitate the natural germen in order to transmit immortal and codified values in which neotenic openness once more shuts itself off in a specific tradition is precisely the characteristic of a degraded culture" (*IP*, 97). What distinguishes the genetic code from tradition, for Agamben, is that the former would save, by repeating blindly, biological properties of the human (or *Homo sapiens*) while the latter would not save any human property at all but transmit the distinctive lack of property that first makes tradition and its elements both necessary and possible. By contrast to genetic code as Agamben figures it, human tradition transmits not

15. Heidegger, *Being and Time*, 43 [21].

"essential characteristics of the species" but that which can in fact never be possessed, "that which has never been possessed as a specific property, but which is, precisely because of this, unforgettable: the being, the openness of the infantile soma, to which only the world, only language is adequate" (*IP*, 98). Of course, to say here that world or language is "adequate" to this infantile soma, a figure of open potential, is to say that it remains, like the being it supplements, while charged with the past, also ever indeterminate and incomplete. For that very reason, it can keep open the place and time of a creation whose work is never done.

To care for such openness, to save a humanity that remains creative because it remains indeterminate and incomplete, requires a temporality that can both guard the heritage of tradition and, at the same time, guard itself from the mechanicity and the closure toward which tradition can tend. The danger is that things will be handed over to self-evidence, and that they will be received not in an authentically creative and living fashion, according to the potential of a futurity not reduced already to presence and actuality, but in an automatic repetition that cancels any future, and any creation, by giving us to know and understand everything ahead of time, beginning with the knowledge or understanding of just who we are and where we stand. In handing things over to self-evidence by means of a codification turned overly programmatic, tradition loses its genuine, living memory and becomes instead a deceptive (or self-deceptive) form of forgetting or negligence—the kind of negligence, indeed, in which we might see religion's opposite.

In order for tradition to hand over creative potential, or an open future, it needs to remember otherwise—to transmit not codified or programmed content but the ground of creative tradition itself, which such codification can tend to close off. It needs to transmit what Agamben calls our infancy, or what Serres calls our constitutive forgetting or deprogramming. As Agamben puts it, what tradition in this sense needs to save in order to remain open and alive is what, in fact, we never have, what cannot ever "itself" be possessed: the indeterminacy, openness, and creative potential of the neotenic, of the human whose nature is to have no nature, whose definition is to elude definition. "Somewhere inside of us," Agamben writes, "the careless neotenic child continues his royal game. And it is his play that gives us time, that keeps ajar for us that never setting openness which the peoples and languages of the earth, each in its own way, watch over in order both to preserve and to hold back—and to preserve only to the extent that they defer" (*IP*, 98). To defer completion, to preserve the infantile: these are the means by which tradition gives—or is given by—the time of creation.

It is along very similar lines that Harrison interprets, quite productively, the notions of authenticity and repetition as these relate to tradition. "Authentic retrieval" of the past, Harrison insists, is not "mimetic repetition," as the genetic is for Agamben, but rather a function of freedom. Freedom, in this sense, is neither "blind rebellion" nor "slavish submission to the dead's authority" but rather the space and time in which the future is kept open by authentic retrieval of the past, which means, at bottom, a retrieval that could—and, again, this seems to me the possibility of all real creation, or genuine birth—also *not* take place. This means, for Harrison, that "authenticity liberates the possibility of choosing one's ancestors"—or that biology, or genetics, insofar as they prove inevitable, do not touch the essential of human inheritance (*DD*, 101–3).

What touches the essential of human inheritance is the freedom of a reception that is not automatic repetition, a retrieval of the past within the horizon of an unprogrammed and unprogrammable future, where we might anticipate—without foreseeing—the birth of possible worlds. The capacity *not* to receive the past here proves indispensable to authentic retrieval, which is creative or birth-giving, and that capacity, like the retrieval it makes possible, cannot do without the human infancy or indetermination in which we keep our lack of property and hence our capacity to be surprised—or awakened. From this perspective, the law of legacy that Harrison elaborates, whose ground in burial and retention he understands according to the logic that he names "lexification," might open a highly suggestive, if perhaps counterintuitive, understanding of human property and its transmission, or tradition, across generations.

A "historial and world-forming" form of "synthesis," lexification is "a retentive relating or binding by which the human mind, like our basic words, continuously accesses the priority into and out of which it is born. In its temporal and historical schematizing, it enables human directedness in the verbal, institutional, and cognitive domains through its synthesis of the law of legacy" (DD, 84–85). In defining lexification thus, Harrison exploits the etymology of law itself, or *lex*, that Vico develops in his *New Science*—where the question of law is always already a question of genealogy and inheritance. As Harrison notes, Vico gathered from the linguistic evidence that "the word *lex* or its root have to do with gathering, binding, relating, and collecting" (*DD*, 79; see *New Science* §240), and he tied such gathering back to its institutional foundations:

> If gathering acorns in the forests [the first meaning Vico assigns to *lex*] is a meaningful and not just a foraging activity, it is because the gatherer is already directed, is already intentionally oriented in his or

her behavior and thinking. Such intentionality is possible only because the gatherer is already humanly related to the predecessor, not merely biologically but institutionally, as it were. The earliest creeds, customs, myths, allegories, poetic characters, and natural languages that philology studies all point to this genealogical law—this being unto the dead, and through them unto the unborn—as the "something extra" that comes first in the gathering of the *lex*. One cannot get back behind the law of legacy. (*DD*, 82)

If we follow Harrison in this reading, then all law is in a basic sense law of inheritance. The property at stake in this inheritance is not first, if at all, private property in a modern capitalistic sense, which begins in Locke with the natural body. It is, rather, the immeasurable fund, both natural and cultural, bequeathed from the dead to the living, and through the living to the unborn—in and through the distributed, transgenerational work of lexification, whose derivation binds it explicitly to the preservation and transmission of property. In developing the term, Harrison notes that he intends by it what Vico understands by the term "authority," whose own original meaning is, for Vico, "property":

> "The term *auctores* was accordingly applied to those from whom we derive the title to property," in other words the ancestors, who were the original title holders of the property they bequeathed as well as the authors of the laws, institutions, and religions that sanctioned the legitimacy of those titles (*New Science* §386). Thus when Vico says of his *New Science* that one of its "principal aspects" is a "philosophy of authority," he does not mean a philosophy of private property but a philosophy of lexification: the relational law by which the dead maintain their hold on the worlds they have handed down to their descendants. We share with the animals our thrownness into gender and into our species-being, but in addition to those determinations we are also thrown into the authority of the past. (*DD*, 85–86)

If indeed we are thrown into our species-being (understood biologically or "naturally"), we need to supplement the analyses both of Harrison and of Agamben by noting that that very being, thanks to emerging technologies which are all, in some real sense, genetic, increasingly becomes a human project, just as our thrownness into the authority of the past (understood "culturally") is a function of the futural human project. The two, natural and cultural, are no longer clearly separable—thanks to a technological being that we can, in line both with recent posthuman discourse and with the traditions of mystical theology, see to be founded in a human lack of property. If lexification, "temporalizing and historicizing that which it conjoins, . . . turns sounds into words, time into ages, and humans into heirs" (*DD*, 85), then it implies what lies at the heart of our passage from infancy to world and language: a lack of property that allows for the reception and transmission of tradition in its vital openness, an oblivion that grounds all memory. The transmission, then, of human "property" in terms of authoritative legacy requires the transmission of what is threatened by tradition even as it is the condition of tradition: the eternal infant, the human lacking property, which is saved only in the measure that we save the capacity *not* to inherit, not to mime or repeat, that which tradition gives. We might say, then, that the neotenic human is necessarily also the neotemnic: to continue the new requires the possible recurrence of that cutting or suspension that might ever renew, ever awaken us in relation to the possibility of our worlds. And we cannot in fact know, with clarity or certainty, when or where prove operative the continuities and when or where the cuts.

⁕

If the tradition of Western metaphysics finds an exemplary formulation in the principle of sufficient reason, which eliminates all possible worlds in favor of the one and best, an unsettling of that tradition opens the thought of possible worlds and their infinity. "Without a why," the principle of insufficient reason, which we might see operative as much in mystical tradition as in the technoscience that Heidegger tied to metaphysics, reawakens the possible beyond the actual, and the actuality of possibility, in terms of infinite creation. As Serres notes, we may be overturning that scenario sketched by Leibniz, in which Theodore is shown by Pallas to the summit of a pyramid where "the actual world, our own, the unique, the best" (*RAM*, 171) sits atop all the possible worlds below, not chosen, left behind. Today, as Serres writes, "the possible worlds that God left below the sole real world, chosen for its excellence, we now throw before ourselves; inverting the creative act, we make spring up before us the range of the virtual in principles ready to be born" (*RAM*, 173). To give birth to possible worlds means to create worlds where birth is made possible, and such making possible can well be taken as a form of love.

. . . when care was crossing a river . . .

As I noted in opening the work now closing, my prior book, *Indiscretion: Finitude and the Naming of God*, moves between the question of a negative theology, which treats the human relation to God as a naming of the unnameable or a thinking of the unthinkable, and the question of a negative anthropology, which treats the finite, mortal existence of the human subject as a Being-toward the possibility of an impossibility—a possibility figured notably by the horizon of a death that remains distinctively mine, and conditions my experience essentially, even as it eludes the full presence or actuality of any thought or language. According to what I named the "apophatic analogy," we can never clearly distinguish nor simply identify the negative logic of such a Being-toward-God and the negative logic of such a Being-toward death because the final term of each relation remains, as figure of the impossible, inaccessible to the thinking and language where any such distinction or identification might be finally secured. In both cases, the dynamism of my thought and language, the open movement and inexhaustible possibility that ground experience, are conditioned by figures of the impossible that prove generous even as their attainment would mean my undoing.

In *The Indiscrete Image: Infinitude and Creation of the Human*, I have attempted to reflect and to build on the insights of *Indiscretion* by developing what I take to be the intimate ties between such a negative anthropology, which here highlights the creative capacity of the human as a function of its relative indetermination or infinitude, and a negative cosmology, according to which our "world," much like the human who dwells in it as indiscrete image, eludes full or final representation—which is to say, any "world picture" or "worldview" that presumes to render the whole intelligible by accounting sufficiently for its origin and its end, its principle and its goal. Such a representation of world, I have emphasized, tends to foreclose the possibility of genuine human creation by giving us to know or comprehend ahead of time, all too securely and without real question, just who we are and just where we stand. While many today will claim, and all too often in the name of religion, to save or to protect the human by finding its reliable definition and its inviolable dignity in "tradition" and in the "values" tradition would keep and transmit, I have argued rather that to define the human is perhaps more to lose it. A crucial determination of the human may well be its indetermination, which itself proves to be an indispensable condition of the creative and technological capacities without which tradition, among other things, cannot live. Rather than understand technological ways of being, then, as a threat to tradition and to the human it sustains, I have argued that tradition and its temporalities rely necessarily on our technological networks, and that the human who needs—and who enables—the technological is defined by its relative lack of definition. Much as I argued previously with respect to revelation and death, where any clear difference between deprivation and generosity can grow obscure,[1] so here the distinction between lack and plenitude can appear unstable, insofar as the emergence of our technological being on the ground of a seeming lack or indetermination is that which opens and enables the immeasurable wealth of our potential inheritance—which, as immeasurable, and like the future it keeps open, cannot be discretely placed or located.

One can develop such a tie between the human's lack of definition and the excess of its creative capacity, I have claimed, both through the resources of theological tradition, specifically in mystical turns often ignored by the self-proclaimed defenders of tradition, and through the resources of more recent thinking about technological humanity, which traditionalists and technophiles alike can fail to see in their religious significance. Highlighting both the importance of technological creativity in the depths of mystical theological tradition, on the one hand, and the religious or mystical character of today's technological culture, on the other, I attempt to show that these two can recall one another, and indeed intersect, in unexpected and illuminating ways.

My reading both of theological tradition and of technological humanity thus stands in some tension not only with reactive and reactionary

1. See especially *Indiscretion*, 231–36.

voices speaking all too loudly of late in the name of "tradition" and of the "human" we would supposedly find there, kept safe and sound, but also with the rightly influential account in which Heidegger elucidates intimate linkages between the ontotheological tradition of an omniscient and omnipotent Creator God and a modern metaphysics and culture of the human subject whose intellectual and technological self-assertion can indeed aspire toward forms of mastery and control much like those of that Creator God. While Heidegger's account remains as compelling as it is far-reaching, it does nonetheless leave room, I've suggested, for these alternative readings both of theological tradition and of technological culture. Taken not only in light of each other but also in their complex interplay as I stage it through an engagement with *Finnegans Wake*, these readings suggest a path along which to think about creativity not in terms of omniscience and omnipotence, conception and production, but in terms of insurmountable ignorance and inexhaustible possibility. To speak of such possibility as irreducible or indeed infinite, I should emphasize, surely does not imply that this creative subject is capable of anything and everything, or that the subject somehow escapes any and all constraints and conditions. To the contrary, the possibility at stake is, like any real possibility, the function of those constraints and conditions attendant to our radical finitude—but it remains also ever open, or infinite, because the subject who dwells creatively within it can never exhaust such possibility by converting it into any present actuality. Beyond the possibility for this or that eventual actuality, which might lend itself to determinate representation, calculation, and management, the possibility of the human as indiscrete image remains indeterminate or infinite. The subject of such possibility remains always yet to be, in excess of the objectified actualities contained or controlled by foresight, and thus that subject's constitutive involvement in processes of creation and self-creation are ever underway, always incomplete, and conditioned by unknowing.

While *Indiscretion* treats such ignorance and possibility by focusing on our Being-toward the horizon of an impossible death—whose generosity, I insist, remains all too often overlooked or denied—the present work highlights their tie with our essentially related Being-toward-birth. To be mortal is, if anything, to be born, as well as the reverse—and one need not look far to see that the power of birth has everything to do with the proximity of death, just as our dying can pointedly recall the labor of birth. The two remain inextricable, and in their coimplication they condition that form of human possibility, or that time of human life, which might resist the kinds of representation, calculation, and management to which an objectified actuality can seem to lend itself. It is this inextricable tie between the mortal and the natal that leads me to conclude, in chapter 6, with a reflection on the "birth of possible worlds." By this phrase I intend both the ongoing creation of worlds exceeding the already actual—those already conceived or represented, in their presumed totality, from origin to end—and worlds that keep open the possibility at stake in birth: a possibility, that is, for the unexpected coming and creation of a gift that could well not have been and could at any moment cease to be.

As I suggested in closing the last chapter, and as I will elaborate in a new project now underway, I suspect that a key to thinking about this birth of possible worlds is to make the question of world, as place and time of open possibility, also the question of a love that we might take to involve, at its heart, the obscure and delicate work—and play— of "making possible." Heidegger himself, perhaps not best known as a thinker of love, nonetheless suggests such a connection in his "Letter on Humanism," where he posits that

> to look after a "thing" or a "person" in its essence means to love it, to favor it [*Sich einer "Sache" oder einer "Person" in ihrem Wesen annehmen, das heißt: sie lieben: sie mögen*]. Thought in a more original way, such favoring means to bestow essence as a gift [*das Wesen schenken*]. Such favoring is the proper essence of enabling, which not only can achieve this or that but also can let something essentially unfold in its provenance, that is, let it be [*Solches Mögen ist das eigentliche Wesen des Vermögens, das nicht nur dieses oder jenes leisten, sondern etwas in seiner Her-kunft "wesen," das heißt sein lassen kann*]. It is on the "strength" of such enabling by favoring that something is properly able to be. (LH, 220 [316]; translation modified)[2]

---

2. The fuller context in Heidegger's "Letter on Humanism" (LH, 220 [316]) suggests that thinking itself can be seen to presuppose the possibility of love:

Thinking comes to an end when it slips out of its element. The element is what enables thinking to be a thinking. The element is what properly enables: it is the enabling [*das Vermögen*]. It embraces thinking and so brings it into its essence. Said plainly thinking is the thinking of Being. The genitive says something twofold. . . . Thinking *is*—this says: Being has fatefully embraced its essence. To embrace a "thing" or a "person" in its essence means to love it, to favor it. Thought in a more original way such favoring [*Mögen*] means to bestow essence as a gift. Such favoring is the proper essence of enabling, which not only can achieve this or that but also can let something actually unfold in its providence, that is, let it be. It is on the "strength" of such enabling by favoring that something is properly able to be. This enabling is what is properly "possible" [*das Mögliche*], whose essence resides in favoring. From this favoring Being enables think-

If indeed it is love that gives being, and if it is love first that enables thinking, then it does so, I bet, by opening and sustaining the kind of possibility
that makes for a world beyond picture.

To develop the question of such a world and its possibility as a question
of love implies also developing the question of love and its possibility as
a question of world. It means, then, among other things, challenging both
those modern human sciences and those theological traditions that have
tended to separate world and love, either by reducing world to picture, thus
making of the world a kind of idolatrous mirror that excludes the open
possibility I take to be at stake in love, or by insisting on a love whose
transcendent bias—for the eternal and immutable—implies, in the end, a
radical separation from, if not a hatred for, the world.

Many in the field of religious studies often think themselves to depart
from theology when, in fact, their assumption that world is, in the first
place, to be thought as "worldview" or as "picture"—which means as a
representation formed, measured, and ostensibly comprehended by the
human subject—may well be the assumption of a distinctively modern,
Western metaphysics of the human subject that itself extends a Christian
theology, or ontotheology, of the Creator God. If world is not, however, to
be captured as view or picture—if world is more that which we inhabit as
the open structure and temporality of a possibility that escapes, even as it
enables, all representation—then the field of religious studies might well
benefit by thinking the creative human as indiscrete image, and world as
place and time of that image. As I suggested in chapter 4, such a figure of
the human, if largely overlooked, actually does appear already—in terms
of the neotenic or pedomorphic—at the heart of social-scientific theories,
crucial to religious studies, of the human as world builder. In the measure
that such a figure of the human entails not only a concept of lack but also
the lack of a concept, in the measure that the human's incompletion and
incomprehension are the conditions of creative capacity, this figure recalls
along the surprising but suggestive paths I've signaled here the anthropology of mystical theological traditions, which trace creative freedom to a
similar negative ground. Among the paths thus opened is one that might

---

ing. The former makes the latter possible. Being is the enabling-favoring, the "may be"
[das "Mög-liche"]. As the element, Being is the "quiet power" of the favoring-enabling,
that is, of the possible.

On relations between this approach to possibility and Cusan theology, see, again, Peter Casarella's very insightful reading in "Nicholas of Cusa and the Power of the Possible," and the similar
but briefer evocation of Cusa and the Heideggerian sense of possibility in Richard Kearney, *The
God Who May Be* (Bloomington: Indiana University Press, 2001), 103–5.

resist the metaphysics of the subject that Heidegger and heirs can rightly see and critique in modernity broadly and, more narrowly, in the human or social sciences. To develop religious studies as the analysis of world building by the human as indiscrete image requires that we abandon the supposition that world is equal to worldview. We thereby reopen the human as ongoing—because creative—question rather than as defined object already accounted for within a totality whose basic principles and goals are already securely decided. In hearing the mystical resonance within the very human who proves to be world builder, or in seeing the human, as indiscrete image, imaged in the world it creates, we can begin to think the human world beyond the closure of modern metaphysics—and hence in deviation from the kind of idolatry one can well read in such metaphysics.

While departing from any idol, however, the indiscrete image may fall short of the icon by contrast to which the idol is often defined. Along these lines, part of the attempt to think through the linkage I want to posit between the human as indiscrete image and world as irreducible to world picture is the effort to situate the indiscrete image between the idol and the icon, or perhaps more in resistance to the clear alternatives they can seem to pose. In evoking these terms I have in mind primarily the meanings they assume in the theological and phenomenological thought of Marion, in which idolatrous consciousness, by making the divine answer to the conditions and capacities of human thought, finds less the divine in its immeasurable excess and more the closure of an invisible mirror where the human subject, through its vision of the divine, actually returns to itself in a kind of economic circle. "The gaze makes the idol," as Marion puts it in *God without Being*, "not the idol the gaze."[3] By contrast to an idolatrous consciousness, where I, through the priority of my intentionality, become measure or indeed maker of all that appears, an iconic consciousness involves a radical reversal of such intentionality through the priority and excess of that which gives itself over that which I can measure or make by means of the categories and concepts already at my disposal. If this distinction between idol and icon concerns in large part a priority of self over other, or, correlatively, an eclipse of the given by the made, the indiscrete image suspends such decision between given and made, just as it figures the relation of self and other by means of a poetic knowing that is perhaps best figured as a cobirth or co-*naissance*.[4] By contrast to any calculated production or to

3. Jean-Luc Marion, *God without Being: Hors-Texte*, trans. Thomas A. Carlson (Chicago: University of Chicago Press, 1991), 10.

4. This is an allusion to Paul Claudel's highlighting the co-*naissance* in *connaissance*, taken

the divine providence that can resemble it, both of which in effect already see and control what is coming—and thus beyond the sway of a modern metaphysics and technological culture that can turn idolatrous insofar as in them "it seems as though man everywhere and always encounters only himself"[5]—in the creativity of birth I am born, ongoingly and in unforeseeable ways, through relation with that to which I also give birth, which includes the enabling constraints of a world that exceeds representation even as it conditions all birth. While unsettling the closure associated with the idol, then, the indiscrete image and its capacity for birth—which is to say, its nature—entails an openness that remains vital thanks to its ongoing relation with, rather than its separation from, the world. It is in this respect, perhaps, that the indiscrete image does not claim the icon's transcendence.

While the logic of such a contrast between idol and icon has many analogues in Heideggerian and post-Heideggerian thought, Marion's much discussed analysis of the icon—and of the human being who, as incomprehensible, answers to the icon or indeed turns iconic—is indebted notably to Emmanuel Levinas's ethical discourse concerning the face of the other as call to responsibility. A significant part of that debt to Levinas, as I suggested in chapter 4, is the extraworldly tendency of the iconic human. Just as for Levinas the face of the other amounts to a "signification without context," so for Marion the iconic human, by contrast to the idolatrous, comes to reflect an invisibility that separates the human from the world. "No longer does the human being distinguish him- or herself from the rest of the world as the 'Platzhalter des Nichts' ('lieutenant of the nothing') or the 'Hirt des Seins' ('shepherd of Being') but as the icon of the incomprehensible. Man's invisibility separates him from the world and consecrates him as holy for the Holy" (PU, 16). However, while Marion's understanding of the icon—and of the human as indefinable insofar as iconic—owes this clear debt to Levinasian ethics and its claim that the significance of the face precedes and transcends any context, and hence any world, the association of iconic precedence and transcendence with a movement of *love* that separates the human from the world is perhaps more in line with Augustinian theology than with Levinasian ethics (where the face of the other actually accuses and persecutes me far more than it loves me).

As I pointed out in chapter 2 while discussing his influential attack on "curiosity" and its roots in a disordered love, Augustine, following Paul

---

up in illuminating ways within Pierre Hadot's rich discussion of the Universe-Poem theme in Western thought and writing. See Hadot, *Le voile d'Isis* (Paris: Gallimard, 2004), 214–18.

5. Heidegger, "Question concerning Technology," 27.

and John, tends to think "world" in terms of a postoriginal fall that results in binding forms of sinful habit that exclude any genuine future by closing us within a form of repetition that imitates, perversely, the unchanging eternity of God. While our true beginning and end, and hence our true life and being, can be found only in the eternal unity of God (who is without beginning and end, without past and future), we are fallen, according to Augustinian thought, into a temporal and alienated condition that gives death by closing off access to that timeless origin and end. Our fallen and deadly love is directed to "this world," which passes away, rather than to the God who abides forever—thus contradicting 1 John's command that we "not love the world or the things in the world" (1 John 2:15). In light especially of my attempt in the preceding chapters to resist overly clear and common distinctions between nature and culture, or between the scientific and the sociopolitical, we should note here that Augustine's interpretation of this command turns in large part on his distinction between a created or "natural" order—the heavens and the earth and the sea—that remains by origin good and a fallen "social" order that corrupts our relation with the natural by encouraging love for the creature instead of the Creator. "For the world," as Augustine writes in his second tractate on the first epistle of John, one of whose central themes is love's relation to world, "is a designation not only of this fabric that God made, the heavens and the earth, the sea, visible and invisible things, but the inhabitants of the world are called the world, as a house is called both the walls and those dwelling in it. . . . For all lovers of the world, because they dwell in the world by their loving, as they dwell in the sky whose heart is on high and yet walk by their flesh on the earth—all lovers of the world, then, are called the world."[6] Such "concupiscence of the world"—whose three main forms are "desire of the flesh," "desire of the eyes," and "the ambition of this age" (ambitio saeculi)[7]—is that from which, according to Augustine, a fallen humanity needs liberation. Thus

6. Augustine, *Tractates on the First Epistle of John*, tractate 2, §12, in *The Fathers of the Church, St. Augustine: Tractates on the Gospel of John 112–24, Tractates on the First Epistle of John*, trans. John W. Rettig (Washington, D.C.: Catholic University of America Press, 1995), 154–55; translation modified. See, within a review of thinking on "world," Heidegger's discussion of this Augustinian take in relation to Pauline and John, in *The Essence of Reasons* [*Vom Wesen des Grundes*, 1929], trans. Terrence Malick (Evanston: Northwestern University Press, 1969), 51–57. Along similar lines, see also the citation and discussion of these passages in Hannah Arendt, *Love and Saint Augustine*, ed. Joanna Vecchiarelli Scott and Judith Chelius Stark (Chicago: University of Chicago Press, 1996), 66.

7. The "ambition of this age" is what Augustine, in exegeting his Old Latin version of the biblical text, gives for "the pride of life" (ἡ ἀλαζονεία τοῦ βίου), which appears in 1 John 2:15 along with "the desire of the flesh" (ἡ ἐπιθυμία τῆς σαρκὸς) and "the desire of the eyes" (ἡ ἐπιθυμία τῶν ὀφθαλμῶν).

liberation here entails a redirection of love from the creature to the Creator, a movement beyond the "river of temporal things."[8]

This extraworldly tendency of love in Augustine and his heirs, like his distinction between the natural and social worlds, relates in a crucial way, I think, to his valuation of our humanity's "becoming a question" to itself. Here it is important to keep in mind the difference I have tried to mark between the mystery of the human in Augustine and the mystery of the human in such mystics as those I engaged in chapter 3. In the latter, I've argued, I am a mystery to myself just insofar as I am a living image of God, whereas in the former I become a question to myself less in my resemblance to God and more through my sinful, deadly fall away from God—itself the function of a love that is disordered because directed to the world. By contrast to a thinker like Cusa—who, as Cassirer notes, and departing from a main tendency of medieval thought, may no longer think redemption as liberation from the world insofar as he "no longer recognized a separation between man and nature"[9]—Augustine understands the rightly ordered love that saves the human to transcend, finally, the human and natural orders that are conditioned by time and its passage. If, as according to Augustine, I become a question to myself owing to sinful estrangement from my true life or being, which rests in the eternal unity of God, then in asking that question, I am beginning my quest to recover such life or being, along with the unending happiness it alone can give. This means, in short, that I am beginning to ask myself "out of the world."[10] And indeed, as I pointed out above, when Augustine notes in the *Confessions* that he has become a question to himself, he does not really affirm or celebrate that question but in fact laments it as an ailment or infirmity about which he prays to God "have pity on me and heal me."[11] To enjoy such healing, for Augustine and his heirs, entails nothing less than finding oneself on the only right side of the question, "What do you want? To have temporal things and to pass away together with time or not to love the world and to live forever with God?"[12]

By contrast to such an Augustinian take on love, world, and the human as question, the project emerging here is to think, in and through the human

8. Augustine, *Tractates on the First Epistle of John*, tractate 2, §10, p. 152.

9. Cassirer, *The Individual and the Cosmos*, 40.

10. As Hannah Arendt well puts it in *Love and Saint Augustine*: "By saying 'I have become a question to myself,' man has begun to ask himself out of the world in his quest for 'true being'" (58).

11. Augustine, *Confessions* 10.33.

12. Augustine, *Tractates on the First Epistle of John*, tractate 2, §10, p. 152.

as indiscrete image, a love that might remain worldly while nonetheless escaping and resisting the closure of idolatry, or the habit of sin, and the repetition of these in a modernity that Heidegger and his heirs rightly critique for its reduction of world to picture and its eclipse of genuine futurity. Not needing, or wanting, to separate or except itself from the world in order to keep a truly open future, nor aiming to comprehend and thus control the world through its objectification and representation, this would be a love enjoyed by the human as indiscrete image for a world that itself proves no less enigmatic, and no more delimited, than the human who dwells co-creatively in it. The task, I think, is to see the incomprehensibility of the human as a function of its inextricable ties, both mortal and natal, with the world—and to see that world, itself no more captured or conquered by picture than is the human, as one in which and for which love opens rather than closes possibility and its temporality. We need, in other words, to "become a question" to ourselves, affirmatively, by asking ourselves "into" the world, and we need to think the birth of world as emerging from a love of it.

To think the love of world as a making possible is indeed to keep open the possibility of birth, which like the possibility of death is one with which we are never done, one never wholly actualized, and thus one that escapes the logic of calculation and management, production and control. By thinking love as making possible, and vice versa, we can perhaps tie love back to a world no longer thought as the objective actuality of all that is or could be—in some presumed presence already conceived or represented—but rather as a totality, or an open whole, of relations that sustain the most fundamental possibility of mortal and natal existence. Not exhausted by any actuality, such a world and existence escape any one image or picture and thus keep open the possibility of a mortal birth that is perhaps also the heart of nature. By situating such love, as making possible, within the world, by making it a condition of the world, this line of thinking might also push us to reconnect those two senses of world that Augustine, along with a good part of Western thought and culture to this day, separated out from one another: the world as our human way of being with others and the world as natural fabric of the heavens and the earth and the sea. We can no longer afford to hold this untenable distinction, for the human way of being in the world, its very possibility, is inextricably woven with that natural fabric. To think these two more fully in their interplay calls for a love of world in its temporality, which is at the same time a love for others in their mortal birth. In this direction, I can perhaps love the anonymous mass of humanity by attending to the most local and concrete places in which I dwell, just as my care for the fabric of the heavens, earth, and sea, globally construed, can become a form of love for the singular individuals with whom I live, and die, most intimately.

There is perhaps no act less loving than to step in for another, or indeed all others, so as to make everything already actual for them, given ahead of time; and there is perhaps no act more loving, or more difficult to define, or quite simply more difficult, than to give another the actuality of possibility itself—to give another time and life. The world of such life and time would be home to the human as indiscrete image, who is not contained by ideals or archetypes, not reflected in the idols placed before it in such a way as to close possibility in the name of the already actual. Not an idol, then, because never finally defined or delimited, the indiscrete image also falls short of that icon whose transcendence entails separation or exception from the world. Neither idol nor icon, the indiscrete image lives in a love that turns, by nature, secular.

BIBLIOGRAPHY

Agamben, Giorgio. *Homo Sacer: Sovereign Power and Bare Life.* Translated by Daniel Heller-Roazen. Stanford, Calif.: Stanford University Press, 1998.

———. *Idea of Prose.* Translated by Michael Sullivan and Sam Whitsitt. Albany: State University of New York, 1995.

———. *Idée de la prose.* Translated by Gérard Macé. Paris: Christian Bourgeois, 1988.

———. *The Open: Man and Animal.* Translated by Kevin Attell. Stanford, Calif.: Stanford University Press, 2004.

———. "The Passion of Facticity." In *Potentialities: Collected Essays in Philosophy,* translated by Daniel Heller-Roazen. Stanford, Calif.: Stanford University Press, 1999.

———. *The Time That Remains: A Commentary on the Letter to the Romans.* Stanford, Calif.: Stanford University Press, 2005.

Agamben, Giorgio, and Valeria Piazza. *L'ombre de l'amour: Le concept de l'amour chez Heidegger.* Translated by Charles Alunni and Joël Gayraud. Paris: Rivages, 2003.

Altizer, Thomas J. J. *The Contemporary Jesus.* Albany: State University of New York Press, 1997.

———. *History as Apocalypse.* Albany: State University of New York Press, 1985.

Aquinas, Thomas. *Summa Theologica.* Translated by Fathers of the English Dominican Province. New York: Benziger Brothers, 1947.

Arendt, Hannah. *Love and Saint Augustine.* Edited by Joanna Vecchiarelli Scott and Judith Chelius Stark. Chicago: University of Chicago Press, 1996.

Atherton, James S. *The Books at the Wake: A Study of Literary Allusions in James Joyce's Finnegans Wake.* Mamaroneck, N.Y.: Paul P. Appel, 1959.

Attridge, Derek, ed. *The Cambridge Companion to James Joyce.* Cambridge: Cambridge University Press, 1990.

———. *Joyce Effects: On Language, Theory, and History.* Cambridge: Cambridge University Press, 2000.

Aubert, Jacques. *The Aesthetics of James Joyce.* Baltimore: Johns Hopkins University Press, 1992.

Augustine. *Confessions.* Translated by R. S. Pine-Coffin. New York: Penguin Books, 1961.

———. *Confessions.* Edited by James J. O'Donnell. Oxford: Oxford University Press, 1992.

——. *Homilies on 1 John.* In *Augustine: Later Works*, edited by John Burnaby. Philadelphia: Westminster Press, 1980.

——. *In Epistolam Joannis ad Parthos.* In *Patrologiae Cursus Completus, Series Latina*, vol. 35, edited by J.-P. Migne. Paris, 1841.

——. *On Christian Doctrine.* Translated by D. W. Robertson Jr. New York: Macmillan, 1958.

Badiou, Alain. *Saint Paul: The Foundation of Universalism.* Stanford, Calif.: Stanford University Press, 2003.

Balsamo, Gian. *Joyce's Messianism: Dante, Negative Existence, and the Messianic Self.* Columbia: University of South Carolina Press, 2004.

——. *Rituals of Literature: Joyce, Dante, Aquinas, and the Tradition of Christian Epics.* Lewisburg: Bucknell University Press, 2004.

Balthasar, Hans Urs von. *Presence and Thought: An Essay on the Religious Philosophy of Gregory of Nyssa.* San Francisco: Ignatius Press, 1995.

Beckett, Samuel. "Dante . . . Bruno. Vico . . . Joyce." In *Our Exagmination Round His Factification for Incamination of Work in Progress.* Edited by Sylvia Beach. Paris: Shakespeare and Company, 1929. Reprint, Norfolk, Conn.: New Directions, 1939.

Beierwaltes, Werner. "Absolute Identity: Neoplatonic Implications in Schelling's 'Bruno.'" In *Contemporary German Philosophy*, vol. 2, translated by Darrel E. Christensen and F. A. Uehlein. University Park: Pennsylvania State University, 1983.

——. "Cusanus and Eriugena." *Dionysius* 13 (1989): 115–52.

——. *Identität und Differenz.* Frankfurt am Main: Vittorio Klosterman, 1980.

——. *Identität und Differenz: Zum prinzip cusanischen Denkens.* Düsseldorf: Westdeutscher Verlag, 1977.

——. "Language and Its Object." In *Jean-Scot Ecrivain*, edited by G.-H. Allard. Montreal: Editions Bellarmin, 1986.

——. "Negati Affirmatio: Welt als Metapher/ Zur Grundlegung einer mittelalterlichen Ästhetik durch Johannes Scotus Eriugena." In *Jean Scot Erigène et l'histoire de la philosophie.* Paris: Éditions du Centre National de la Recherche Scientifique, 1977.

——. "The Revaluation of John Scottus Eriugena in German Idealism." In *The Mind of Eriugena*, edited by John J. O'Meara and Ludwig Bieler. Dublin: Irish University Press, 1973.

——. *Visio Facialis: Sehen ins Angesicht, Zur Coincidenz des endlichen und unendlichen Blicks bei Cusanus.* Munich: Verlag der Bayerischen Akademie der Wissenschaften, 1988.

Benjamin, Walter. "The Work of Art in the Age of Mechanical Reproduction." In *Illuminations*, edited by Hannah Arendt. New York: Schocken Books, 1968.

Berger, Peter. *The Sacred Canopy.* New York: Garden Books, 1967.

Bergson, Henri. *The Two Sources of Morality and Religion.* Translated by R. Ashley Audra and Cloudesley Brereton. Notre Dame, Ind.: Notre Dame University Press, 1977.

Bishop, John. Introduction to *Finnegans Wake.* New York: Penguin Books: 1999.

——. *Joyce's Book of the Dark: Finnegans Wake.* Madison: University of Wisconsin Press, 1986.

Blanchot, Maurice. "Literature and the Right to Death." In *The Station Hill Blanchot*

Reader: Fiction and Literary Essays, edited by George Quasha. Barrytown, N.Y.: Station Hill Press, 1999.

Bloom, Harold, ed. *Modern Critical Views: James Joyce*. New York: Chelsea House, 1986.

Blumenberg, Hans. *The Legitimacy of the Modern Age*. Translated by Robert Wallace. Cambridge, Mass.: MIT Press, 1983.

Bolk, Louis. "La genèse de l'homme." *Arguments* 4, no. 18, 2nd trimester (1960).

————. *Das Problem der Menschwerdung*. Jena, 1926.

————. "Le problème de la genèse de l'homme." *Revue Française de Psychanalyse*, March/April, 1961.

Borges, Jorge Luis. *Atlas*. Translated by Anthony Kerrigan. New York: E. P. Dutton, 1985.

————. "A Defense of the Kabbalah." In *Selected Non-Fictions*, edited by Eliot Weinberger. New York: Penguin Books, 1999.

————. "Everything and Nothing." In *Everything and Nothing*, translated by Donald A. Yates et al. New York: New Directions, 1999.

————. "A Fragment on Joyce." In *Selected Non-Fictions*, edited by Eliot Weinberger. New York: Penguin Books, 1999.

————. "From Someone to Nobody." In *Selected Non-Fictions*, edited by Eliot Weinberger. New York: Penguin Books, 1999.

————. "Joyce's Latest Novel." In *Selected Non-Fictions*, edited by Eliot Weinberger. New York: Penguin Books, 1999.

————. "Joyce's *Ulysses*." In *Selected Non-Fictions*, edited by Eliot Weinberger. New York: Penguin Books, 1999.

————. "The Nothingness of Personality." In *Selected Non-Fictions*, edited by Eliot Weinberger. New York: Penguin Books, 1999.

————. "The Total Library." In *Selected Non-Fictions*, edited by Eliot Weinberger. New York: Penguin Books, 1999.

Bossuet, Jacques-Bénignee. *Traité de la concupiscence*. Edited by Ch. Urbain and Eug. Levesque. Paris: Éditions Fernand Roches, 1930.

Boyle, Marjorie O'Rourke. "Cusanus at Sea: The Topicality of Illuminative Discourse." *Journal of Religion* 71, no. 2 (April 1991).

Brient, Elizabeth. *The Immanence of the Infinite: Hans Blumenberg and the Threshold to Modernity*. Washington, D.C.: Catholic University of America Press, 2002.

Brown, Norman O. *Closing Time*. New York: Random House, 1973.

Bruno, Giordano. *Cause, Principle, and Unity and Essays on Magic*. Edited by Richard J. Blackwell and Robert de Lucca. Cambridge: Cambridge University Press, 1998.

————. *De la cause, du principe et de l'un*. Vol. 3 of *Oeuvres complètes*. Edited by Giovanni Aquilecchia. Paris: Belles Lettres, 1996.

————. *De l'infini, de l'univers et des mondes*. Vol. 4 of *Oeuvres complètes*. Edited by Giovanni Aquilecchia. Paris: Belles Lettres, 1995.

————. *The Expulsion of the Triumphant Beast*. Translated by Arthur D. Imerti. Lincoln: University of Nebraska Press, 1964.

Brüntrup, Alfons. *Können und Sein: Der Zusammenhang der Spätschriften des Nikolaus von Kues*. Munich and Salzburg: Verlag Anton Pustet, 1973.

Cabassut, André. "Curiosité." In *Dictionnaire de spiritualité ascétique et mystique*, vol. 2, pt. 2. Paris: Beauschesne, 1953.

Cadava, Eduardo, Peter Connor, and Jean-Luc Nancy, eds. *Who Comes After The Subject?* New York: Routledge, 1991.

Cage, John. *Roaratorio: Ein Irischer Circus über "Finnegans Wake."* Mainz: Ars Acustica, 1994.

———. *Silence.* Middletown: Wesleyan University Press, 1961.

———. *Writing for the Second Time through Finnegans Wake (Ausschnitt).* In *Roaratorio: Ein Irischer Circus über "Finnegans Wake."* Mainz: Ars Acustica, 1994.

———. *Writing through Finnegans Wake.* Tulsa: University of Tulsa Press, 1978.

Caputo, John D. *Deconstruction in a Nutshell: A Conversation with Jacques Derrida.* New York: Fordham University Press, 1997.

———. *More Radical Hermeneutics: On Not Knowing Who We Are.* Bloomington: Indiana University Press, 2000.

———. *The Mystical Element in Heidegger's Thought.* Athens: Ohio University Press, 1978.

———. *The Prayers and Tears of Jacques Derrida: Religion without Religion.* Bloomington: Indiana University Press, 1997.

Carlson, Thomas A. "Blindness and the Decision to See: On Revelation and Reception in Jean- Luc Marion." In *Counter-Experiences: Reading Jean-Luc Marion,* edited by Kevin Hart. Notre Dame, Ind.: University of Notre Dame Press, 2007.

———. "Consuming Desire's Deferral." In *Practices of Procrastination,* edited by Paul Bowman, Joanne Crawford, and Alison Rowley. *Parallax* 10 (January-March 1999).

———. *Indiscretion: Finitude and the Naming of God.* Chicago: University of Chicago Press, 1999.

———. "Locating the Mystical Subject." In *Mystics: Presence and Aporia,* edited by Michael Kessler and Christian Sheppard. Chicago: University of Chicago Press, 2003.

Carraud, Vincent. *Pascal et la philosophie.* Paris: Presses Universitaires de France, 1993.

Carrier, Michelle. "D'un Prométhée oublié." http://www.er.uqam.ca/nobel/mts123/carrier.html/.

Casarella, Peter J. "Nicholas of Cusa and the Power of the Possible." *American Catholic Philosophical Quarterly* 64, no. 1 (Winter 1990).

Casey, Edward S. *The Fate of Place: A Philosophical History.* Berkeley and Los Angeles: University of California Press, 1997.

Cassirer, Ernst. "Giovanni Pico della Mirandola: A Study in the History of Renaissance Ideas." *Journal of the History of Ideas* 3 (1942): 123–44 (pt. 1), 319–46 (pt. 2).

———. *The Individual and the Cosmos in Renaissance Philosophy.* Translated by Mario Domandi. New York: Harper and Row, 1963. Reprint, Mineola, N.Y.: Dover, 2000.

———. *Individuum und Kosmos in der Philosophie der Renaissance.* Darmstadt: Wissenschaftliche Buchgesellschaft, 1962.

Certeau, Michel de. "The Gaze of Nicholas of Cusa." *Diacritics* 17, no. 3 (1987).

———. "What We Do When We Believe." In *On Signs,* edited by Marshall Blonsky. Baltimore: Johns Hopkins University Press, 1985.

Christiani, Marta. "Le problème du lieu et du temps dans le livre Ier du "Periphyseon." In *The Mind of Eriugena,* edited by John J. O'Meara and Ludwig Bieler. Dublin: Irish University Press, 1973.

Christie, Yves. "Influences et retentissement de l'oeuvre de Jean Scot sur l'art médiéval: Bilan et perspectives." In *Eriugena Redivivus*, edited by Werner Beierwaltes. Heidelberg: Carl Winter-Universitätsverlag, 1987.

Cicero. *De natura deorum*. Translated by H. Rackham. Loeb Classical Library Edition. Cambridge: Cambridge University Press, 1933.

Clark, Andy. *Being There: Putting Brain, Body, and World Together Again*. Cambridge, Mass.: MIT Press, 1997.

———. *Natural-Born Cyborgs: Minds, Technologies, and the Future of Human Intelligence*. Oxford: Oxford University Press, 2003.

Cordier, Pierre-Marie. *Jean Pic de la Mirandole, ou "La plus pure figure de l'humanisme chrétien."* Paris: Nouvelles Éditions Debresse, 1957.

Corrigan, Kevin. "Ecstasy and Ectasy in Some Early Pagan and Christian Mystical Writings." In *Greek and Medieval Studies in Honor of Leo Sweeney, S.J.*, edited by William J. Carrol and John J. Furlong. New York: P. Lang, 1994.

Cortázar, Julio, "Axolotl." In *End of the Game and Other Stories*, translated by Paul Blackburn. New York: Harper and Row, 1967.

———. "Axolotl." In *Final del juego*. 1985. Madrid: Punto de Lectura, 2003.

Dante Alighieri. *De vulgari eloquentia*. Edited and translated by Steven Botteril. Cambridge: Cambridge University Press, 1996.

Daston, Lorraine, and Katherine Park. *Wonders and the Order of Nature*. New York: Zone Books, 2001.

Deming, Robert H. *James Joyce: The Critical Heritage*. Vol. 1, *1902–1927*. Vol. 2, *1928–1941*. London: Routledge and Kegan Paul, 1970.

Derrida, Jacques. "Deux mots pour Joyce." In *L'Herne: James Joyce*. Paris: Éditions de l'Herne, 1985.

———. "Faith and Knowledge: The Two Sources of 'Religion' at the Limits of Reason Alone." In *Religion*, translated by Samuel Weber, edited by Jacques Derrida and Gianni Vattimo. Stanford, Calif.: Stanford University Press, 1998.

———. "Force of Law: The 'Mystical Foundation of Authority.'" In *Deconstruction and the Possibility of Justice*, edited by Drucilla Cornell. New York: Routledge, 1992.

———. *Ulysse gramaphone: Deux mots pour Joyce*. Paris: Éditions Galilée, 1987.

———. "Violence et métaphysique." In *L'écriture et la différance*. Paris: Éditions du Seuil, 1967.

———. *Voyous*. Paris: Éditions Galilée, 2003.

Derrida, Jacques, and Giani Vattimo, eds. *La religion*. Paris: Éditions du Seuil, 1996.

Descartes, René. *Discours de la méthode: Texte et commentaire par Étienne Gilson*. Vrin, 1925.

———. *The Philosophical Writings of Descartes*. Vol. 1. Edited by John Cottingham, Robert Stoothof, and Dugald Murdoch. Cambridge: Cambridge University Press, 1985.

———. *Selected Philosophical Writings*. Edited by John Cottingham, Robert Stoothof, and Dugald Murdoch. Cambridge: Cambridge University Press, 1988.

de Vries, Hent. "In Media Res: Global Religion, Public Spheres, and the Task of Contemporary Comparative Religious Studies." In *Religion and Media*, edited by Hent de Vries and Samuel Weber. Stanford, Calif.: Stanford University Press, 2001.

———. *Philosophy and the Turn to Religion*. Baltimore: Johns Hopkins University Press, 1999.

Diderot, Denis. "Curiosité." In *Encyclopédie, ou Dictionnaire raisonné des sciences, des arts, et des métiers*, vol. 10. Berne: Société Typographique, 1782.

Duclow, Don. "Divine Nothingness and Self-Creation in John Scotus Eriugena." *Journal of Religion* 57, no. 2 (April 1977).

Dufour, Dany-Robert. *Lacan et le miroir sophianique de Boehme*. Paris: Cahiers de L'Unebévue, 1998.

———. *Lettres sur la nature humaine à l'usage des survivants*. Paris: Calmann-Lévy, 1999.

———. *On achève bien les hommes: De quelques conséquences actuelles et futures de la mort de Dieu*. Paris: Denoël, 2005.

Dupré, Louis. *Passage to Modernity: An Essay in the Hermeneutics of Nature and Culture*. New Haven, Conn.: Yale University Press, 1993.

Dupuy, Jean-Pierre. *The Mechanization of the Mind: On the Origins of Cognitive Science*. Translated by M. B. DeBevoise. Princeton, N.J.: Princeton University Press, 1994.

Eco, Umberto. *The Aesthetics of Chaosmos: The Middle Ages of James Joyce*. Translated by Ellen Esrock. Cambridge, Mass.: Harvard University Press, 1989.

———. *The Open Work*. Translated by Anna Cancogni. Cambridge, Mass.: Harvard University Press, 1989.

Eliade, Mircea. *The Sacred and the Profane: The Nature of Religion*. Translated by Willard R. Task. New York: Harcourt Brace Jovanovich, 1959.

Eriugena, John Scotus. *De imagine*. Edited by M. Cappuyns. *Recherches de Théologie Ancienne et Médiévale* 32 (July–December 1965): 205–62.

———. *Patrologiae Cursus Completus, Series Latina*. Vol. 122, *Ioannes Scotus Eriugena*. Edited by J. P. Migne. Turnhout, Belgium: Brepols Editores Pontificii.

———. *Periphyseon (The Division of Nature)*. Translated by I. P. Sheldon Williams, revised by John J. O'Meara. Montreal: Editions Bellarmin, 1987.

Feuerbach, Ludwig. *The Essence of Christianity*. Translated by G. Eliot. New York: Harper Torchbooks, 1967.

Foucault, Michel, and Ludwig Binswanger. *Dream and Existence*. Edited by Keith Hoeller. Atlantic Highlands, N.J.: Humanities Press, 1993.

Freud, Sigmund. *The Interpretation of Dreams*. Translated by James Strachey. New York: Avon Books, 1967.

Fukayama, Francis. *Our Posthuman Future: Consequences of the Biotechnology Revolution*. New York: Farrar, Straus, and Giroux, 2002.

Funkenstein, Amos. *Theology and the Scientific Imagination: From the Middle Ages to the Seventeenth Century*. Princeton, N.J.: Princeton University Press, 1986.

Gadamer, Hans-Georg. "Nikolaus von Kues im Modernen Denken." In *Nicolo' Cusano: Agli inizi del mondo moderno*. Florence: G. C. Sansoni Editore, 1970.

Gandillac, Maurice de. *Nicolas de Cues*. Paris: Ellipses, 2001.

———. "Pascal et le silence du monde." In *Blaise Pascal: L'homme et l'oeuvre*. Paris: Éditions de Minuit, 1956.

———. *La philosophie de Nicolas de Cues.* Paris: Aubier, 1941.

Garr, W. Randall. *In His Own Image and Likeness: Humanity, Divinity, and Monotheism.* Leiden: Brill, 2003.

Gehlen, Arnold. *Man: His Nature and Place in the World.* Trans. by Clare McMillan and Karl Pillemer. New York: Columbia University Press, 1988.

———. *Der Mensch.* Frankfurt: Athenaion, 1974.

Gifford, Don. *Ulysses Annotated: Notes for James Joyce's "Ulysses."* Berkeley: University of California Press, 1988.

Gopnik, Adam. "Chatter: Orange and White." *New Yorker*, March 3, 2003.

Gould, Stephen Jay. "A Biological Homage to Mickey Mouse." In *The Panda's Thumb: More Reflections in Natural History.* New York: W. W. Norton, 1980.

———. "The Child as Man's Real Father." In *Ever Since Darwin: Reflections in Natural History.* New York: W. W. Norton, 1973.

Grassi, Ernesto. *Heidegger and the Question of Renaissance Humanism: Four Studies.* Binghamton, N.Y.: Medieval and Renaissance Texts and Studies, 1983.

A Greek-English Lexicon. 9th ed. Edited by H. G. Liddell and R. Scott. Oxford: Oxford University Press, 1995.

The Greek New Testament. 3rd ed. Edited by Kurt Aland et al. Stuttgart: United Bible Societies, 1983.

Gregory of Nyssa. *La création de l'homme.* Translated by Jean Laplace. Paris: Éditions du Cerf, 1944.

———. "On the Making of Man." In *Nicene and Post-Nicene Fathers*, ser. 1, vol. 5, *Gregory of Nyssa: Dogmatic Treatises, etc.*, edited by Philip Schaff and Henry Wace. Peabody, Mass.: Hendrickson, 1994.

———. περὶ κατασκευῆς ἀνθρώπου, or *De hominis opificio.* In *Patrologiae Cursus Completus, Series Graeca*, edited by J.-P. Migne et al., vol. 44. Turnhout, Belgium: Brepols Editores Pontificii.

Greenberg, Gary. "After Nature: The Varieties of Technological Experience." *Harper's*, March 2004, 91–96.

Haar, Michel, ed. *Cahier de L'Herne: Heidegger.* Paris: Éditions de l'Herne, 1983.

Habermas, Jürgen. *The Future of Human Nature.* Cambridge, UK: Polity Press, 2003.

Hadot, Pierre. *Le voile d'Isis.* Paris: Gallimard, 2004.

Haraway, Donna. "Deanimations: Maps and Portraits of Life Itself." In *Picturing Science Producing Art*, edited by Caroline A. Jones and Peter Galison. New York: Routledge, 1998.

Harries, Karsten. *Infinity and Perspective.* Cambridge, Mass.: MIT Press, 2001.

Harrison, Robert P. *The Dominion of the Dead.* Chicago: University of Chicago Press, 2003.

———. *Forests.* Chicago: University of Chicago Press, 1992.

Hart, Clive. *A Concordance to Finnegans Wake.* Corrected edition. Mamaroneck, N.Y.: Paul P. Appel, 1963.

Hart, Kevin, ed. *Counter-Experiences: Reading Jean-Luc Marion.* Notre Dame, Ind.: Notre Dame University Press, 2007.

———. *Trespass of the Sign: Deconstruction, Philosophy and Theology.* Cambridge: Cambridge University Press, 1989.

Hart, Ray L. *Unfinished Man and the Imagination*. New York: Herder and Herder, 1968.

Hartman, Geoffrey. *Scars of the Spirit: The Struggle against Inauthenticity*. New York: Palgrave, 2002.

Hayles, N. Katherine. *How We Became Posthuman: Virtual Bodies in Cybernetics, Literature, and Informatics*. Chicago: University of Chicago Press, 1999.

Hayman, David. *Joyce et Mallarmé: Les éléments mallarméens dans l'oeuvre de Joyce*. Paris: Lettres Modernes, 1956.

———. *Joyce et Malarmé: Stylistique de la suggestion*. Paris: Lettres Modernes, 1956.

Hegel, G. W. F. *Lectures on the Philosophy of Religion: The Lectures of 1827*. One-volume edition, edited by Peter C. Hodgson. Berkeley and Los Angeles: University of California Press, 1988.

Heidegger, Martin. "Age of the World Picture." In *The Question concerning Technology and Other Essays*. Translated by William Lovitt. New York: Harper Torchbooks, 1977.

———. *Being and Time*. Translated by John Macquarrie and Edward Robinson. Oxford: Basil Blackwell, 1962.

———. *Beiträge zur Philosophie (vom Ereignis)*. Vol. 65 of *Gesamtausgabe*. Frankfurt am Main: Vittorio Klostermann, 1989; rev. ed. 1994.

———. "Brief über den Humanismus." In *Wegmarken*, vol. 9 of *Gesamtausgabe*. Frankfurt am Main: Vittorio Klostermann, 1967; rev. ed. 1996.

———. *Contributions to Philosophy (from Enowning)*. Translated by Parvis Emad and Kenneth Maly. Bloomington: Indiana University Press, 1999.

———. *Einführung in die Metaphysik*. Vol. 40 of *Gesamtausgabe*. Frankfurt am Main: Vittorio Klostermann, 1983.

———. *The Essence of Reasons: A Bilingual Edition, incorporating the German text of Vom Wesen des Grundes*. Translated by Terrence Malick. Evanston, Ill.: Northwestern University Press, 1969.

———. "Die Frage nach der Technik." In *Vorträge und Aufsätze*. Stuttgart: Neske, 1954.

———. *The Fundamental Concepts of Metaphysics: World, Finitude, Solitude*. Translated by William McNeill and Nicholas Walker. Bloomington: Indiana University Press, 1995.

———. *Die Grundbegriffe der Metaphysik: Welt-Endlichkeit-Einsamkeit*, Vol. 29/30 of *Gesamtausgabe*. Frankfurt am Main: Vittorio Klostermann, 1983.

———. *Heraclitus Seminar*. Translated by Charles H. Seibert. Evanston, Ill.: Northwestern University Press, 1993.

———. *Introduction to Metaphysics*. Translated by Ralph Manheim. New Haven, Conn.: Yale University Press, 1959.

———. "Letter on Humanism." In *Basic Writings*, rev. ed., edited by David Farrell Krell. San Francisco: Harper Collins, 1993.

———. "Memorial Address." In *Discourse on Thinking*. New York: Harper and Row, 1966.

———. "The Origin of the Work of Art." In *Basic Writings*, rev. ed., edited by David Farrell Krell. San Francisco: Harper Collins, 1993.

———. *Phänomenologie des religiösen Lebens*. Vol. 60 of *Gesamtausgabe*. Frankfurt am Main: Vittorio Klostermann, 1995.

———. *The Phenomenology of the Religious Life.* Translated by Matthias Fritsch and Jennifer Anna Gossetti-Ferenci. Bloomington: Indiana University Press, 2004.

———. "The Question concerning Technology." In *Basic Writings*, rev. ed., edited by David Farrell Krell. San Francisco: Harper Collins, 1993.

———. *The Question concerning Technology and Other Essays.* Translated by William Lovitt. New York: Harper Torchbooks, 1977.

———. *Sein und Zeit.* 16th ed. Tübingen: Max Niemeyer Verlag, 1986.

———. The *Spiegel* Interview. In *Martin Heidegger and National Socialism*, edited by Günther Neske and Emil Kettering. New York: Paragon House, 1991.

———. *Was ist Metaphysik?* In *Wegmarken*, vol. 9 of *Gesamtausgabe*. Frankfurt am Main: Vittorio Klostermann, 1967; rev. ed. 1996.

———. "Die Zeit des Weltbildes." In *Holzwege*. Frankfurt am Main: Vittorio Klostermann, 1950.

Hopkins, Jasper. *A Concise Introduction to the Philosophy of Nicholas of Cusa.* Minneapolis: University of Minneapolis Press, 1978.

———. "Nicholas of Cusa (1401–1464): First Modern Philosopher?" *Midwest Studies in Philosophy* 26 (2002): 13–29.

Hughes, Thomas P. *Human-Built World: How to Think about Technology and Culture.* Chicago: University of Chicago Press, 2004.

Huizinga, Johan. *Homo Ludens: A Study of the Play Element in Culture.* Boston: Beacon Press, 1950.

Hutchins, Edwin. *Cognition in the Wild.* Cambridge, Mass.: MIT Press, 1995.

Janicaud, Dominique. *On the Human Condition.* Translated by Eileen Brennan. New York: Routledge, 2005.

Jaspers, Karl. *Anselm and Nicholas of Cusa: From The Great Philosophers.* Vol. 2. Edited by Hannah Arendt. New York: Harcourt, Brace, Jovanovich, 1966.

Jaurretche, Colleen. *The Sensual Philosophy: Joyce and the Aesthetics of Mysticism.* Madison: University of Wisconsin Press, 1997.

Joyce, James. *Critical Writings.* Edited by Ellsworth Mason and Richard Ellmann. Ithaca, N.Y.: Cornell University Press, 1989.

———. *Finnegans Wake.* Introduction by John Bishop. New York: Penguin Books, 1999.

———. *James Joyce's Scribbledehobble: The Ur-Workbook for Finnegans Wake.* Edited by Thomas E. Conoly. Evanston, Ill.: Northwestern University Press, 1961.

———. *Ulysses.* Edited by Hans Walter Gabler. New York: Random House, 1986.

Kass, Leon. *Human Cloning and Human Dignity: The Report of the President's Council on Bioethics.* New York: Public Affairs, 2002.

———. *Life, Liberty, and the Defense of Dignity: The Challenge for Bioethics.* San Francisco: Encounter Books, 2002.

Kaufman, Gordon D. *In the Beginning . . . Creativity.* Minneapolis: Fortress Press, 2004.

Kearney, Richard. *The God Who May Be: A Hermeneutics of Religion.* Bloomington: Indiana University Press, 2001.

Kierkegaard, Søren. *The Concept of Anxiety.* Translated by Reider Thomte. Princeton, N.J.: Princeton University Press, 1980.

———. *The Present Age and Of the Difference between a Genius and an Apostle.* Translated by Alexander Dru. New York: Harper Torchbooks, 1962.

————. *The Sickness unto Death*. Translated by Edna Hong and Howard Hong. Princeton, N.J.: Princeton University Press, 1983.

Kisiel, Theodore. *The Genesis of Heidegger's Being and Time*. Berkeley: University of California Press, 1993.

Kolbert, Elizabeth. "The Climate of Man." *New Yorker*, April 2005.

————. *Field Notes from a Catastrophe: Man, Nature, and Climate Change*. New York: Bloomsbury, 2006.

Koyré, Alexandre. *From the Closed World to the Infinite Universe*. New York: Harper and Brothers, 1957.

Kristeller, Paul Oskar. Introduction to the "On the Dignity of Man." In *The Renaissance Philosophy of Man*, edited by Ernst Cassirer, Paul Oskar Kristeller, and John Herman Randall Jr. Chicago: University of Chicago Press, 1948.

Lapassade, Georges. *L'entrée dans la vie*. Paris: Éditions Economica, 1997.

————. "Présentation de Louis Bolk." *Arguments* 4, no. 18, 2nd trimester 1(960).

Levin, Harry. "On First Looking into *Finnegans Wake*." Review from *New Directions* (1939). Reprinted in *James Joyce: The Critical Heritage*, vol. 2, *1928–1941*, edited by Robert H. Deming. London: Routledge and Kegan Paul, 1970.

Levinas, Emmanuel. *Ethics and Infinity: Conversations with Philippe Nemo*. Pittsburgh: Duquesne University Press, 1985.

————. "Heidegger, Gagarin, and Us." In *Difficult Freedom: Essays on Judaism*, translated by Seán Hand. Baltimore: Johns Hopkins University Press, 1997.

————. *Otherwise than Being, or Beyond Essence*. Translated by Alphonso Lingis. Boston: Martinus Nijhof, 1981.

Mahnke, Dietrich. *Unendliche Sphäre und Allmittelpunkt*. Stuttgart-Bad Canstatt: Friedrich Frommann Verlag, 1966 (Faksimile-Neudruck der Ausgabe Halle, 1937).

Mallarmé, Stéphane. "Un coup de dés jamais n'abolira le hasard." In *Oeuvres complètes*. Paris: Gallimard, 1998.

————. "Le livre, instrument spirituel." From the Web site Mallarme.net. http://www.mallarme.net/site.php?n=Mallarme.LeLivreInstrumentSpirituel/.

Margel, Serge, *Logique de la nature*. Paris: Éditions Galilée, 2000.

Marion, Jean-Luc. *Being Given: Toward a Phenomenology of Givenness*. Translated by Jeffrey L. Kosky. Stanford, Calif.: Stanford University Press, 2002.

————. *La croisée du visible*. 1991. Paris: Presses Universitaires de France, 1996.

————. *Dieu sans l'être: Hors texte*. Paris: Fayard, 1982.

————. *Etant donné: Essai d'une phénoménologie de la donation*. Paris: Presses Universitaires de France, 1997.

————. *God without Being: Hors-Texte*. Translated by Thomas A. Carlson. Chicago: University of Chicago Press, 1991.

————. *The Idol and Distance*. Translated by Thomas A. Carlson. New York: Fordham University Press, 2001.

————. *L'idole et la distance*. Paris: Grasset, 1977.

————. "L'interloqué." In *Who Comes after The Subject?* edited by Eduardo Cadava, Peter Connor, and Jean-Luc Nancy. New York: Routledge, 1991.

————. "*Mihi magna quaestio factus sum*: The Privilege of Unknowing." *Journal of Religion* 85, no. 1 (January 2005).

———. *On Descartes' Metaphysical Prism.* Translated by Jeffrey L. Kosky. Chicago: University of Chicago Press, 1999.

———. *Le phénomène érotique.* Paris: Éditions Grasset, 2003.

———. *Reduction and Givenness: Investigations of Husserl, Heidegger, and Phenomenology.* Evanston, Ill.: Northwestern University Press, 1998.

———. *Réduction et donation: Recherches sur Husserl, Heidegger, et la phénoménologie.* Paris: Presses Universitaires de France, 1989.

———. *Sur le prisme métaphysique de Descartes.* Paris: Presses Universitaires de France, 1986.

Mazzotta, Giuseppe. *The New Map of the World: The Poetic Philosophy of Giambattista Vico.* Princeton, N.J.: Princeton University Press, 1999.

McGinn, Bernard. *The Foundations of Mysticism.* Vol. 1 of *The Presence of God: A History of Western Christian Mysticism.* New York: Crossroad, 1991.

———. *The Growth of Mysticism.* Vol. 3 of *The Presence of God: A History of Western Christian Mysticism.* New York: Crossroad, 1994.

———. *The Harvest of Mysticism in Medieval Germany.* Vol. 4 of *The Presence of God: A History of Western Christian Mysticism.* New York: Crossroad, 2005.

———. "The Negative Element in the Anthropology of John the Scot." In *Jean Scot Erigène et l'histoire de la philosophie.* Paris: Éditions du Centre National de la Recherche Scientifique, 1977.

———. "The Originality of Eriugena's Spiritual Exegesis." In *Iohannes Scottus Eriugena: The Bible and Hermeneutics,* edited by Gerd Van Riel, Carlos Steel, and James McEvoy. Leuven: University Press, 1996.

McHugh, Roland. *Annotation to "Finnegans Wake."* Rev. ed. Baltimore: Johns Hopkins University Press, 1991.

McKibben, Bill. *Enough: Staying Human in an Engineered Age.* New York: Henry Holt, 2003.

McLuhan, Marshall. *The Interior Landscape: The Literary Criticism of Marshall McLuhan, 1943–1962.* Edited by Eugene McNamara. New York: McGraw-Hill, 1969.

———. *The Medium and the Light: Reflections on Religion.* Edited by Eric McLuhan and Jacek Szklarek. Toronto: Stoddart, 1999.

McLuhan, Marshall, and Quentin Fiore. *The Medium is the Massage: An Inventory of Effects.* Madera, Calif.: Gingko Press, 2001.

Meehan, Bernard, ed. *The Book of Kells: An Illustrated Introduction to the Manuscript in Trinity College Dublin.* London: Thames and Hudson, 1994.

Mendieta, Eduardo. "We Have Never Been Human, or How We Lost Our Humanity: Derrida and Habermas on Cloning." *Philosophy Today.* SPEP suppl., 2003.

Merchant, Carolyn. *The Death of Nature: Women, Ecology, and the Scientific Revolution.* San Francisco: Harper Collins, 1980.

Milbank, John. *The Religious Dimension in the Thought of Giambattista Vico, 1668–1744.* Pt. 1, *The Early Metaphysics.* Pt. 2, *Language, Law and History.* Lewiston, N.Y.: Edwin Mellen Press, 1991–92.

Miner, Robert. *Truth in the Making: Creative Knowledge in Theology and Philosophy.* New York: Routledge, 2004.

Mirapaul, Matthew. "Arts Online; Making an Opera from Cyberspace's Tower of Babel." *New York Times*, December 10, 2001.

Moran, Dermot. *The Philosophy of John Scottus Eriugena*. Cambridge: Cambridge University Press, 1989.

Nancy, Jean-Luc. *La création du monde, ou La mondialisation*. Paris: Éditions Galilée, 2002.

———. "La déconstruction du christianisme." *Les Etudes Philosophiques*, no. 4 (1998).

Nicholas of Cusa (Nikolaus von Kues). *De apice theoriae (Concerning the Loftiest Levels of Contemplative Reflection)*. In *Nicholas of Cusa: Metaphysical Speculations*, vol. 1, translated by Jasper Hopkins. Minneapolis: Arthur J. Banning Press, 1998.

———. *De beryllo (On [Intellectual] Eyeglasses)*. In *Nicholas of Cusa: Metaphysical Speculations*, vol. 1, translated by Jasper Hopkins. Minneapolis: Arthur J. Banning Press, 1998.

———. *De coniecturis (On Surmises)*. In *Nicholas of Cusa: Metaphysical Speculations*, vol. 2. Translated by Jasper Hopkins. Minneapolis: Arthur J. Banning Press, 2000.

———. *De possest (On Actualized Possibility)*. In *A Concise Introduction to the Philosophy of Nicholas of Cusa*, 3rd. ed., translated by Jasper Hopkins. Minneapolis: Arthur J. Banning Press, 1986.

———. *Dialogus De ludo globi (The Bowling Game)*. In *Nicholas of Cusa: Metaphysical Speculations*, vol. 2, translated by Jasper Hopkins. Minneapolis: Arthur J. Banning Press, 2000.

———. *On Learned Ignorance*. In *Nicholas of Cusa: Selected Spiritual Writings*, edited by H. Lawrence Bond. New York: Paulist Press, 1997.

———. *On the Vision of God*. In *Nicolas of Cusa: Selected Spiritual Writings*, edited by H. Lawrence Bond. New York: Paulist Press, 1997.

———. *Philosophisch-Theologische Werke, Lateinisch-Deutsch*. Hamburg: Felix Meiner Verlag, 2002.

Nietzsche, Friedrich. *Nachgelassene Fragmente* (1884), 25 (428), *Werke* 7.2. Edited by Colli-Montinari. Berlin and New York, 1974.

Nobel, Philip. "First Take: Philip Nobel on Ben Rubin." *Artforum*, January 2002.

Norris, Margot. *The Decentered Universe of Finnegans Wake: A Structuralist Analysis*. Baltimore: Johns Hopkins University Press, 1974.

Novum Testamentum Latine. Edited by Kurt Aland and Barbara Aland. Stuttgart: Deutsche Bibelgesellschaft, 1984.

Oberman, Heiko A. "Some Notes on the Theology of Nominalism, With Attention to its Relation to the Renaissance." *Harvard Theological Review* 53, no. 1 (January 1960): 47–76.

O'Regan, Cyril. *Gnostic Apocalypse: Jacob Boehme's Haunted Narrative*. Albany: State University of New York Press, 2002.

———. *Gnostic Return in Modernity*. Albany: State University of New York Press, 2001.

———. *The Heterodox Hegel*. Albany: State University of New York Press, 1994.

Origen. *Contra celsum*. Translated by Henry Chadwick. Cambridge: Cambridge University Press, 1953.

Otten, Willemien. *The Anthropology of Johannes Scottus Eriugena*. Leiden: Brill, 1991.

————. "The Dialectic of Return in Eriugena's *Periphyseon.*" *Harvard Theological Review* 84, no. 4 (1991): 399–421.

Oxford Latin Dictionary. Edited by P. G. W. Glare. Oxford: Oxford University Press, 2005.

Pico della Mirandola, Giovanni. *De hominis dignitate.* In *Oeuvres complètes,* edited by O. Boulnois and G. Tognon. Paris: Presses Universitaires de France, 2004.

————. *Dignità dell'uomo [De hominis dignitate].* 3rd ed. Translated by Bruno Cicognani. Florence: Le Monnier, 1943.

————. *Of the Dignity of Man.* Translated by Elizabeth Livermore Forbes. *Journal of the History of Ideas* 3 (1942).

————. "Oratio." In *Pluralità delle vie: Alle origini del Discorso sulla dignità umana di Pico della Mirandola,* edited by Pier Cesare Bori. Milan: Feltrinelli, 2000.

————. "Oration on the Dignity of Man." Translated by Elizabeth Livermore Forbes. In *The Renaissance Philosophy of Man,* edited by Ernst Cassirer, Paul Oskar Kristeller, and John Herman Randall Jr. Chicago: University of Chicago Press, 1948.

————. *Über die Würde des Menschen, Lateinisch-Deutsch.* Translated by Norbert Baumgarten. Hamburg: Felix Meiner Verlag, 1990.

Picq, Pascal. "L'humain à l'aube de l'humanité." In *Qu'est-ce que l'humain?* by Pascal Picq, Michel Serres, and Jean-Didier Vincent. Paris: Le Pommier, 2003.

Plato. *Protagoras.* In *Plato: The Collected Dialogues,* edited by Edith Hamilton and Huntington Cairns. Princeton, N.J.: Princeton U. Press, 1961.

————. *Protagoras.* In *Plato II,* edited by G. P. Goold. Loeb Classical Library. Cambridge, Mass.: Harvard University Press, 1999.

Riccati, Carlo. *"Processio" et "Explicatio": La doctrine de la création chez Jean-Scot et Nicolas de Cues.* Naples: Bibliopolis, 1983.

Roques, René. "'Valde Artificialiter': Le sens d'un contresens." *Annuaire de l'Ecole Pratique des Hautes Etudes — Sciences Religieuses* 77 (1969–70): 31–72.

Santner, Eric. *On Creaturely Life: Rilke, Benjamin, Sebald.* Chicago: University of Chicago Press, 2006.

Saward, John. "Towards an Apophatic Anthropology." *Irish Theological Quarterly* 41, no. 3 (July 1974): 222–34.

Scholem, Gershom, *Major Trends in Jewish Mysticism.* New York: Schocken Books, 1974.

Schürmann, Reiner. *Meister Eckhart, Mystic and Philosopher.* Bloomington: Indiana University Press, 1978.

Serres, Michel. *Angels: A Modern Myth.* Paris: Flammarion, 1995.

————. *Atlas.* Paris: Flammarion, 1996.

————. *Le contrat naturel.* Paris: Éditions François Bourin, 1990.

————. *Hermès I: La communication.* Paris: Éditions de Minuit, 1968.

————. *Hermès II: L'interférence.* Paris: Éditions de Minuit, 1972.

————. *Hermès III: La traduction.* Paris: Éditions de Minuit, 1974.

————. *Hermès IV: La distribution.* Paris: Éditions de Minuit, 1977.

————. *Hermès V: Le passage du Nord-Ouest.* Paris: Éditions de Minuit, 1980.

————. *Hermes: Literature, Science, Philosophy.* Baltimore: Johns Hopkins University Press, 1982.

———. *Hominescence*. Paris: Le Pommier, 2001.

———. *L'incandescent*. Paris: Le Pommier, 2003.

———. *Rameaux*. Paris: Le Pommier, 2004.

———. *Récits d'humanisme*. Paris: Le Pommier, 2006.

———. "Le temps humain: de l'évolution créatrice au créateur d'évolution." In *Qu'est-ce que l'humain?* by Pascal Picq, Michel Serres, and Jean-Didier Vincent. Paris: Le Pommier, 2003.

Serres, Michel, and Bruno Latour. *Conversations on Science, Culture, and Time*. Ann Arbor: University of Michigan Press, 1995.

Silesius, Angelus. *The Cherubinic Wanderer*. Translated by Maria Shrady. New York: Paulist Press, 1986.

Sloterdijk, Peter. *Regeln für den Menschenpark: Ein Antwortschreiben zu Heideggers Brief über den Humanismus*. Frankfurt am Main: Suhrkamp Verlag, 1999.

Stiegler, Bernard. *La technique et le temps*. Vol. 1, *La faute d'Épiméthée*. Paris: Éditions Galilée, 1994.

———. *La technique et le temps*. Vol. 2, *La désorientation*. Paris: Éditions Galilée, 1996.

Stock, Gregory. *Redesigning Humans: Our Inevitable Genetic Future*. New York: Houghton Mifflin, 2002.

Taylor, Mark C. *About Religion: Economies of Faith in Virtual Culture*. Chicago: University of Chicago Press, 1999.

———. *Confidence Games: Money and Markets in a World without Redemption*. Chicago: University of Chicago Press, 2004.

———. *Erring: A Postmodern A/theology*. Chicago: University of Chicago Press, 1984.

———. *Hiding*. Chicago: University of Chicago Press, 1997.

———. *The Moment of Complexity: Emerging Network Culture*. Chicago: University of Chicago Press, 2001.

———. "p.s. fin again." In *Tears*. Albany: State University of New York Press, 1990.

———. "Returnings." Introduction to reissued *Journeys to Selfhood: Hegel and Kierkegaard*. New York: Fordham University Press, 2000.

Theall, Donald. "Beyond the Orality/Literacy Dichotomy: James Joyce and the Prehistory of Cyberspace." *Postmodern Culture* 2, no. 3 (May 1992).

———. *James Joyce's Techno-poetics*. Toronto: University of Toronto Press, 1997.

Tillich, Paul. *The Courage to Be*. New Haven, Conn.: Yale University Press, 1952.

Tindall, William York. *A Reader's Guide to "Finnegans Wake."* Syracuse, NY: Syracuse University Press, 1969.

Tomasic, Thomas. "Negative Theology and Subjectivity: An Approach to the Tradition of the Pseudo-Dionysius." *International Philosophical Quarterly* 9, no. 3 (September 1969): 406–30.

Toulmin, Stephen. *Cosmopolis*. Chicago: University of Chicago Press, 1990.

Trinkaus, Charles. *In Our Image and Likeness: Humanity and Divinity in Italian Humanist Thought*. Vol. 2. Chicago: University of Chicago Press, 1970.

Ullman, Ellen. "Programming the Posthuman: Computer Science Redefines 'Life.'" *Harper's* 305, no. 1829 (October 2002).

Van Buren, John. *The Young Heidegger: Rumor of the Hidden King*. Bloomington: Indiana University Press, 1994.

Verene, Donald Philip, ed. *Vico and Joyce*. Albany: State University of New York Press, 1987.

———. *Vico's Science of Imagination*. Ithaca, N.Y.: Cornell University Press, 1981.

Vico, Giambattista. *The Autobiography of Giambattista Vico*. Translated by Max Harold Fisch and Thomas Goddard Bergin. Ithaca, N.Y.: Cornell University Press, 1944.

———. *New Science*. Translated by David Marsh. New York: Penguin Books, 1999.

Vincent, Jean-Didier. "L'homme interprète passionné du monde" In *Qu'est-ce que l'humain?* by Pascal Picq, Michel Serres, and Jean-Didier Vincent. Paris: Le Pommier, 2003.

Watts, Pauline Moffitt. *Cusanus: A Fifteenth-Century Vision of Man*. Leiden: E. J. Brill, 1982.

Weber, Max. "Science as a Vocation." In *From Max Weber: Essays in Sociology*, edited by H. H. Gerth and C. Wright Mills. New York: Oxford University Press, 1946.

———. "Wissenschaft als Beruf." In *Gesammelte Aufsätze zur Wissenschaftslehre*, edited by Johannes Winckelmann. 1922. Tübingen: J. C. B. Mohr, 1988.

Weber, Samuel. *Mass Mediauras: Form, Technics, Media*. Stanford, Calif.: Stanford University Press, 1996.

Wexler, Philip. *Mystical Society: An Emerging Social Vision*. Boulder: Westview Press, 2000.

Winter, Jochen. *La création de l'infini*. Paris: Calmann-Lévy, 2004.

Wyschogrod, Edith. *Saints and Postmodernism: Revisioning Moral Philosophy*. Chicago: University of Chicago Press, 1990.

⚜

INDEX

General

absence, 68, 133, 156, 187
absens, or *absenthéisme*, 133, 135
absolute, the, 41, 97, 99, 101, 103, 105n62,
     107, 108n69, 110, 112, 114, 117, 124,
     132n25, 156, 187
abyss, 169, 183
acosmism, 147
activity, 30n46, 38, 128, 136, 140, 145, 203;
     bustling, 56–57, 62, 69; creative, of God,
     13; creative, of human, 29, 78, 93n36, 96,
     104–5, 107, 114, 138, 143, 194; projective,
     60, 197; and representational thought,
     41, 43; synthetic and/or retentive and/or
     formative, 25, 190, 193, 195–97
actual, the, or actuality, 2, 47, 63, 99, 113,
     155–56, 192, 202, 208–9; of possibility
     itself, 156. *See also* possibility: reduction
     of to actuality
Adam, 122, 127, 166–67, 181. *See also* atom
adoption, 137, 142
affirmation, 29, 30n46, 86, 88, 92n34, 93n36,
     99, 107n67, 108, 115, 127n18, 176, 178
Agamben, Giorgio, 26–27, 31, 64–66, 113,
     119–20, 137n33, 199–204
agency, 15, 136, 138; distributed, 137, 141.
     See also mind: distributed; networks
alienation, 42, 51, 122, 150
Allself, 180–81
Altizer, Thomas J. J., 155–56, 180n59
amazement, 51, 62, 132–33
ambitio saeculi, 213
anabasis, 171
angelic, or angels, 30, 172, 180–81
animal, or animals, 79–81, 84, 106n66, 116,
     122–23, 126, 182, 199
annihilation, 178
anonymity, 158, 160, 180, 184; divine,
     107n67; human, 24, 70–71, 74, 76, 179,
     215. *See also* culture: mass; God: naming
     of; polyonymy; religious: diversity
Anthropocene age, 144
anthropocentrism, 122
anthropology, 9, 89, 100, 123, 129, 195.
     See also negative anthropology
anxieties, or anxiety, or anxious response, 5,
     36, 37, 48, 57, 62, 152, 159, 185–86, 188
anything, 35, 45, 86, 114–15, 160, 174, 183,
     208. *See also* everything; human: unpro-
     grammed; nothing

anywhere, 51, 175, 181
apolis, 68
apolitical, 67. *See also* political
apophasis, 108
apophatic, 179; analogy, 1, 206; anthropol-
     ogy, 18n24, 34–35, 77, 78, 81, 91, 114;
     ascent, 176; attitude, 107; cosmology, 114;
     cosmos, 159; erasure, 88n26; theology, 9,
     12, 34–35, 78, 81, 85, 91
apparatus, 142
appareil, or *appareillage*, 142
Aquinas, Thomas, 51, 171n44
archaic, 158, 180
archetype, 23, 31, 33, 41, 77, 82–83, 126, 176,
     216
Arendt, Hannah, 214n10
Aristotle, Aristotelian, 30n46, 92, 96, 123,
     133
art, 52, 104–6, 145; machine, 149; work of,
     33, 138, 153. *See also* God: as infinite art;
     human: self-creative
aspiration, 171
atheism, 12–13. *See also* humanism
Athena, 79
atom, 166–67, 178, 181. *See also* Adam
attentiveness, 162n26
Augenblick, der, 23
Augustine, Saint, or Augustinian, 18n24,
     40, 48, 51–64, 76, 157–58, 171n44,
     195–96n10, 212–15
Aupers, Stef, 192n6
aura, 145
autarchy, 66
authentic, or authenticity, 36, 39, 62, 66, 72,
     154, 158, 203
authority, 71n48, 147, 204
autoimmunity, 135n30
automatic, or automaticity, 71, 198–99.
     See also machination
axolotl, 26–28, 169
awakening, 166, 187

babble, or Babel, 160, 163
Badiou, Alain, 137n33
Balsamo, Gian, 162n26, 180n59
banality, 149, 154
bavardage, 55
Beckett, Samuel, 30–31n47, 156–57, 182, 187
becoming, 115
Begreifen-Können, 112. *See also* mind:
     being-able-to-conceive